Clark Howard's

# LIVING LARGE
## IN LEAN TIMES

# Clark Howard's

# LIVING LARGE

# IN LEAN TIMES

*250+ Ways to Buy Smarter,*
*Spend Smarter, and Save Money*

## Clark Howard

*with Mark Meltzer and Theo Thimou*

AVERY
*a member of Penguin Group (USA) Inc.*
*New York*

Published by the Penguin Group

Penguin Group (USA) Inc., 375 Hudson Street, New York, New York 10014, USA • Penguin Group (Canada), 90 Eglinton Avenue East, Suite 700, Toronto, Ontario M4P 2Y3, Canada (a division of Pearson Penguin Canada Inc.) • Penguin Books Ltd, 80 Strand, London WC2R 0RL, England • Penguin Ireland, 25 St Stephen's Green, Dublin 2, Ireland (a division of Penguin Books Ltd) • Penguin Group (Australia), 250 Camberwell Road, Camberwell, Victoria 3124, Australia (a division of Pearson Australia Group Pty Ltd) • Penguin Books India Pvt Ltd, 11 Community Centre, Panchsheel Park, New Delhi–110 017, India • Penguin Group (NZ), 67 Apollo Drive, Rosedale, North Shore 0632, New Zealand (a division of Pearson New Zealand Ltd) • Penguin Books (South Africa) (Pty) Ltd, 24 Sturdee Avenue, Rosebank, Johannesburg 2196, South Africa

Penguin Books Ltd, Registered Offices: 80 Strand, London WC2R 0RL, England

Most Avery books are available at special quantity discounts for bulk purchase for sales promotions, premiums, fund-raising, and educational needs. Special books or book excerpts also can be created to fit specific needs. For details, write Penguin Group (USA) Inc. Special Markets, 375 Hudson Street, New York, NY 10014.

Library of Congress Cataloging-in-Publication Data

Howard, Clark, date.
Clark Howard's living large in lean times : 250+ ways to buy smarter, spend smarter, and save money / Clark Howard with Mark Meltzer and Theo Thimou.
p.      cm.
ISBN 978-1-58333-433-1
1. Finance, Personal—United States.    2. Consumer education—United States.
3. Thriftiness—United States.    I. Meltzer, Mark.    II. Thimou, Theo.    III. Title.
HG179.H6853        2011                      2011012420
332.02400973—dc22

Printed in the United States of America
7   9   10   8

BOOK DESIGN BY AMANDA DEWEY

Neither the publisher nor the authors are engaged in rendering professional advice or services to the individual reader. The ideas, procedures, and suggestions contained in this book are not intended as a substitute for consulting with your physician. All matters regarding your health require medical supervision. Neither the authors nor the publisher shall be liable or responsible for any loss or damage allegedly arising from any information or suggestion in this book.

This publication is designed to provide accurate and authoritative information in regard to the subject matter covered. It is sold with the understanding that the publisher is not engaged in rendering legal, accounting, or other professional services. If you require legal advice or other expert assistance, you should seek the services of a competent professional.

While the authors have made every effort to provide accurate telephone numbers and Internet addresses at the time of publication, neither the publisher nor the authors assume any responsibility for errors, or for changes that occur after publication. Further, the publisher does not have any control over and does not assume any responsibility for author or third-party websites or their content.

To Lane, Rebecca, Stephi, Grant, Gretchen, and Gayle, who always bring a smile to my face and are as proud of me as I am of them.
—CLARK

For Gina. Gracias por tu amor y apoyo.
—MARK

To Cynthia, Mason, Patricia, Paul, and Nick. Thanks for believing in me.
—THEO

# Contents

# Introduction

Every day people ask me when I think the economy is going to come back. My response always stuns the questioner. I believe that it could take another five to ten years for us to heal. Neither you nor I can control the economic cycle of the United States or the world. But you can take charge of your own life.

We as a country got into trouble step-by-step, living beyond our means using borrowed money. It was a team effort. Government at all levels promised and spent money it didn't have, banks behaved recklessly and brought great harm to the entire globe, and consumers were happy to borrow themselves into oblivion. If you go back to the 1970s, the typical American carried debt of 65 cents to each dollar they earned. On the eve of the Great Recession in 2007, the average person had debt of $1.36 for each dollar they earned. Today, the debt is down to $1.24 and still falling, but we are only about halfway back to more reasonable levels.

I can't predict when the nation will get healthy. But I can help you empower yourself so that you have your personal financial house in order. That way you can survive and ultimately prosper regardless of the country's progress. You do it one step at a time, fixing your finances and then building the path to independence and ultimately, dare I say, wealth.

Every day on my syndicated radio show and every weekend on my HLN TV show, I guide you toward saving more, spending less, and avoiding getting ripped off.

I have been serving my listeners and viewers since 1987. Over the years I have written eight books pushing people to become active, not passive, with their wallet. Since 1997 my website, ClarkHoward.com, has provided up-to-the minute guidance for more than 25 million consumers each year. In 1993, I founded TeamClark, our consumer action center, staffed with 155 volunteers who answer people's questions forty-five hours per week and give callers a booster shot of confidence to stand up for themselves and take charge.

*Living Large in Lean Times* is your guide for this uncertain, difficult era. I know there are those, when times are tough, who believe things will never get better. I don't buy it. When times turn, this book will help you to be better positioned for success.

There are so many ways to reduce debt, buy smarter, and build a future. Follow my lead. I will get you there.

A word about how I've structured this book: I have broken it down into thirteen chapters. In the first chapter, I give you twenty-five tips that highlight things you can do right away to make an immediate difference in your finances. I call this section "Help Me Now, Clark: Improve Your Personal Finances in One Week."

The next ten chapters constitute the meat of the book and have more than 250 pieces of my best advice on a range of topics from cars to homes to travel. Within each of these ten chapters, you'll find plenty of ways to start packing a real punch in your wallet.

Throughout these chapters, I've included anecdotes from people who've written to me and wanted to share how they've used specific pieces of my advice to save more, spend less, and avoid rip-offs. If you like the advice in this book and put it to good use, maybe you can be featured in my next book!

Another thing you'll see throughout this book: a notation that a particular tip is flagged as either "Clark's Greatest Hits" or "A Clark Favorite."

The tips I've called Clark's Greatest Hits are classics that I've told people about for years, the bedrock of my money-saving philosophy. These include ideas such as having a used car inspected by a mechanic before purchase, or refinancing your mortgage into a fifteen-year rate, or starting a Roth IRA to have the benefit of tax-free spending in retirement.

A Clark Favorite is a tip that I love, but that I acknowledge might be a little "out there" for some readers. So you have things like the idea of flying with a carry-on only to beat luggage fees, or firing your home phone provider and making all your phone calls over the Internet. Likewise, I describe a technique I have to make disposable razors last months and even years so I don't have to spend much on shaving. Plus, I'll tell you how to get ultra-cheap prescription eyeglasses starting at $7 that have lenses ground in China! Just give some of these wacky ideas a try and see how they work for you.

*Living Large in Lean Times* winds down with what I call "Clark's Graveyard." Ultimately, I believe that talking about money should be funny and entertaining. So this section compiles some of the money-saving ideas I loved that "died" in the marketplace ahead of their time. You'll get a real laugh when you read about bygone vending machines that sold eggs and diapers; busted airlines that offered $9 seats; and even my favorite, a three-wheel car that had no reverse gear!

Finally, the book's very last chapter is a recap of important websites mentioned throughout the manuscript, all compiled in one place for easy reference.

—*Clark Howard*

# Help Me Now, Clark

Improve Your Personal Finances in One Week

Some consumer problems can be daunting and discouraging. Digging out from under a pile of credit card debt can take years. Saving for retirement is a slow process. But there are a lot of things you can do right away to make an immediate difference in your finances. Then you will have more money to pay off debt, save for the future, or take that vacation you've always wanted but couldn't afford. I've chosen twenty-five of my very best tips for this section, with a special emphasis on ones you can put to use today. Try a few, and you'll get instant satisfaction that will motivate you to try more of the money-saving tips in this book.

### 1. Search for unclaimed money in your name.

Do you have money in a bank or brokerage house account that hasn't been touched in a while? Or let's say you're the unknowing beneficiary of an insurance policy that's floating around out there, or maybe a late relative you never met left you some stock in a will. After a period of time, the state eventually rules those accounts or policies dormant, and the money is sent to an unclaimed-property office. Which state office it is sent to depends on where the company holding the money is based or where the deceased person lived.

*USA Today* reports that certain states suffering from budget problems have decided it's okay to steal these leftover funds from you. Washington, Delaware, Alabama, Oregon, South

Carolina, Louisiana, and Kentucky all changed their laws to make it legal to seize unclaimed money and not give it back. But there's good news. There's a way to find out whether you have dormant money so you can claim it before the state does! A website called MissingMoney .com allows you to type in your name and see if you are due a refund. You can also check for relatives, but only they can claim money in their name. Do a multistate search to include the state you live in and the states that include the headquarters of all your previous employers. In addition, always search in Delaware and Connecticut, as most stock brokerage and insurance companies are based in those two states.

Another website to check is Unclaimed.org. And if you've ever had an FHA loan, be sure to see if there are leftover assets waiting for you at HUD.gov. (Read "See If You're Owed a HUD Refund on an FHA Mortgage" on page 132 for more details on the latter.)

You could be a hero to a loved one, or be the beneficiary of money you didn't even know you had!

### 2. Start enjoying free TV and movies.

If you're like most Americans, you're probably paying $60 per month or more for cable or satellite TV service. It's not uncommon to pay more than $100. That's upward of $1,200 annually. Who *couldn't* use that money back in their pocket?

The high price of pay TV has forced more than 1 million Americans to disconnect their satellite or cable service, according to *The Wall Street Journal.* Are they going TV-less? No, they're getting TV content on the Web or with "rabbit ears" antennae instead.

That's right, you can fire your pay TV provider and use a simple pair of rabbit ears and a modestly priced digital converter box ($40–$60) to get over-the-air TV absolutely free. The picture you get over the air is actually superior to what you get when your satellite or cable provider gets done compressing its signal for distribution.

But getting your TV signal over the air means you're going to receive only the local broadcast channels. If you still want to get your cable fix, try going to websites such as Fancast.com or YouTube.com for free programming. Websites like Boxee.tv and Clicker.com act as virtual program guides to let you know what's playing where in cyberspace. Most of the major networks also have free programming available at their own websites.

Hulu.com was the real breakthrough service in this arena. It was like a poor man's DVR, where you could watch what you wanted when you wanted on demand with commercials. Of course, they've now changed their strategy to a "freemium" model: There's only a limited amount of programming available for free, and the rest can't be accessed until you pay $7.99 each month for their Hulu Plus pay service.

Certain cable channels have not yet made their content available on the Internet. But they'll ultimately have to do so or risk losing the advertising base of tech-savvy, high-income viewers. If there are specific programs you can't live without, you can always rent them from Netflix.com or a similar service.

I've been talking for three years about people disconnecting from the cable and satellite companies. Now that I've been with Netflix on demand for a year, I can tell you it's a real deal. My family almost never watches regular TV anymore. We simply use a Wi-Fi–enabled Blu-ray player to get the programming from Netflix to our TV. Netflix is $7.99 each month.

Ratcheting up the competition, Amazon has introduced unlimited streaming video as a feature of its Amazon Prime loyalty program. The main attraction of Amazon Prime was originally the offer of free two-day shipping on most online purchases, with no minimum order size for hardcore Amazon customers who wanted to pay $79 for annual membership. But the free streaming has been thrown in as a carrot to entice more casual customers to join. Right now there are only 5,000 programming choices on Prime, but that's expected to grow quickly. The monthly charges work out to be a little less than $6.60. Visit Amazon.com/Prime for more details.

I love the idea of competition creating innovation and more choice for you. When you think about how many more competitors will be coming to market soon, you realize it's going to become routine to watch video in a whole new way for very little dough.

### 3. Get unlimited texting and e-mailing for $10 per month.

Have you ever tried to use a smartphone and wound up feeling really dumb? Today's mobile devices are packed with so many features that it's easy to get confused when using one. That's where a handheld device called Peek comes in. The Peek is a supersimple-to-use mobile device for e-mail and texting at rock-bottom prices.

The Peek was originally marketed to tweens and teens because it's an e-mail-only device that does not feature any calling capability—we all know how young people actually think using a phone to talk is something only old folks do! But that approach missed a more valuable market segment. Now they've modified their business plan to cater to small businesses. Corporate types may not know how much their CrackBerry or iPhone costs each month if their company is paying for it. But entrepreneurs who are struggling to make a profit need to watch every penny.

The Peek Pronto sells for $70 in charcoal gray for businesspeople. (There's also a black cherry–colored model that would appeal to tweens.) Monthly service starts at $10. And there's never a contract! Think of it as a poor man's BlackBerry. If you have a teen whose texting is eating up your wallet, the Peek could present a solution. One thing Peek doesn't offer, however, is the ability to use your existing phone number. Visit GetPeek.com for more details.

Kajeet.com is another service that's geared to parents who want to monitor what their teens are doing with their mobile devices. This service has a full suite of parental controls that let you restrict certain numbers for incoming and outgoing calls and texts, select when the phone can be used, and more. Refurbished Kajeet phones are available for as little as $24.99. Monthly service with unlimited text messaging and sixty minutes of talk time starts at $14.99.

In addition, Kajeet allows parents to track the movement of their teens with a built-in locator for an additional $8 per month. Unlike Peek, Kajeet does allow you to move a phone number you already have over to their service.

### 4. Get a 2 percent cash-back card with no strings attached.

When the new credit card rules went into effect February 2010, the banks that issue the majority of cards in the United States were prohibited from practicing many of their common rip-offs. But that hasn't meant that the rip-offs have stopped completely; to the contrary, the banks have instead switched to cooking up new legitimate gouge fees, especially annual fees on cards that previously had no annual fees.

That's put a lot of people into the market for a new credit card. Fortunately, one respected low-cost brokerage house has stepped up to offer what I call the best credit card deal in America: Fidelity Investments.

Their Fidelity Retirement Rewards American Express Card takes your 2 percent cash back and deposits it directly into your IRA, 529 college savings plan, or Fidelity brokerage account. This is not 2 percent cash back only when you charge $500 on the third Tuesday of every other month; this is every single charge—no games, no gimmicks, no annual fees, and no limits on what you can earn back. Visit Fidelity.com or call 800-343-3548 for more details.

Notice that I didn't say a word about the interest rate of this card. I don't even know what the interest rate is! That's because this card should really be used only by people who do *not* run a monthly balance.

If you do run a balance, try hunting around for a credit card at your local credit union.

If you want another option, I also like the Pentagon Federal Credit Union Platinum Rewards card. I was alerted to this card by a website called CreditCardTuneUp.com, which I discuss later in the book. (See "Find the Best Reward Card for You" on page 183.)

Membership to Pen Fed Credit Union is usually limited to the Army, Air Force, Coast Guard, Homeland Security, other U.S. military and government organizations, and related groups and institutions. But anyone can join if they first join the National Military Family Association, a nonprofit advocacy organization for military families that requires only a onetime tax-deductible fee of $20 for entry. You don't even have to keep your membership active to remain in Pen Fed Credit Union. Visit PenFed.org or call 800-247-5626 for more details.

### 5. Check all your monthly statements line by line.

There's something brewing right now that I consider a national scandal. The cell phone companies are in cahoots with rip-off artists and they're stealing your money, doing courtesy billing for third-party crooks who push a variety of text messaging services.

I know that cell phone bills are impossible to understand. My last cell phone bill was fifty-six pages long! But I go through it page by page each month. I'll find something that's not legit about once every four months. Look for deceptive terms such as "Premium Content" or "Direct Bill Charge" (sometimes referred to as "DBC" on your bill).

Recently, I found a $2.95 charge for a ring tone that the provider's website claimed was free. I called my carrier and got my money back.

Too often, people today just get bills of all kinds charged to their credit card and never see a statement. Don't be one of them! Get a paper statement each month and scrutinize it line by line. But if you want to go green, you can also review your full bill online each month. Just don't fall into the trap of thinking you'll get around to viewing it online and then never do it.

Businesses are a major target because their phone bills can be pages and pages long. But this is war. Carriers think they can get away with stealing your money, but they can do so only if you allow it.

Sadly, the danger isn't limited to the world of telecommunications.

Christa DiBiase, the executive producer of my radio show, is completely obsessive-compulsive when it comes to checking her brokerage account online every day. Several years ago, she logged in and noticed that every single holding she owned had been liquidated, the address on her account was changed, and there were instructions to wire the money out of the country. She reported it immediately and was able to reverse all the damage. Her vigilance foiled a crime in progress.

Be sure to check your online brokerage or mutual fund account at least three times a week. After the fact, there is no protection under the law if your account is fraudulently accessed. You've got to be proactive.

When it comes to your credit card statement, you should go through it carefully on a monthly basis. You're allowed a full sixty days to dispute any fraudulent charges.

### 6. Start a Roth IRA.

If you're a regular listener or viewer of my radio or TV show, you hear me talk about the Roth IRA account all the time. In fact, Christa often refers to this wonderful investment option as my "girlfriend" because of my bias for it. Yet despite my enthusiasm, only about one in five Americans has a Roth account.

I think people are unnecessarily confused by the Roth. I want to demystify it for you.

With a Roth, you make regular contributions each pay period, just like you would with a 401(k) at work. You can even set up automatic payroll deductions like with a 401(k). But unlike a 401(k), a Roth gives no tax break up front; the benefit is that every single penny you put in can be spent tax-free after age fifty-nine and a half! And you can contribute up to $5,000 annually, unless you're over fifty, in which case you can contribute $6,000. Where do you put Roth money? Just about anywhere you want: in a bank, credit union, or no-load ("no load" means no commission) mutual fund; with a full-commission or discount stockbroker or a financial planner. When you are young and starting out, you should put the money with a discount broker or in a no-load mutual fund because then you're reducing management fees. I want all your money working for you.

It's important to know that a Roth is just an empty shell or a vacant house and you've got to put some "furniture" in it. One of my favorite pieces of furniture is a total stock market index—where you own tiny little slices and dices of thousands of companies across the spectrum of capitalism.

Roths can be flexible, depending on which company you choose to invest with. You can start with $50 and put in as little as $50 each month. (See "Start a Roth with $100 or Less" on page 193 in the Personal Finance chapter.) If you already have a regular IRA or a 401(k) at work, don't think it's an either/or proposition with a Roth. You can have all three types of retirement savings accounts without any conflict.

### 7. Fire your bank and join a credit union.

It's often been said that there are no free lunches. But I think that credit unions come pretty darn close.

I have been a member of four different credit unions over the years. I first learned about them in the early 1970s while working as a civilian employee in the Air Force. At the time, I overheard an officer speaking about the great loan rates the credit union offered, and I had to check it out for myself.

What exactly is a credit union? It's like a bank in which you are a shareholder. In other words, you own the place! Membership is basically available to anyone, based on where you live or what profession you have. There's a nominal fee to become a member and once you join, it's like you've taken a step up to the "mezzanine" of the financial world with a ton of great products at your disposal. For example, my credit union currently offers car loans at 2.99 percent interest to those with good credit. Home equity loans are available at 4 percent for five years.

You have access to all the usual services you would with a giant bank, including ATM cards, savings instruments like CDs, and more. And while credit unions might still have rip-off charges for overdrafts on your savings or checking accounts, they're usually lower than elsewhere.

In addition, credit unions offered interest rates on credit cards that were 8 percent cheaper on average than the giant monster mega-banks' rates, according to recent figures from Datatrac. That alone can add up to big bucks each month if you carry a monthly balance.

Customer service is outstanding at most credit unions—with some limited exceptions. The one thing you *don't* get with a credit union is convenience. Credit unions typically don't have as many branches as the giant monster mega-banks and they may be fewer and farther between.

Visit CUNA.org or FindaCreditUnion.com to find a credit union to join.

**8. Raise the deductible on your insurance.**

Insurance is one of those things in life that nobody wants to buy, but we do it because it's necessary. I have a way you can save on it, and it doesn't even involve switching your insurer or making any other scary changes.

Pick up the phone and raise the deductible on your insurance policy. Do this for both your automobile and homeowners insurance policies.

The typical auto insurance customer can save fifteen to thirty percent on their premium for collision coverage by bumping their deductible up from $250 to $500, according to the lastest numbers I've seen from *Consumer Reports*. Those savings jump—on average to forty percent—if you make the leap to a $1,000 deductible.

When it comes to homeowners insurance, we've come a long way from the $500 deductible of yesteryear. You should raise the deductible to either $1,000 or $2,500, regardless of whether you're in a house, a townhouse, a co-op, or a condo. Some mortgage lenders may have a cap on how high you can set your deductible. Check with yours about any limitations.

By doing this, you'll pay less in premiums, but more important, you'll reduce the risk that your insurer will cancel your coverage because you made too many claims. Today homeowners insurance can be used only in the case of a catastrophic loss. It's a "use it and lose it" proposition.

And I recommend that you update your coverage for the value of your home and its contents every five years, if needed. Don't wait until *after* a catastrophic loss to find out there's no way you could rebuild and replace with what the insurer is offering.

One final word about car insurance. If you have an old "beater" car that's of little value, you may be unsure if you should get collision and/or comprehensive insurance. The general rule of thumb is that if the cost of full coverage annually is greater than 10 percent of the car's value, you'd be better-off dropping both collision and comprehensive coverage and having only liability on your policy.

**9. Avoid extended warranties.**

For years, I've been trying to convince people that extended warranties are garbage. I felt like the lone wolf in the wilderness until *Consumer Reports* started backing me up.

Electronics seldom fail, according to the magazine. In fact, TVs fail at a rate of only 3 percent in the first four years of ownership. Why would anyone buy a warranty when you have a 97 percent chance that your TV will work for numerous years?

In the world of flat screens, VIZIO was once the king of off-brands and their failure rate was only 3 percent. Ditto for Sharp. Samsung, a premium brand, has only a 4 percent failure rate. So whether you're talking name brand or off-brand, the failure rate all around is minuscule.

In addition, extended warranties are extremely expensive relative to the cost of the item you're buying, and that makes them a poor investment. *The New York Times*, for example, found a popular Nikon camera with a warranty that was 27 percent of the purchase price at Best Buy! A netbook they looked at had a warranty that was nearly a third of the purchase price!

But that still hasn't convinced everyone they should avoid extended warranties. The *Hartford Courant* reports that sales of extended warranties were up 10 percent toward the end of the last decade, and almost 50 percent of consumers bought extended warranties on computer purchases.

You never want to insure a rapidly depreciating asset. And no products depreciate faster than electronics or computers. You get back only 8 to 15 cents out of every warranty dollar, after you account for depreciation and how quickly technology becomes outdated.

Luckily, there is a free way to extend a manufacturer's warranty. Many credit card issuers will double the manufacturer's original warranty up to one additional year if you use their card to make your purchase. (See page 34 of the Cars chapter for my take on extended auto warranties.)

### 10. Switch to a cheap no-contract cell phone provider.

It seems like every week there's a new price point being set in the telecommunications world. As I write this, there's an all-out war going on between the traditional Big Four wireless carriers—AT&T, Sprint, Verizon, and T-Mobile—and smaller operators such as MetroPCS, Cricket, Boost Mobile, Virgin Mobile, Straight Talk, and others. When one drops the price on its rate plans, the others are sure to follow. (T-Mobile has agreed to be purchased by AT&T, but the deal has yet to be approved by federal regulators.)

The Big Four have historically pushed expensive "bucket of minutes" business models with twenty-four-month contracts. That's allowed the smaller operators to carve out a market niche by offering cheaper unlimited calling plans with no contracts.

Which would you rather have?

I recently switched from a Big Four carrier to Straight Talk. I'm paying $45 each month for an unlimited calling/texting/Web plan and I love it. There's also a monthly plan for $30 that comes with 1,000 minutes, 1,000 text messages, and 30 MB of data for Web surfing and free 411 calls. Visit StraightTalk.com for more details or a participating Walmart store near you.

Straight Talk actually uses Verizon's and AT&T's networks to place calls. So you can go with Verizon or AT&T and pay around $100 each month for unlimited calling and texting, or you can go with Straight Talk and use AT&T's and Verizon's infrastructure for $45 monthly. You decide.

More recently, I've been testing an Android-based phone manufactured by Huawei on the MetroPCS network. It sells for $100 with no contract for now. Monthly service with almost unlimited everything is $50. (And I want you to know that when I test something, I buy it. I don't accept *any* freebies from manufacturers or carriers *at all*, because I want you to know I'm unbought and unbossed.)

Do I like the MetroPCS Huawei as much as my current main phone, the EVO 4G from Sprint? No way. That EVO is so amazing it practically makes my breakfast in the morning!

But if I wasn't spoiled by the EVO, I would love this particular MetroPCS phone. Metro-PCS has a reliable network that works in about ninety percent of the United States. And unlike the EVO, the Huawei actually has good battery life. Visit MetroPCS.com for more details.

If you don't do a lot of calling, Virgin Mobile has what I think is the best plan in America at this time. You get basic unlimited everything for $25 month with one qualifier: A scant 300 minutes of calling each month. This could be a great option for Web-, e-mail-, and text-happy people who don't do a lot of talking, like my daughter Stephanie. Visit VirginMobile-USA.com for more details.

### 11. Change your landline service to POTS.

Are you *still* paying for a landline? If so, you've got to know about the tariff rate.

The tariff rate—aka Plain Old Telephone Service (POTS)—is an ultra-cheap regulated rate set by your state's local telephone monopoly. You get a basic dial tone with no frills or extra features. Monthly service typically costs between $7 and $18. But you'll still have to pay additional junk fees of $10 to $13 each month.

To get it, just call your monopoly phone company and ask for the "state-regulated tariff rate" or the "POTS line." If the representative you speak to feigns ignorance, ask to be transferred to a supervisor and make your request.

I have a landline at home that my wife will not allow me to drop. In my home state of Georgia, the POTS costs us a little more than $29 each month. So we still throw away $360 each year—even though we use that phone only about two minutes each month. I'd call that getting ripped off at a discount. So I skip eating a couple of days each month to make up for it! (Just kidding.)

### 12. Get free phone service for life for $200.

For many years, people have been looking for a better way to make landline calls than through their monopoly phone company. Vonage was a real game-changer on this front and then other Voice over Internet Protocol (VoIP) services like Skype came along. But you still had to put up with pesky monthly charges.

Well, what if you could have free home phone service for life with no monthly fees? You can with Ooma.

The Ooma device looks like a house intercom. You plug a cable for your Internet into it; you plug your traditional landline phone into it; and suddenly you have phone service! The makers of Ooma claim they have a built-in processor that makes their sound quality comparable to monopoly phone service. The calls do sound great.

When I first discussed Ooma on my radio show in 2007, many of my staffers were speculating about how long it would take for Ooma to end up in Clark's Graveyard—that repository of all those wacky, entrepreneurial ideas I love so much that never find their footing in the marketplace and go broke. (See the Clark's Graveyard chapter at the end of this book.)

But fast-forward to today and Ooma is still around—with a new cheaper price! When Ooma first launched, it was priced around $400. Now that has dropped to $200 to $249, depending on where you get it. I've even seen it at Costco Wholesale for $179. And that's it. No more monthly fees ever, though you will pay about $11 annually for an FCC charge.

Of course, "lifetime service" means the lifetime of the company, not your lifetime! But at $200 or less, that's a price point at which I am willing to take a leap of faith. Visit Ooma.com for more info.

### 13. Exit a cell phone contract without early termination fees.

Cell phone contracts are rapidly becoming a thing of the past as more and more people switch to noncontract carriers. But maybe you recently re-upped your service or switched to a more expensive phone with one of the Big Four carriers. That likely means you have a fresh pair of twenty-four-month handcuffs known as a contract. Happily, there is a way to pull a Houdini and get out of that stinking contract!

CellSwapper.com and CellTradeUSA.com are two websites that offer you the chance. For about $20, both services will allow you to trade your phone and contract to someone who wants it. You can also take over someone else's contract, which will allow you to avoid the $35 activation fee on a new phone.

Of course, the type of phone you have is very important when you're looking to swap out—that is, the "hotter" your phone, the more likely someone else will want it. Sprint contracts are typically the hardest to exit. The reason is twofold: First, they have abysmal customer no-service. Second, many of their phones lack the coolness factor and that makes them harder to unload. On the flip side, if you're looking to take an existing contract over from someone else, you might have luck with Sprint users.

Finally, there's always the poor man's way to get out of your existing contract. When you get some mice-type in the mail saying the service fees are changing, that is your opportunity to exit from your contract without paying a cancellation fee.

### 14. Supplement your income with a legitimate work-at-home job.

The conventional wisdom about education and employment—that as your level of education rises, the less likely you are to be affected by layoffs—was completely flipped on its head during the Great Recession. The recession knew no boundaries in terms of education, skill level, training, or years on the job.

If you have skills of a certain nature, you can try picking up some consulting work or freelancing on a per-job basis. The Internet offers a variety of sites that hook freelancers up with employers. Some of the more popular ones I read about in the *San Francisco Chronicle* include crowdSPRING.com, eLance.com, Guru.com, and oDesk.com.

Then there's a service called Fiverr.com, through which people share things they're willing to do for $5. You might be able to hire someone to review your résumé, design a website, improve a PowerPoint presentation, or even write your maid-of-honor speech—for just $5! The low price is really just a loss leader that allows work-at-home types to attract a client base for their particular area of expertise.

I read about one of the wackier gigs out there on Fiverr.com on the MSN Money website. Apparently there's a resident of Newport Beach, California, who will write whatever personal messages you want in the sand, take a picture, and then e-mail it to you for $5. It's a business that brings in about $300 dollars a month, according to MSN Money . . . just for playing in the sand!

Think about it in your life: What can *you* do to earn extra income? At ClarkHoward.com, I have a list of companies offering work-at-home opportunities that I believe are legitimate, Many of them involve being a virtual call center operator. You typically need a phone, a computer, and an Internet connection to do this kind of work. Visit my site and search keyword "work at home" to see the complete list.

### 15. Reduce your withholding.

People will often come up to me around tax time and happily ask for advice on what to do with their giant refund. They treat it like it's found money or some kind of windfall. But it's not.

I'd prefer that you get no refund at all. If you are getting one, it means that you've made an interest-free loan to the government and your money has been working for them—not you—all year long.

Doesn't Uncle Sam already get enough of your money? Why give him more? Many people try to justify their tax refunds by saying it forces them to save money. Nice try. While I agree that saving money is a valid concern, I believe there's a better way to accomplish that goal. Let's say you typically get a refund of $1,200 every year. Try reducing your withholding at work by $100 each month and have your bank or credit union automatically transfer that $100 into a savings account. You never see it, so you never miss it. But the end result is that you'll build your savings *and* earn interest all year long.

You can talk to your human resources department or a payroll specialist at work to reduce your withholding. I want you to be even-steven when it comes time to do your taxes—neither a borrower nor a lender (to the government) be.

### 16. Lower your student loan payment.

At the end of the last decade, a radical new change on the student loan front took place that could potentially benefit a lot of borrowers. Income-Based Repayment (IBR) plans became available to those with federally guaranteed student loans such as Stafford Loans and Direct PLUS Loans for graduate students.

Under this new repayment program, your monthly payment is based on your current income and family size. In fact, it could be an unprecedented zero dollars! For example, a single person earning $16,245 annually would have a zero-dollar payment under the program's terms, according to the Project on Student Debt (PSD) website.

The IBR plan is something you have to apply for; a deal like this won't simply come to you! Start by contacting the lender or lenders who hold your student loan(s) for more details on the application process.

Unfortunately, I've been hearing from callers who say their lenders are ignoring them when they ask about the IBR plan. Many lenders simply don't have any info up on their websites. It's difficult to say whether the lenders are incompetent or purposely playing dumb to avoid losing revenue. Let's hope it's just an oversight.

Fortunately, the PSD has a nonprofit info site called IBRInfo.org to help you navigate through any difficulty you might have getting into an IBR plan. The site even offers a beta calculator with a detailed Q&A that will help you figure what you need to pay to stay current on your student loans.

I can't overstate the importance of staying current on student loans. In particular, if you have private student loans in default, the lender is allowed to seize your wages and empty your account without proving that you owe the money. Don't let that happen to you if you fall on hard times. Get going with an IBR instead.

### 17. Comparison shop for health care.

One of my big beefs with medicine is how hard it is to figure out the cost of medical care *before* you actually receive it.

If you don't have health insurance, or you have big out-of-pocket expenses with health insurance—say you're in a high-deductible plan and it really matters what you're going to be charged—there's a website called PriceDoc.com. It allows you to put doctors and providers into competition with one another to provide the best cash prices for your medical care.

If you have insurance and like to comparison shop, ZocDoc.com is a new website that allows you to locate doctors by specialty and the kind of insurance they accept. You can also read user-generated reviews of doctors and make an appointment online instantly with their office. As I write this, ZocDoc is available only in Chicago, Dallas, New York, San Francisco, and Washington, D.C.

Over the next five years, medicine is going to be brought kicking and screaming into the era of actually having to post prices—much as the doc-in-a-box retail clinics that I love so much do. This should have happened a long time ago. But if you need to know what a procedure is going to cost now, these are a couple of ways for you to do it and shop around for the best price.

### 18. Let online pharmacies bid for your business.

There are so many ways to attack the high price of prescriptions, but I want to share one listener-suggested tip: BidRx.com offers a new way to shop for medication by letting pharmacies bid for your business.

There are actually two benefits to the BidRx model. First, you enter the name of your desired name-brand medication and BidRx will give you a list of generic alternatives. That in itself can represent a savings to you. Be sure to contact the doctor who wrote your original prescription to see if any of the suggested generics would work for you.

The second benefit is what really makes BidRx unique. It puts your prescription—whether generic or brand name—up for electronic bid among independent pharmacies. You get instantaneous price quotes right there on your computer.

This is a completely free service that requires you only to register at the site. Use "clark" as the referral code. (Don't be thrown off by the wording you'll see online, saying that a referral code comes from an "approved marketing agent." In no way, shape, or form do I receive any money from BidRx. They simply set up "clark" as the referral code because their traffic spiked after I talked about them on my radio show and website.)

We are in an era when there are so many breakthroughs in medication. But I still think you should be wary of seeking out the latest and greatest drugs. You don't want to be a guinea pig for a pharmaceutical sales rep who convinces doctors to write scripts for a hot new drug that later turns out to harm your health.

The safe choice is to stick with a time-tested and well-proven generic of a long-issued brand name. The only exception to this rule might be if you have an unusual condition that does not respond to existing medications.

### 19. Consider medical tourism.

For several years now, people have been going overseas to places like Thailand, India, Costa Rica, Brazil, and other far-flung locations to save money on surgeries. This practice is known as medical tourism.

While there are some inconveniences in going far away for care, the cost differences can be enormous. For example, a hip replacement that might run you $60,000 in the United States could be $12,000 to $15,000 overseas.

I'll be the first to admit that I'm a complete idiot when it comes to most medical issues, but I think if you're grappling with the cost issue alone, this is a no-brainer.

The number of Americans who are medical tourists is rising 20 percent per year, according to a recent report in the *Financial Times* of London. While the savings may be extraordinary, the big question remains, "What kind of care will I get overseas?"

While the quality does vary, many places overseas have first-rate hospitals that cater to foreigners. The *Financial Times* reports that Singapore is the best place to go overseas for Western-quality medical care. You'll save substantial amounts there—up to 50 percent off— and have a private nurse twenty-four hours a day.

Far from being a possible insurance risk, medical tourism is actually encouraged by some insurers. Several Southern California insurers have provisions for treatment in Mexico that can save 40 percent on insurance premiums. Meanwhile, a couple of insurers in the state of South Carolina offer care at Bumrungrad International Hospital in Bangkok.

Just beware that if you go abroad for medical treatment, you'll typically have no liability protection or recourse in the event of malpractice, plus there's limited availability of aftercare.

You'll want to vet facilities carefully before you go. Check the credentials of the doctors and surgeons who will treat you. Are they trained or board certified in the United States or another Western country? And be sure the hospital or facility you're thinking about using is certified by Joint Commission International, a division of the major U.S. accreditation organization of the same name.

If you plan to work with a medical tourism company, such as Medical Tours International or Planet Hospital, to handle the arrangements of your trip, be sure that the hospital recognizes the company and that the company has carefully vetted the hospital.

### 20. Buy prescription eyeglasses for as little as $7.

Eyeglasses don't have to cost hundreds of dollars. ZenniOptical.com is just one of several websites that offer prescription eyeglasses starting at $7 per pair with shipping costs of $5.

How can they be so cheap? Zenni grinds its lenses in China and offers absolutely no service after the sale. That's led some of my listeners to become disenchanted with Zenni.

But I've used them multiple times and never had a problem. You can even order only the frames at half off Zenni's already low prices!

If you plan on ordering, get your vision checked by an eye doctor first to determine your prescription. You'll also want to find out your pupillary distance (PD)—the space between the center of your pupils, expressed in millimeters. Certain frames will not work with certain PDs because the center of the lenses will either be too wide or too narrow. You need a fit that's just right.

When my ten-year-old daughter recently needed glasses, my wife wanted to go to Costco Wholesale. But I nearly had a coronary when I looked at the price of the frames and lenses my daughter liked—they were $80! I quickly suggested Zenni, prompting my wife to blow her top and tell me not to be so cheap. We soon reached an agreement: My daughter got the pair of glasses at Costco, but she got a spare pair from Zenni for $19. It turns out that she likes the pair from Zenni better than the one from Costco!

Some people wonder how Zenni glasses can be any good if they're so cheap. I have a friend who is an investigative reporter for an Atlanta TV station. A couple of years ago, he did a story about eyeglasses in which he compared Zenni and a number of other more expensive brands. The Zennis had perfect prescriptions compared with the glasses that were filled at well-known U.S. optometry chain stores. Buying cheap glasses does not automatically mean you'll get bad quality.

A host of Zenni competitors including EyeBuyDirect.com, GlassesUnlimited.com, and GlassesShop.com also offer prescription eyeglasses at a similarly low price point.

### 21. Enroll at a hospital gym.

If you're like most people, you overindulge in calories during the holidays and then make a New Year's resolution to eat better and exercise more. Here's a word of warning to avoid getting eaten alive by gym salespeople.

The health club industry basically has two business models. In the good one, you pay monthly or quarterly with no contract. The sleazy business model, however, involves long-term contracts designed to give your checking account a workout.

With the sleazoids, the downfall begins when they offer you a free tour of the facilities. The tour is done by a commissioned salesperson with the intention of getting you to sign a multiyear contract. Once you sign that contract, the gym does what's called "moving paper."

They sell off the contract to a finance company that will take the note on for pennies on the dollar. That creates additional incentive for the club to sign up more members—and hope that none of them ever show up to work out all at once!

In a recent filing with the Securities and Exchange Commission, Bally Total Fitness disclosed that the average member visits the club one half of one time per week. You'd be hard-pressed to find any fitness expert who recommends a full workout only once every two weeks!

There is, however, a better way for health clubs to do business: by allowing customers to pay month to month or quarterly with no real contract. That creates incentive for the club to help you stay on a healthy regimen so you'll keep coming back. They win and you win!

I recommend checking out hospital-affiliated fitness centers. They're usually rehab-based or geared toward the hospital staff. They're clean, well run, and don't force contracts on you. Best of all, most will sell memberships to the public. Visit the hospital nearest you to see if this kind of gym facility exists in your neighborhood.

Another option I've noticed popping up in vacant storefronts around the country is the ultra-low-cost no-frills gym that is open twenty-four hours and tends to price out at around $15 each month with no contract. But beware: These gyms might not have showers for you to use; they simply offer the use of exercise equipment at rock-bottom prices.

### 22. Use coupon code sites to save when shopping online.

The use of online coupon codes always sees a boost during the holiday season. Both Black Friday and Cyber Monday—those days that follow Thanksgiving and mark the start of the holiday shopping season—have helped popularize the use of online coupon code sites. But these sites also offer a really great way to save money all year long.

Some popular coupon code sites include RetailMeNot.com, CouponCabin.com, and BradsDeals.com. When you visit them, they'll reveal secret codes you can enter for extra savings when checking out at a retailer's website.

In fact, it's a good idea before checking out at any website to enter that retailer's name plus the words "coupon code" into a search engine and see what's out there.

When it comes to buying online, it's very important to read the website's return policy. Some online retailers have awful policies, while Amazon and Zappos.com generally have favorable ones.

Here's another tip: Christa DiBiase, the executive producer of my radio show, always checks to see if she can get credit for her child's college savings account by clicking through to an online retailer via UPromise.com or BabyMint.com. In six years of doing that, she estimates her online purchases have contributed about $1,100 to her daughter's future educational expenses!

### 23. Buy three copies of the Sunday newspaper.

It's amazing to think that the use of coupons was very uncool before the recession. But I've never been about cool; I just like to save money. Many Americans jumped aboard the coupon train when the Great Recession hit.

Coupons are the kinds of low-hanging fruit that I really encourage you to grab because they're so easy. Here's how to do it: First, I want you to buy three copies of the Sunday newspaper just for those glossy RedPlum and SmartSource coupon circulars. As an alternative, you can also visit RedPlum.com and SmartSource.com to print coupons for free, though you may find some variation between what's available online and what's in your Sunday paper.

Once you've gathered all your coupons, visit a site like CouponMom.com that breaks down weekly sales by state and explains which coupons to use where and when for maximum savings.

The second key here is to know your prices. You don't need a complicated price book. Just track the prices of your top ten items. Keep an eye on them for a month and a half or so. If you know the regular prices of your ten most common purchases at local stores, then you'll know when to stock up on something when it goes on sale. If you have a coupon at that point, so much the better! MyGroceryDeals.com will notify you when items of your choice go on sale.

Third, be flexible. Brand loyalty will cost you money. If you have a coupon for a brand you're not familiar with, why not give it a try and see if you like it? You may be surprised.

Finally, there's one last step to saving money with coupons: Know your store's policy. Some grocers will double manufacturers' coupons up to 50 cents every day and others will actually accept competitors' coupons. So a coupon worth 50 cents could actually be more valuable to you than a coupon worth 75 cents if your grocery store will double the first coupon.

When it comes to food shopping, a little coupon strategy will go a long way!

One side note here: There's been a big push to get consumers to use electronic coupons. I loaded an e-coupon app on my smartphone but soon deleted it because I found I never used it. E-coupons have been something of a bust so far. That will likely change in the future, but right now Americans still prefer clipping traditional newspaper coupons.

### 24. Buy private label groceries at the supermarket.

There's no better way to instantly save up to 30 or 40 percent off your grocery bill than buying a store brand. You won't even have to change where you shop.

Before you balk at this particular tip, know that store brands are much better than they once were. Remember those plain packages marked "cola," "potato chips," or "potted meat product" branded with big, black NO FRILLS logos that were the kiss of death? They're gone.

But Americans have been slow to buy private label groceries as readily as shoppers in most other developed countries. Canadians, for example, have always had a strong focus on no-frills goods. They've even perfected premium-style store brands that look like they're name brands. President's Choice—one outstanding Canadian private label—has managed to create a sense of high-quality products at a low price. That name, of course, is a bit ironic considering that Canada has a parliamentary government headed by a prime minister!

We're now seeing widespread market segmentation of store brands here at home, with up to three different versions of a particular generic product—each with a different price point and different packaging. One product might be superior to the brand name; another could be equivalent in quality but 30 percent cheaper; and a third will be low quality for a dirt-cheap price, much like the original no-frills goods of the late 1970s and early 1980s.

If you're not yet buying store brands, here's my advice: Grab a store brand and your favorite national brand and compare the ingredients. They're very similar in most cases. So why not give the no-name a try? If it turns out you don't like it, you've bought a piece of garbage just once. But if it's good, you can buy it moving forward and save each time.

### 25. Make your razor blades last longer.

In February 2006, a gentleman called my radio show and told me he'd been using the same razor for a year. The caller, a metallurgist, revealed that blades don't degrade from shaving but instead corrode over time from the moisture that collects on them.

The man said he uses a blow dryer to dry his razor after each use. His call prompted others to share their tricks for maximizing a razor's life.

At first I was incredulous. Using a disposable razor for even a month sounded crazy—let alone a year. But then I got inspired by the discussion (and the expense of shaving blades) and decided to take a single 17-cent razor and make it last for twelve months.

I didn't dry my razor with a blow dryer but instead took the lazy man's approach of just blotting it dry on a towel.

The razor actually lasted for a whole year, and I was very pleased not to have to throw away money on blades anymore. And no, I didn't cut myself even once. The moment I bleed, that razor is out of my life!

After my experiment was well under way, I opened a drawer under my sink and found two fifty-five-count bags of double-edged razors that I'd gotten on clearance at a warehouse club. One bag was open and had fifty-one shavers left, while the other was completely sealed. Using one blade a year, I'd have to live past one hundred to use up the package that was already open. I'd have to live to 158 years to use both bags. I don't expect to live that long, so I'll be donating that unopened package to a shelter where my wife and I volunteer.

# Cars

For most people, buying a car is the second-largest expense they'll ever undertake—after you consider the cost of housing. The topic of car buying is also one that results in some of the most painful calls on my show.

I hate hearing about people who get taken when they're shopping for a vehicle—be it new or used. So in this chapter, we'll cover everything from researching a sensible ride to arranging financing to actually making the purchase. Plus, I have special pointers on the dangers of leasing, extended auto warranties, and much more.

## DOING YOUR RESEARCH BEFORE A PURCHASE

### CLARK'S GREATEST HITS

#### *Buy a used vehicle instead of a new one*

When you're considering a new car versus a used car, I want you to think about the bigger picture of car ownership costs. It's more than just the sticker price and the expense of gas. AAA reports that the true annual cost of owning and operating a new car is $9,369.

Ouch! That painful figure takes into account hidden costs such as depreciation, insurance, maintenance, and interest on a car loan.

With a used car, however, somebody else has already taken a hit on the depreciation, which is really just a fancy way of saying that new cars lose a ton of value the minute they are driven off the dealer lot. When you buy used, you let some other poor soul absorb that loss up front.

Buying used, however, can be fraught with danger. In my radio work, we have something informally known as "Car Call Mondays." Every Monday, my staffers have to ration the number of car calls that get on the air. People flood the phone lines after buying suspect used vehicles over the weekend.

With used car purchases, you buy "as is"—no matter what condition the car is in. The vehicle and all its warts become your problem. If it comes with any warranty, it's usually very limited. Yet if you know how to buy safely, your wallet will smile at you, I promise! Visit CarGurus.com to get some help sorting through the critical mass of used cars in your area. (See "Have a Certified Mechanic Inspect a Used Car Before Purchase" on page 28.)

## Check a car's repair record before buying

Buying a used car involves a little more risk than buying a new car because you never know how the previous owner treated that vehicle. One way to minimize that risk is to buy used car models that have proven to be reliable.

The best place to get that information is in *Consumer Reports*. The magazine publishes its Annual Auto Issue every April, containing a rundown of all its top picks for the new model year. Near the back of the April issue, you'll also find detailed information on used cars.

The Auto Issue lays out *Consumer Reports'* top used car picks by price category ("Less than $4,000," "$4,000–$6,000," and up). There are also detailed reliability ratings for the past six model years on every possible nameplate, which are compiled from reports about seventeen common trouble spots in more than a million cars on the road. This latter feature gives you a great vantage point on long-term reliability.

Another helpful feature is the magazine's list of "Used Cars to Avoid" and a companion tally called the "Worst of the Worst" list. You *never* want to buy one of the stinkers on these lists!

If you stick with *Consumer Reports'* used vehicle recommendations, odds are good that you won't have any major problems. You shouldn't have to buy an extended warranty.

Visit ConsumerReports.org to purchase onetime access or read the April issue for free at your local library.

*I've always been a "thrifty" person, and at times have been ridiculed for it, so imagine my delight when I first listened to Clark Howard. I bought my first new car in 1991, a 4-door Geo Metro, and named him Herschel (after the rock group "Swim Herschel Swim" because I used to take Herschel 4-wheeling and through streams). I had researched cars for months, and got the car with the highest mpg and one that also fit my string bass and two cellos, plus several violins and violas. Clark says to pay it off and then keep your car until it dies. I did both. I traded my car in only last year when I finally got a new car. Yes, that's 1991 to 2009. I lost track of how many times the speedometer flipped, but with regular oil changes and good care, that little car still gave me up to 42 mpg. I only gave it up because it had died a few times in the middle of traffic and as I drive for a living, I had to have a reliable car. The new auto dealer gave me $800 for it, and it wouldn't even pass state inspection. They said someone bought it right away off the car lot too.*

*Thank you Clark! By the way, my new car is almost paid for too! I love my Red Pontiac Vibe. His name is Red Flash.*

*Tristan A., UT*

## Know a potential purchase's total operating cost

When you're in the market for new wheels and you've narrowed it down to one or two different vehicles, I want you to step back and consider the total operating cost of your top contenders.

Many people think of the vehicle's expense as the price tag alone, but there's also the cost of insurance, gas, and maintenance. Beyond that, the real cost of a new car is depreciation, which is how much it loses in value during the initial years of ownership.

KBB.com (*Kelley Blue Book*) said that half of all 2010 model year vehicles were expected to maintain less than 20 percent of their initial value after five years. So consider that before buying a fancy new car. Why not buy a not-so-fancy used car instead and let somebody else handle the depreciation?

If you're still set on buying new, there's a "total operating costs" interactive tool at

NewCarBuyersGuide.com that lets you compare the costs of ownership for up to four different vehicles over the course of five years.

The way to really save money is to drive your new car long past five years—at least ten years to absorb all the depreciation. The interactive tool is a start to get you thinking in the right direction about total operating cost.

## Consider a hybrid vehicle with early payback

People often wonder what the payback is on fuel-efficient vehicles. A few years ago, it would have been hard to find a true payback. But that math has changed significantly. More often than not, a hybrid or diesel will save you money, even though you spend more up front.

A recent report from IntelliChoice.com—a company that specializes in automotive ownership cost and value analysis—found that the most economically efficient vehicle is a clean diesel: the VW Jetta TDI. Over a five-year cycle (or 70,000 miles), it's more than $6,000 cheaper to own this than a gas engine version of the same car—even though the diesel costs $2,000 more up front.

In all, IntelliChoice.com graded fifty-one hybrids and clean diesels on the cost of fuel, maintenance, and repair; retained value; insurance; and taxes and licensing fees over the first five years of ownership. Thirty-five of those vehicles offered a better cost of ownership versus their gas engine counterparts.

Another standout vehicle is the GMC Sierra 1500 crew cab hybrid 2WD, which costs about $500 more up front but is more than $5,000 cheaper to own over five years. Other top picks include the Toyota Prius (versus the Camry) and the Chevy Silverado 1500 crew cab hybrid 2WD.

On the flip side, one car that is an absolute bomb as a hybrid and should be avoided is the Lexus LS 600 H. Over the first five years, you will lose almost $25,000 compared with the gas engine version!

There are still some concerns about the reliability of hybrids and clean diesels. Those will be worked out in time.

For me, I buy alternative-fuel vehicles because I want to be part of the process of reducing our dependence on foreign oil. So I'm happy to be an early adopter of new car technologies because I believe that it's important for our national security—even if it means taking a financial hit.

I recently outfitted my Prius with an aftermarket conversion kit that turns it into a plug-in hybrid. Now when I'm driving up to 50 miles per hour on streets, I do it as an electric-only vehicle, with no gas assist whatsoever. (The cost of the electricity is a little over a penny per mile.) A gas assist is still necessary when I'm traveling at freeway speeds. I'm averaging about ninety miles per gallon now, which is actually a little less than I expected.

The cost of the conversion kit? After a recent price reduction, it's dropped to $7,000. But I paid $9,000 when I bought the kit before the reduction. At $9,000, I'll almost *never* make my money back. But again, I'm happy to be at the forefront of alternative-fuel vehicles because I believe they are important to our future. Visit PlugInSolutions.net for more info about the conversion kit I bought.

## Vet out problem cars online

In the aftermath of Hurricanes Katrina and Rita, I gave warnings about flood cars entering the used car market. At that time, hundreds of thousands of vehicles were rebuilt and had their titles "washed." This is a recurring problem that happens anytime we have a major hurricane season or flooding.

Dishonest people take flooded vehicles into certain states where they can easily wash titles. That action removes any evidence that the vehicle was ever in a flood. Cars with washed titles can then be sold to any dealership across the country that either doesn't know or doesn't care that they're buying a flood vehicle.

These cars often end up in the hands of "curb stoners," illegal dealers who run ads in the paper. They pretend they're selling their sister's car or their mother's car and they hope you don't know what they know. About 20 percent of these cars go to unsuspecting people overseas. The other 80 percent stay right here at home.

To the naked eye, you can't tell that anything is amiss with these cars. But you'll know you've got a flood car when you encounter failed electrical systems throughout the vehicle.

A lot of people will pay CARFAX.com $35 to run the vehicle identification number (VIN) to check for title problems, liens, odometer rollback, salvage history, and more. That's a good idea. But I want you to be doubly sure by also running the VIN through a free database operated by the National Insurance Crime Bureau at NICB.org.

Even if the car checks out in both databases, you should still have the vehicle inspected by a diagnostic mechanic before you buy (as I explain below). If the used car you want checks out in CARFAX and NICB, and it passes a diagnostic inspection, you can be confident it is a good car.

## A CLARK FAVORITE
### *Have a certified mechanic inspect a used car before purchase*

I was recently reminded of the dangers of used car buying when an unfortunate motorist broke down and had to pull into my driveway! Can you imagine the irony? I spend a lot of my days warning people not to buy used car lemons and here I had just such a drama playing out in front of my eyes.

In this particular instance, the motorist was a member of the U.S. Air Force who had bought the used car from a Craigslist seller. The airman had just picked up the car and didn't even make it home before the vehicle broke down.

I bring this story up to show you that all used cars are sold "as is," whether by a private seller or a licensed dealer—unless they come with a written warranty. Worse yet, the seller is not required by law to be honest about the condition of the vehicle. Whatever representations they make about the car can be false.

On my radio show, I talk to so many people who are duped when buying a used car. We call them "razor blade calls" because they're so painful to hear. There's usually nothing I can do to help.

Here's my key rule for used car buying: Have the car inspected by a certified diagnostic mechanic of your choice as a condition of purchase. You can leave a deposit if you wish but specify in writing that the money must be returned to you if the car doesn't check out. You can eliminate nine out of ten used car buying disasters this way.

You want an ASE-certified (Automotive Service Excellence) mechanic. Garages that participate in the Blue Seal of Excellence Recognition Program typically retain the most highly trained ASE-certified mechanics. Visit ASE.com to find one near you.

# FINANCING AND THE PURCHASE PROCESS

## *Prearrange your auto loan financing*

You might have spent hours researching a potential car purchase thoroughly, but did you do the same when it came to getting your loan? One of the biggest mistakes people make when buying a car is to not arrange financing before they walk into a car dealership.

Dealers are entitled to make money on a loan if you don't do your homework and get prequalified elsewhere. Credit unions offer interest rates on car loans that can be one to three percentage points lower than other lenders. You may also want to check online lenders. Even your auto insurer may be able to give you a competitive interest rate.

The real money in car dealerships is made in the F&I (finance and insurance) department, where the F&I man (or woman) sells extended warranties and writes car loans.

When you fill out a credit application at a dealership, the dealer goes out to wholesale the money for you. They might get money at 4 percent, but they could write the loan at up to 7 percent or even higher—especially if they con you into thinking you have bad credit. The younger you are, the likelier it is that you'll be conned into thinking you aren't good for the money and they are heroes to get a loan for you!

By prequalifying elsewhere, it will change the whole equation at the dealership. You can then go in and tell them the interest rate you've been prequalified for. If the F&I department can beat the deal you have, fine, give them a chance to make some money originating the loan. But don't let them make money by gouging you on the markup of a loan.

I want *you*, not the F&I man, in the driver's seat.

## Never finance for longer than forty-two months

During a recent flight, I was talking with a seatmate who sold gap insurance for the automotive industry. This woman was telling me how people borrow so much on their cars and how the great service she sells helps them if they're upside down in their vehicle (owing more on the auto loan than the vehicle is worth) when it's stolen or destroyed. She had the solution to a problem that you shouldn't let happen in the first place. You should not buy a car with no money down because of the rapid level of depreciation. The average auto loan is now more than sixty months long. So it's very difficult to close the gap between your rapidly depreciating car and the amount of your loan.

The longest auto loan you should ever take out is forty-two months. If you can't afford the payment on a forty-two-month loan, then you should buy a cheaper car.

The right way to buy a car is to save money first. Of course, it's probably unrealistic to think that you can pay for a new car entirely in cash; estimates suggest only 1 percent of Americans are able to do so. But by saving a down payment of 20 percent, for example, you can have a shorter loan and pay less interest.

## Avoid "the grind" at car dealerships

One thing you should never do when buying a car, new or used, is to go to the dealership and negotiate the purchase of your car then and there. Doing so means you risk facing "the grind."

The grind happens after you've test driven the vehicle and kicked the wheels on the lot. When you're ready to talk financing, the nice salesperson says he or she will go talk to the manager about getting you the best deal on your intended vehicle.

Instead they go watch TV for five minutes and eat a ham sandwich. Then they come back looking defeated while telling you that they really went to bat for you, but the manager couldn't help out with a better price despite their best efforts on your behalf.

This is total baloney.

What they're hoping for is that you'll agree to a higher price. When it comes to price, you've got to understand that they have the home field advantage because they sell cars every single day. You, on the other hand, might buy only a handful of vehicles during your lifetime.

That's why it's so important to get a direct no-hassle price online, as I explain in the next tip, or perhaps at a warehouse club through their negotiated-rate car-buying program. If you have that price in hand, you're not going to agree to pay a higher price at a dealership. If the dealer wants your business, they'll have to offer a competitive price. You want to play in your ballpark, not theirs.

## Get a direct no-hassle price online

A few years ago, after seeing one episode of Bravo's reality TV show *The Real Housewives of Atlanta*, I thought it was a continuous train wreck, with a cast of women who had clashing personalities that were just unreal. Not to mention the way most of the women spent money!

Kim Zolciak, one of the cast members, was a prime example. In one episode, Kim wanted a new giant SUV, but she did not negotiate the purchase. She simply bought it on the spot for what seemed like a zillion dollars.

Her polar opposite was Kandi Burruss, another cast member who is unique on the show for being fiscally responsible. She's a Grammy-winning singer/songwriter/producer and seemed to be the only show participant who did not think of her money as a joke to be spent frivolously. Around the peak of the show's popularity, Burruss appeared on my radio show to explain how she became conservative with a buck. When the conversation took a turn to Zolciak's SUV-buying fiasco, Burruss told me that she herself was leery of the whole car-buying process and didn't like it.

Of course, she's not alone in her sentiments. But it's now possible to do everything without stepping into a dealership. In the past, I've talked about how CarsDirect.com and the wholesale clubs' auto buying programs can help you in this respect.

Now there's a new kid on the block known as Zag.com. Much like CarsDirect.com, Zag .com gives buyers instant guaranteed up-front prices from a network of certified dealers. It also offers an easy delivery process that helps you avoid "the grind" at a dealership. (See "Avoid 'the Grind' at Car Dealerships" on page 30.)

But Zag.com distinguishes itself by offering the benefit of various organizations' large membership bases. As I write this, the service is available to members and customers of American Express, Bank of America, *Consumer Reports*, Overstock.com, Sallie Mae, and USAA.

So will Zag.com or CarsDirect.com get you the lowest possible price? Well, it's a very good price, and you should definitely use it as a starting point for others to beat. In some cases, a quote from CarsDirect or Zag will be the best price. However, a dedicated hardworking shopper might be able to find a slightly better deal on his or her own.

## Never trade in a car you still owe money on

Picture this scenario: You have a car and you're still paying off the note. You decide to trade it in and get a newer vehicle, taking out a new loan in the process.

Several months later, you are contacted by the lender *on your last car* about missed payments. What happened? The dealership never paid off your loan when you traded your car in . . . and you don't have the vehicle anymore. Unfortunately, you are still responsible for payments on the car that you no longer own. Your credit is damaged because of the missed payments, and your new car may be repossessed if you can't meet both loans!

The Associated Press has reported this happening all over America during the Great Recession. The car dealerships that took trade-ins and did this were not initially trying to cheat customers. But when they hit hard times and went insolvent, they weren't worrying about paying off your note.

There's actually a real double whammy here. If someone had the misfortune of buying the car you traded in, that person could have it repossessed because your original loan is outstanding. And they would still have the obligation on the loan they took out! Talk about a train wreck.

Be sure you're not buying a used car with an outstanding note on it by doing a free title search at CARFAX.com or by checking with your local Department of Motor Vehicles. Until state legislatures pass bonding laws to protect consumers, we'll continue to have this problem.

So the takeaway is this: Do not trade in a car you still owe money on—period. Pay it off before dumping it.

# LEASING

## Don't lease a vehicle

People often ask me, when is it okay to lease a vehicle?

The answer is: almost never. Leasing is usually a bad deal because manufacturers and dealers like to trick people into getting more car than they can actually afford. They do that by using up-front fees to create ultra-low monthly payments. That disguises the true cost.

There are only two circumstances when leasing a car is acceptable. The first is if you like new wheels all the time and want to worry only about gas, oil changes, and routine maintenance on your vehicle. Then it's okay to lease a new car every two or three years, but no longer than that.

The second instance is when luxury automakers offer factory-subsidized leases for which they eat a lot of the cost. The luxury nameplates hate to cheapen their brands with a bona fide "sale," so often they offer such leases to help move extra product.

But other than in these two circumstances, don't lease. It may seem cheaper than buying, but you're mortgaging your future. After a few years of leasing a vehicle and making payments, you own nothing. And stay away from four- or five-year leases unless you want to face financial Armageddon.

## Minimize the negatives of leasing

If you are going to lease a car, one key bit of advice I have is to stick to leasing terms of 36,000 miles over three years. Any longer than that and you're really doing yourself financial harm.

What can you do if you're already in over your head with a lease? You may want to try getting approval for a qualified person to take over your lease. LeaseTrader.com is one website where you can begin your search. Just be realistic: If you have a giant gas-guzzling SUV and gas is expensive, you probably won't find many takers willing to get you out of your lease!

One other way you can minimize the damage of leasing is to refinance if you have good credit. Visit LowerMyLease.com to see if this is an option for you. This service takes your lease and shops it around among national financial institutions. If they find a better offer, LowerMyLease.com will pay off your existing lease and write you a re-lease under new, more favorable terms.

Of course, if you're already in a manufacturer-subsidized lease, it's unlikely that you'll find a better deal. Also remember that you never want to extend the length of the lease, regardless of whether you get a lower rate.

## Beware of leasing gotchas

I don't know how to get the point across any better—leasing is my least favorite way for you to get in a car!

But if you do lease, make sure your lease agreement doesn't come with an exceedingly low mileage allowance, and beware of excessive wear-and-tear assessments when you turn in the vehicle. The average leased vehicle gets hit with wear-and-tear charges to the tune of nearly $2,000.

When you lease a vehicle, take extensive photographs of the interior and exterior so there's no question that you're returning it in top shape. And if you do spill something in the car or tear the upholstery, fix it before returning the car. It will be one-fifth cheaper for you to have it repaired on your own than to let the dealer charge you their inflated repair prices.

Finally, before you return the leased vehicle, make sure you've gotten a third party to do a thorough inspection of the car. This alone could save you up to $1,500 in unnecessary turn-in fees.

And let me take a moment to address a really messy situation—when your leased vehicle gets totaled in an accident. You could be responsible for a giant gap between the amount the insurance company will pay and the stated residual in the lease. Ask the dealer when you lease for free gap insurance to protect you.

# MAINTENANCE AND REPAIR

### Don't buy an extended warranty from a third-party company

Cars are the second largest expense in most people's lives following housing. So it's only natural that people would want some peace of mind when making a vehicle purchase, be it used or new. Sometimes they see that peace of mind in an extended warranty.

But please, don't ever buy an extended warranty on your vehicle from a third-party company. Odds are you'll be overcharged and the company may disappear when you need help.

For several years, USfidelis was perhaps the most heavily marketed extended auto warranty in the country, with a lot of ads on bad late-night TV featuring NASCAR champion Rusty Wallace. *Consumer Reports* investigated this popular outfit and warned people about them at the end of the last decade. I want to go one step further and warn people about all extended auto warranties except in limited circumstances.

According to *Consumer Reports*, USfidelis failed to respond to more than one thousand complaints registered with the Better Business Bureau. Among the complaints were gripes about the difficulty of canceling a warranty; obtaining a refund; the nature of the company's misleading ads; their misrepresentation of coverage; and their failure to remove customer names from mailing lists.

In addition, *Consumer Reports* revealed that USfidelis told them customers were not allowed to see their contract until *after* they purchased it. You just know that signals somebody is up to no good.

Of course, many of these problems are not necessarily specific to USfidelis. They also plague the smaller players in the extended auto warranty business. USfidelis just happened to be the top dog at the time of the *Consumer Reports* exposé, so that's why it was singled out. The company has since filed for bankruptcy and no longer sells extended warranties. "Customers who purchased a vehicle service contract can rest assured that their claims are still being adjudicated and paid by the top rated providers USfidelis represents," according to a statement on the company's website.

Here's my longstanding advice: If you can afford the potential cost of a car repair, you should never buy an extended warranty. But if you're unable to budget and save for repairs, then you should consider buying only the manufacturer's warranty. If trouble happens, the manufacturer should be there to stand behind its warranty. A third-party company usually will not.

If you stick to *Consumer Reports'* annual recommended list of vehicles, you shouldn't have to buy an extended warranty at all—even if you have budgeting difficulties. The odds are such that their recommended vehicles won't have severe problems over time.

## Money-back car warranties are a real ruse

I've gotten calls from people who are being offered a unique kind of extended vehicle warranty that seems to be a real bargain. They're told they can purchase a warranty, and then if they never use it, they'll get back the money they paid. Unfortunately, it turns out this is just a ruse.

*The Kansas City Star* wrote a story about a lawsuit that went on for six years concerning the sale of these money-back warranties. The plaintiffs, obviously, were having difficulty getting their money back! A court ruled that the warranty company in question should give the money back, but—surprise—the company had already filed for bankruptcy. Good luck getting your money back then!

Here's the lay of the land when it comes to cash-back warranties: The warranty companies market directly to dealers and get them to sell their warranties—instead of a manufacturer's own, as I prefer—at huge profit margins to both parties.

But the warranty company doesn't even have enough underwriting to pay for repairs. They just collect money with no intention of paying it back. Then they do what's called a "bust-out" in law enforcement circles: They abandon their operations overnight and disappear with the money, leaving the lights on and all the office furniture in place.

The end result is that you as a consumer are stuck holding a worthless warranty. So don't believe the claim that you'll get your money back in the end. It has only a marketing company backing it up and isn't worth the cost of the paper it's written on.

## Negotiate on a manufacturer's extended warranty price

As you can probably tell by now, I'm something of an agnostic when it comes to extended auto warranties.

But I also recognize that in some cases an extended auto warranty can be a good thing. Fortunately, the cost of an extended warranty purchased through a manufacturer is open to negotiation. These typically have a markup of between 400 and 1,000 percent! Though they don't want you to know it, manufacturers have a lot of wiggle room when it comes to the final price of a warranty.

The best way I've found to negotiate is to call your insurer for a quote and then use that as a negotiating tool with the manufacturer. Of course, if the insurer proves to be more expensive, do the opposite. Tell them what the manufacturer is asking and see if they'll beat it. Just be sure to compare costs and coverage apples to apples.

Finally, never make a decision about an extended warranty on the day you're purchasing your car. Take some time to sleep on it. With most extended warranty providers, you usually have at least twelve months from the date you purchase the car to make a decision.

## Check for service bulletins and recall notices

The year 2009 will long be remembered for the sudden acceleration problems that prompted Toyota's massive recall of millions of vehicles. The heavy publicity around the debacle really shone a light on recalls, and that's a good thing, for a number of reasons.

A breakdown of your vehicle might be part of a defect in the model that affects other car owners. You might be able to negotiate a lower repair price or receive a reimbursement for repair work if the vehicle has been cited in a recall or in what's called a technical service bulletin (TSB).

Many times when there's no official recall, there still might be a TSB from the manufacturer. Thousands of TSBs are issued each year, as automakers become aware of systemic problems reported by mechanics and consumers. You can preview both full-blown recalls and TSBs for your vehicle by make, model, and year at the Center for Auto Safety website at AutoSafety.org and at ALLDATAdiy.com.

In one relatively benign example, I had an issue with a gas cap that would not open on one of my vehicles. So I went online to investigate and found that this was a widespread problem. I printed out some supporting material and went to the dealer, fully expecting some kind of push-back from them. But the dealer was happy to replace the cap for me once they pried it off!

Until recently, only one out of three people complied when notified about a recall and brought a vehicle in for the necessary fix. But I'm betting that number spiked after the Toyota controversy.

## Get a second opinion on expensive repair estimates

We're in an era in which more and more people are holding on to their old cars and repairing them instead of buying new. As a result, the repair and maintenance business is booming.

The best time to find a mechanic is before your car breaks down. If you're at a loss picking a shop, consult websites with user-generated reviews like Yelp.com or Kudzu.com for guidance.

Members of AAA have access to the motor club's Approved Auto Repair program that connects them with AAA-approved repair facilities. If you have any problem with the work done, AAA has a process to handle the dispute, and the mechanic must abide by what they say, though you're not bound by the decision.

In general, you always want to talk with the mechanic doing the work on your car. I'm not a fan of the traditional dealer service model where you talk only to the service ticket writer, not the mechanic actually doing the work.

If you choose to deal with the service writer, be sure he notes the symptoms you're seeing in your vehicle, not the remedy. Too often they'll just write "do a tune-up" when you're saying the car is intermittently losing punch while driving. The problem then becomes your signing your name to authorize a tune-up while the true nature of the problem remains undiagnosed.

If the estimate is large, don't accept it as the final word. Take your car to another garage for a second opinion on the repair cost. If your car is not drivable, have it towed for a second estimate. Even after the cost of a tow, you could save yourself a bundle in the long run.

For foreign nameplates, I like going to single-brand independent shops that are not affiliated with the dealer. These kinds of shops service only one brand of vehicle, such as Honda or Toyota.

If you're in need of auto body work, try a service called DentBetty.com, which allows you to upload a digital photo of your dents and have local auto body shops bid on the job. This service is available only in select areas. But it's an ingenious idea because the pricing at body shops is dynamic, based on the volume of jobs they have during any given week.

> *Back when I lived in Atlanta traffic, I listened to Clark every day. I drove a Honda and the horn button was broken. I originally contacted the dealer and they estimated the repairs to be around $170 and said the airbag would need to be re-packed. Based on Clark's advice to another listener, I went to a Honda-only salvage yard in an Atlanta suburb. They found the part I needed, charged me a dollar and it took me about 30 seconds to attach it!!! I honked my horn all the way home in tribute to Clark. Thanks, Clark!!!*
>
> *Kati W., MO*

## Fill up with regular unleaded gas

We Americans have very short memories. When the price of a barrel of oil hit a record high of $147 in July 2008, I took a ton of calls from people who wanted to dump their SUVs and buy a hybrid or other fuel-efficient vehicle. But as prices subsided, Americans resumed their love affair with bigger vehicles.

It's been the same trend with the sale of premium gas. According to the U.S. Energy Information Administration, premium gas sales dropped to an all-time low—7 percent of all gas sold in the United States—when the price of oil was at its peak in July 2008. That's a big drop when you consider premium gas has accounted for up to 20 percent of all gas sold in the last twenty years.

But you know the story; now that $4-a-gallon gas is a distant memory, sales of premium have begun to climb.

I'm here to tell you that premium gas is, for most people, a waste of money. Most cars will run just fine on regular gas—even a Porsche! And unless your vehicle specifically requires premium, using higher-octane gas may actually harm it. If you're not sure, just check your owner's manual to see what your car or truck needs.

Ultimately, you want to use whatever the manufacturer specifies, even if that means premium gas.

## Comparison shop for gas online

When gas prices at wholesale drop significantly in short time periods, you'll probably notice big differences in the price of a gallon from station to station in most metro areas.

The price difference ranges from 15 to 20 cents, but it's possible to see disparities of around 35 cents per gallon from station to station.

Why the almost double spread? It's all about delivery cycles and the volume of business at filling stations. Stations known as "pumpers" in the lingo of the trade might get three deliveries a day. By comparison, slower stations that don't sell as much gas might get a delivery only once every few weeks.

So during times of falling wholesale prices, the high-volume stations cycle through deliveries every day and reflect market prices quicker and more accurately. But during times of rising gas prices, the whole cycle is reversed and the low-volume stations have the best prices because they're still selling gas from a week or two before the run-up in price at wholesale.

Pay attention to prices as you're driving around and fill up when you see a deal. You can use websites like GasPriceWatch.com and GasBuddy.com to help you comparison shop for gas prices.

But remember, it costs around 58 cents per mile to operate a vehicle, when you consider fuel, maintenance, depreciation, and other factors. So beware of driving too far out of your way to get cheap gas. It defeats the purpose.

And finally, you need to know that there's no difference in the quality of gas between a brand-name and a no-name filling station. The only difference is the price. So save your money!

## Go five thousand miles between oil changes

It's a message that has been steered at drivers for years: Change your engine oil every three thousand miles. Mechanics say you could be damaging your engine if you don't. Yet *Consumer Reports* says it's a waste of money.

To reconcile the differing opinions, you've got to consult your owner's manual and use a little bit of common sense. Most owner's manuals for newer vehicles will tell you it's acceptable to go five thousand miles between oil changes under normal conditions. But you should drop to three thousand miles if you drive under severe conditions.

What exactly are severe conditions?

One oil change technician I spoke to said that "jackrabbit" stops and starts—the kind people tend to do when racing from traffic light to traffic light—are a prime example. An AAA spokesman I heard from cited other factors, including extreme heat and using your vehicle to tow others.

If you're just driving back and forth to work during the week and soccer fields and baseball games during the weekend, then there's really no sense in changing your oil every three thousand miles. A *Consumer Reports* study put the brakes on three-thousand-mile oil changes a few years ago. They found no noticeable difference in engine protection whether you changed the oil every three thousand or six thousand miles.

Ultimately, this one has to be a personal decision. Maybe you're comfortable changing every three thousand miles and think five thousand is too long to wait. Then why not split the difference and do it every four thousand miles? You'll be saving a third of the cost of oil changes by going that extra 1,000 between oil changes.

Experts tell me a $20 oil change is the best preventative maintenance you can do. So the interval is really up to you as long as you don't exceed what's recommended in your owner's manual.


## Avoid fancy wheels/tires on a car purchase

Have you gotten sticker shock when you've needed replacement tires for your car? Chances are you could have expensive nonstandard tires. It's not at all unusual when you have to replace tires on your new car to have to pay maybe five times more than you paid to replace them on your last car.

Are we being gouged by tire makers? No, we're being gouged by ourselves.

Automakers create multiple lines of a single vehicle at different price points. One of the up-sells they add to the pricier lines is fancy wheels that require larger-than-usual tires.

Some models even have speed-rated tires that are designed to perform at 149 mph or higher. We've all seen the commercials with stunt drivers tearing it up on closed roads. It's the James Bond syndrome! But how often do you drive even 100 mph? Do you really need those high-performance tires?

So I recommend you check out the tire size and type before you buy a car. Or simply ask the dealer about the replacement tire price. Of course, for many people style is king and they don't care if they have to pay extra.

But if you do care, use TireRack.com to price out the different tire sizes that are possible on the car you're thinking of buying. When you see the price difference from cheapest to most expensive, that might change what wheels you buy on that new vehicle you're purchasing. Your wallet will smile on you for years.

## A CLARK FAVORITE
### Find free street parking

I have always been cheap, which I define as being willing to accept lower quality for a lower price. That's just me. But sometimes, my cheap tendencies have come back to bite me.

For example, I hate to pay for parking. So I often park in questionable areas where I can find free parking. My reward for being that cheap? Five smash-and-grabs through the years that have required me to replace the car window each time.

I could have paid for a lot of parking at that rate. In fact, I've had vehicles broken into in four countries—Holland, Spain, Canada, and here at home—because of my insistence on free parking.

But you're not necessarily safe in paid parking areas, either. A couple of years ago, my wife, Lane, had parked her car in a paid lot and came back to find the window smashed. The thief or thieves were after a $99 GPS unit that I had bought during Christmas. So they smashed a $350 window to get a used electronics item that you could pawn for maybe $20.

I look at this story as a justification of my cheapness. And I think I'll keep parking in shady neighborhoods. Maybe next time I'll just leave my doors unlocked and make sure there's nothing of value in the car.

My associate producer, Joel Larsgaard, has a favorite story about how my cheapness with parking doesn't pay.

When we were traveling for the show in Appleton, Wisconsin, there was a parking lot right next to our hotel that cost $1 to park. Not $10 or $5, but ONE dollar. But I decided to park a half-mile down the road across the railroad tracks.

In the morning, I got to the car and there was a ticket on it—a $25 parking ticket. I tried my best to fight the ticket, but there is an ordinance that doesn't allow street parking from 2:00 to 5:00 a.m. in the whole city of Appleton. I had to pay the ticket, plus an extra $1 processing fee. Talk about adding insult to injury!

Another time, I wound up getting my rental car crushed by falling debris when I opted for free street parking in Manhattan. Oh, when am I going to learn?! Sometimes it just doesn't pay to be cheap. . . .

# Computers and Internet

I love gadgets and computers. The Internet has literally changed the world we live in, opening up communication and allowing us to shop, bank, and research anything online. It has also presented opportunities for crooks to steal your identity and rip you off.

In this chapter, I talk about how to save money on your Internet service; how to get a cheap but effective computer for well under $300; some ways to cash in on your gently used electronics; and how to stay safe while using popular social networks like Facebook and Twitter.

## BUYING ELECTRONICS AND ACCESSORIES

### Buy current technology—not state of the art

It's amazing how many things that used to be so precious and expensive are unbelievably cheap today. I recall buying the first computer for my travel agency back in 1982. At the time, I needed specialized software to do travel accounting, plus specific hardware. The price? $25,000 used! And that was considered a deal back then!

Now my $19 Casio watch has more capability than that old computer. Unlike some other consumer items, technology actually gets cheaper over time. Last year, I bought a new Acer laptop for $299. Now even that price is high by today's standards. But a cheap computer today is more sophisticated than what was used to put a man on the moon more than forty years ago.

Computers are getting so affordable that they're almost becoming impulse purchases. What a world of difference from the beginning of this decade, when buying a computer was a major financial decision.

When it comes to electronics, you don't want to buy state-of-the-art products. Buy current products or ones that are a little behind the times. Remember, early adopters always get their wallets emptied out for them. They pay big money to deal with the bugs of something that's new so the rest of us can benefit from it down the road at cheaper prices. It pays to be un-hip! You'll get a great deal if you just wait a little while.

## A CLARK FAVORITE
### Shop for electronics on sites that sell one item a day

I love a bargain, and few places are better to find one than the Internet. A slew of new websites have cropped up in recent years that offer one item for sale per day for extra cheap. I mean between 50 to 75 percent off retail! These include Woot .com and 1SaleaDay.com and they typically do most of their volume in electronics and tech gadgets. (For a more complete list of these "deal a day" sites, check DODTracker.com.)

Shipping varies but usually is only $5 per order no matter what you buy—even if it's a laptop computer or a big-screen TV. Once the deal of the day is gone on these sites, it's gone; you have to wait until midnight for the next day's product to be posted. Once or twice a month, however, Woot will bend that rule and immediately start selling another item after the day's initial offering runs out. That's called a "Woot-Off."

I purchased an easy-to-use handheld video camera for my daughter on Woot that usually prices out around $100. But I bought it for $59, which gives you a good idea of the deals you can steal.

Two caveats here about these kinds of websites. First, there's typically no customer service after the sale. Second, some users on my website have reported that the electronics they sell might be refurbished. But that's okay with me; I'm perfectly willing to accept lower quality for a lower price!

Finally, are you an eBay addict looking for a more efficient way to steal a deal online? LastMinute-Auction.com scours eBay for auctions that are ending in sixty minutes or less and are still priced at $1 or less. Sure, you'll find some worthless items, but there's an occasional gem to be had at a rock-bottom price.

*From time to time, Woot will sell a "bag of crap" that is a true crapshoot as to what you'll*

*get. I was lucky enough to get one and here's what they sent me:*

*1 Hamilton Beach Stay Cold blender*

*1 Perfect Pull-up (As Seen on TV)*

*1 set of six Star Wars bobble-head dolls*

*1 paper bag with trademark Woot! Bag of Crap (BOC) question mark printed on it.*

*1 hand-written note that read:*

   *"We apologize for any inconvenience this may cause you, however your last item will*

*not fit in this box and will be shipped separately. Thanks for your understanding."*

*So the last item remained a mystery . . . I didn't see a tracking number for it on Woot's site.*

*Then it arrived unannounced. In one final moment of anxiety, the FedEx door sticker said*

*it was left at the address next door. So I go knock. They didn't know what I was talking*

*about. Uh oh. But all was well. The FedEx guy had left it at the house on the other side and*

*just took a swag on the number. So my neighbors opened the garage door and . . . voila! A*

*32" 1080p LCD. Vizio model VOJ320F1A. "Recertified" (naturally). Street price: $375!*

                                                                    *Andrew C., GA\**

---

### *Shop online for the best computer deals*

When you're shopping online for computer gear, you want the best price—but you also want to know you're buying from a reliable retailer. That's why I love a site like DealNews.com.

This site aggregates deals from across the Web by searching more than two thousand online retailers each day and verifying that each deal they post is valid. Deals are updated about twice an hour and each deal is graded based on how hot it is; the more orange circles, the hotter the deal, on a scale of zero to five circles. No more guesswork as to whether you're paying a great price or a mediocre one.

---

\* Editor's note: Andrew's results may be atypical. As Woot founder/CEO Matt Rutledge told us, "[We] would not want to over-promote the Random Crap event to a cautious consumer. We have a lot of fun mixing up contents and enjoy our members' reactions, but unfortunately we can only confirm the 'Random Crap' contents to be a bag of some sort and some crap. To expect otherwise would encroach on the spirit of the event!"

> The site has become such a one-stop shop for cheap tech gadgets that they've adopted the tagline "Where every day is Black Friday." Indeed, it can be with DealNews.com.
>
> As I write this, DealNews.com is offering a Toshiba Satellite AMD Dual Core 2. 1GHz 16" Laptop for $299, plus $25 shipping and handling. That got four orange circles. And an Acer Aspire One Intel Atom 1.66GHz 10" LED Netbook for $245 with free shipping. That got three orange circles.
>
> Of course, these deals won't be there when you check DealNews.com—hopefully you'll find even better ones!

## Buy a cheap netbook for basic computing needs

The netbook trend that has taken the market by storm really started with the vision of one techno-optimist named Nicholas Negroponte. This MIT professor started a nonprofit called One Laptop per Child that aimed to make small, inexpensive laptops available to Third World children.

The for-profit computer manufacturers responded quickly by rolling out their own versions of ultra-cheap lightweight mini-laptops when they caught wind of MIT's nonprofit plan.

One of the first companies to make money with netbooks was Asus with the Eee (pronounced "triple E") PC. Today a basic Eee model starts at just under $200 when you find it on sale.

Other manufacturers like Hewlett-Packard, Dell, and Acer all have their own netbooks. The typical screen size is about nine or ten inches and they generally operate on Windows XP or Linux. These "wundercomputers" are designed for the basics and not much else: Web surfing, e-mailing, word processing, and cheap VoIP service.

So for around $200, a business traveler can take a two-pound netbook as a substitute for a regular laptop instead of paying $2,000 for a traditional one and having to lug around ten or fifteen pounds of extra baggage.

The neat thing is that netbooks are suddenly out, and the hip and in thing is the iPad and competing tablets. Consequently, netbooks are seen as the redheaded stepchild of the industry and have dropped severely in price. For my money, though, I still want a physical keyboard.

A word about the tablet market: If you're looking for a cheaper alternative to the iPad, it's still too early. Give it at least six months and you'll be rewarded with very nice tablets at very nice prices.

I expect tablets to be priced so low they'll become impulse purchases by the middle of 2012. One of the key indicators telling me so is that VIZIO is entering the tablet market. VIZIO is the number-one seller of TVs and the company that's had the most to do with driving down the cost of HDTVs. When VIZIO enters a market, it builds stuff of very high quality, at lower prices than anybody else says is possible.

Tablets that run on the Android platform will be the real bargain, not Apple tablets. With tablets, people get hung-up on screen size, but the real key is to know what version of Android a tablet is running before you buy it. As new versions come out, people will dump their older-version Androids, and you may steal a deal on a used tablet, but it's up to you to make sure the version it's running will do everything you want.

## Sell your gently used electronics

If you're like most Americans, you have gently used electronics lying around your house that you wouldn't really miss. A couple of websites have now popped up that will give you the opportunity to turn your e-trash into cash in an environmentally responsible way.

Gazelle.com is just about the most popular of these "cash for old gadgets" ventures. You simply log on to Gazelle and enter the make and model of your electronics—everything from cell phones, MP3 players, computers, and cameras to GPS systems and gaming consoles.

If they see resale value in what you've got, the service then makes you an offer. Customers are sent a box to ship their item(s) in and Gazelle even pays for the postage. It typically takes about a week before you're paid once they receive your package. Gazelle says they remove all personal info from your devices before selling them off to wholesalers and retailers.

If what you've got isn't worth anything, they'll still take your e-trash off your hands and recycle it for free.

Many major retailers are now partnering with Gazelle. That means you can log on to the websites of Costco Wholesale, Walmart, and Sears to do your transaction. If you go that route, payment is remitted in store gift cards.

Other websites that offer a similar service to Gazelle include MyBoneYard.com, which offers Visa gift cards for laptops, desktop PCs, cell phones, and flat-panel monitors; and

TechForward.com, which requires a fee to lock in a guaranteed value. A couple of newer entries into the marketplace are eBay's Instant Sale program and EcoSquid.com. The latter acts like an aggregator of various recycling programs across the Web.

Finally, I've used Best Buy's recycling program over the years. You can turn in up to two old electronics items at the Geek Squad counter and they'll take them off your hands for free. There can be a charge of up to $10 for certain items, but then you get a store gift card for $10.

Of course, the possibility of a pay option is more enticing, right?

## Consider the cost of replacement ink when buying a new printer

With computers being an undeniably popular item year after year, I want to share a tip that can help you save money on one important accessory.

A printer is the kind of purchase that I see people making based on price sensitivity. Few understand that the real cost of a printer is not its up-front expense but rather the cost of replacement ink over its lifetime.

One study I've seen from the University of Wisconsin–Green Bay suggests that the cost of printer ink is nearly $10,000 per gallon. Wow is all I can say!

Hewlett-Packard—the dominant printer company—is the perfect example of the traditional printer business model. They lose on every HP printer they sell, but they make a zillion dollars on ink cartridges. It's an idea borrowed from Gillette, which takes a haircut on razor handles but makes a profit on replacement blades.

One printer company has flipped this business model on its head. Kodak makes money on its printers and sells ink at rock-bottom prices. This approach has won Kodak only about a 2 percent market share in the printer business. But it can mean long-term savings for you if you're willing to pay the $150 or so for a Kodak printer up front.

I bought an early-generation Kodak printer that was so-so on quality, but now I have a newer one that I really like. Some people have complained to me about recommending Kodak printers; however, I haven't had any problems with my new one. And I really love the cost of replacement cartridges, which can be as little as $9. You get a *lot* of pages for that $9. I usually buy cartridges in multipacks at Sam's Club.

Regardless of what kind of printer you have, there's an easy way to save money on ink. Buy generic cartridges if available for your printer from your store of choice. The major office supply stores all offer their own in-house brands.

You'll find much cheaper prices on eBay, but be warned that sometimes the cartridges don't work!

## Beware of bait-and-switch when buying cameras online

The online sale of cameras and accessories can often be a tricky business. Toward the end of the last decade, the attorney general of the state of Texas brought charges against two online retailers—Broadway Photo, L.L.C., and Starlight Camera & Video, Inc.—that were accused of the old bait-and-switch routine.

Consumers who would make a purchase that was advertised as new would often receive refurbished or used gear. In 2011, both companies were fined by the Texas attorney general. Starlight had to pay $5,000 up-front and must dissolve as a corporation—or pay another $250,000! And Broadway Photo got hit with $100,000 in fines right off the bat, but can keep doing business in the Lone Star State.

Here's some advice for those who are going to buy just about anything on the Internet. First, stick only to sellers that have multiple positive ratings—not just one or two glowing postings from family and friends. You can use Epinions.com to vet out potential vendors. Or use a search engine like Google or Bing and enter the vendor's name plus the words "rip-off" or "scam" to see what kind of gripes are out there in cyberspace.

Many times I'm willing to pay more to buy from a reputable seller.

Second, pay only with a credit card—not a debit card or a check or a PayPal account linked to a checking account. With a credit card, you have the right to dispute the charge within sixty days if your merchandise never shows up or is not what was advertised.

Sometimes a deal is not a deal, particularly if you're dealing with hoodlums.

## Get free software online for office use

If you have a small business, you know that software can be expensive. For many years, Microsoft enjoyed a virtual monopoly in the world of office productivity suites and was able to charge sky-high prices for Microsoft Office. But the software giant's primacy has been challenged in recent years by free services from OpenOffice.org and Docs.Google.com.

Surprisingly, only 6 percent of people have ever used software alternatives to Microsoft Office. I'm not one of those anti-Microsoft people, but I'd rather you save the dough.

OpenOffice works like traditional software that you download to your computer and is interoperable with Microsoft Word. Google Docs, however, works via "cloud computing." That is a fancy way of saying that your documents are stored not on your computer but in a password-protected "cloud" on the company's server. The benefit is that documents can be accessed from any computer, anywhere in the world. Visit Docs.Google.com for more info.

In fact, I worked with my coauthors on this book using another free office productivity suite at Zoho.com. The service is free for up to three people and allows easy collaboration without having to e-mail documents to one another.

Not wanting to fall behind the times, Microsoft recently introduced a a new business model, called Office 365, that borrows from cloud computing and makes it more affordable to everyone. All the programs are password protected and available from any computer, anywhere. Best of all, it's available via a subscription model. You pay $6 per user each month for up to twenty-five users. So a one-person company would be $72 per year. Visit Office365.Microsoft.com for more details.

# GETTING ONLINE

## Consider naked DSL

For a long time if you wanted your high-speed Internet from a phone company, you had to purchase a landline as a prerequisite. The phone monopolies thought they were smart pushing obsolete landline technology on consumers who wanted modern DSL.

But now there is another option called "naked DSL." The term was originally coined by Qwest Communications to describe high-speed Internet access without a landline.

Naked DSL typically appeals to younger generations like my college-age daughter or my twenty-seven-year-old assistant producer, Joel Larsgaard. But it's also great for older consumers who have dropped landline phone service.

The nation's two big traditional phone monopolies—AT&T and Verizon—each have their own versions of naked DSL. A basic version of AT&T's FastAccess DSL is available for $15 to $20 per month with a twelve-month contract. Verizon, meanwhile, charges you $10 more a month (with a two-year annual contract) to go naked.

As a result of its purchase of NBC, Comcast is now required to sell high-speed stand-alone Internet without having you buy a landline or cable service. The Comcast offer looks like it's pricing out around $20 per month with a six-month contract right now. But check on these offers often; the providers are always trying to attract more market share, and you never know what you'll find.

Visit ATT.com, Verizon.com, and Comcast.com for more details.

## Talk to customer retention at your ISP to get a better deal

Are you thinking about firing your high-speed Internet service provider (ISP) because it's too expensive? Don't do it before trying to negotiate to see if your ISP can offer you a better deal. Essentially what you want to do is play one provider against another and make them compete for your business.

The trick is simple: Research what other deals the marketplace is offering and present them when you speak to the customer service representative. You can use a website like WhiteFence.com to get quotes. Once you have those quotes in hand, share them with your current provider and ask them to make it worthwhile for you to be their customer. It's just a matter of calling up and negotiating.

You'll likely be switched to the customer retention department. Sometimes if you threaten to fire them as a company, you'll magically be offered a cheaper deal that might be unpublished elsewhere.

Several years ago, I was paying the outrageous price of $43 per month for high-speed Internet. When I told the customer retention specialist that I was about to cancel, she offered me three months for $9.99 per month. She also told me to call back again in ninety days to see if I could get the same deal.

Well, I was so excited about saving $100 in a four-minute phone call that I went on my show and blabbed about it to the world. Then my *SmartMoney* magazine arrived in the mail days later and knocked me down a notch. The issue said not to take any three-month offers and to keep fighting for more. In fact, the reporter was able to get a discount on service for an entire year.

Now that's some real negotiating!

*Having been a loyal Media-Com subscriber for 15 years, I thought maybe they would offer*
*me a good-customer discount. After playing phone tag for several minutes, I got a*
*supervisor and pleaded my case. She suggested that I sign up for a yearly subscription*

*instead of the month-to-month service. (I did not know they even offered it and they do not advertise it.) My monthly rate was $120 (Internet, cable, phone, etc.) but after signing the contract, my bill is now $84 per month, saving me $36 per month or $432 per year. The catch? There is a $45 penalty if I cancel anytime before one year. Let's see—it might cost me $45 but I could save $432 over a year . . . duh! Loyalty pays off, but you have to ask!*

*Gerald M., IA*

## Drop the cable and telephone monopolies as ISPs

Much of America has suffered under the shared duopoly of the local phone companies offering DSL and the cable giants offering cable modem service. But those who live in distant suburbs or rural areas might have access to only one or even none of those choices.

Now things are about to change.

CLEAR—a technology that sends out a blanket high-speed Internet signal to cover an entire metro area—is available in most cities across America. With CLEAR, you can have either floating or fixed wireless Internet. The former allows you to access the Internet when traveling at speeds of about seventy miles per hour—hopefully as a passenger rather than as a driver!

I used a first-generation version of CLEAR (then called "Clearwire") at my Florida beach home and was very impressed with it. Now I'm on the new CLEAR and it is amazing, much faster. I pay about $24 per month and have been impressed by its reliability over the course of nearly five years. But keep in mind that prices will likely fluctuate as CLEAR rolls out to more markets. The entry of a third player is always a game changer in a capitalist system.

One word of caution: Be wary of your current Internet service provider trying to lock you into a long-term contract ahead of CLEAR's arrival in your market. With the way technology changes, you definitely don't want to be locked in!

## Beware of subsidized electronics offers

As netbooks and tablets have become hot items, I've noticed more and more subsidized offers promising to put these tiny cutting-edge computers that weigh practically nothing into your hands for as little as $49. AT&T, Sprint, and Verizon have all stepped up with offers of this sort in past Christmas selling seasons.

Sounds like a great deal, right? Actually, no, it's not.

If you accept the offer, the subsidized electronics devices come with a contract for an overpriced two-year data plan. You'll pay massive overage fees if you exceed the data cap. So while you might save yourself $80 to $100 on the up-front costs of a netbook or a tablet, you could wind up paying as much as $1,500 extra over two years because of the restrictive data agreement.

This marketing push is very similar to what we saw in the 1990s when AOL, CompuServe, and others offered a free computer in return for signing a three-year contract for dial-up service. You'll be better served today by competitively shopping for the electronics item you want using a site like DealNews.com (mentioned earlier in this chapter) and going with an unlimited Internet service plan of your choosing.

# MAINTENANCE AND REPAIR

## Make minor computer repairs yourself

Imagine you have a gadget, a gizmo, or even an appliance that's sitting unloved in your home because it's broken. Instead of junking it or hiring someone to fix it, you might want to consider repairing it yourself.

Now, there is nothing I'm capable of repairing myself, but I know there are lots of you out there who are pretty handy. It turns out there is a website devoted to you called iFixIt.com that I've been getting a kick looking through.

iFixIt.com offers repair manuals, step-by-step instructions, and diagnostic tools to help you troubleshoot problems, with an emphasis on electronics repair. It also offers links to any parts you might need for the repair. What's more, the site is truly collaborative. Users can post additional information and fix-it tips with each article.

Historically, the choice to fix or trash electronics has been a tough one. Once an electronics item is out of its initial manufacturer's warranty, it never pays to have it repaired because electronics depreciate so quickly in value. But that's not a viable answer for someone who is short on cash and cannot afford a replacement but is motivated to try the do-it-yourself route.

So next time, instead of running to the electronics repair shop, give it a go yourself with iFixIt.com.

## Don't buy a Windows recovery disc from a store

Several years ago, Best Buy and the now defunct Circuit City came up with a new way to rip off customers buying computers—and it has nothing to do with extended warranties! According to *PC World*, these retailers were trying to get customers to pay for Windows recovery discs.

These backup discs are rarely needed, but retailers have found a way to boost profits by tapping into the "what if?" fear of consumers who may not know a lot about computers. It turns out that you can make these discs yourself or buy them from the manufacturer for half of what the stores charge you.

*PC World* got so fired up over the whole issue that they sent in secret shoppers to get the real scoop. The shoppers found that Circuit City pushed them hard to pay an extra $30 for the store-made recovery discs. At Best Buy, three out of five stores visited told the secret shoppers that it's not possible to make the backup discs yourself.

Very often a recovery disc will be included with your new computer, so be sure to check the packaging thoroughly. If not, Acer, Dell, Gateway, Hewlett-Packard, and Lenovo all say that you can create your own recovery disc using the preinstalled software on your store-bought PC. All Acer and HP notebook models come with instructions and software for creating the recovery discs.

## Shake your printer cartridge for maximum value

I really hate to waste things. So I was excited when I read a TechWorld.com report about how manufacturers of the cartridges we all use in our printers give you a notice that your cartridge is empty when nearly 60 percent of the ink is still left. If you throw it out at that point, more than half the ink you pay for goes unused!

So when your computer tells you to replace the cartridge, instead just pull it out and shake it. You'll probably get several weeks more use out of it. Manufacturers have a clear financial incentive to shortchange you and make you buy more of their product. What you pay to print per page skyrockets if you throw that cartridge out or recycle it too early.

Multi-ink cartridges are the worst because they have individual ink banks for up to three or four colors. Any one of them can run out before the others do. Another way to save money on ink cartridges is to get them refilled. Manufacturers hate it when you do this. The studies I've seen haven't yet shown decisively if the refilled ink is of a good quality or not.

So just shake it up, baby!

Meanwhile, Samsung is one of the few companies that makes printers with a toner saver button that can reduce the amount of ink you use per page by 40 percent. Over time, that becomes a great savings.

Another way to reduce your ink use is to change the font you use to print. The general consensus out there seems to be that Century Gothic is just about the most economical font.

## Avoid extended warranties on computers

I hate extended warranties in general but no more so than on computers. The profit margins for retailers are huge, and it never makes financial sense to insure a rapidly depreciating asset like a computer.

Let's run through one scenario: Say you buy a warranty that extends your coverage on a new laptop purchase to three years. And let's say that computer finally croaks . . . at two years, eleven months and twenty-nine days. You're feeling great because you're covered for repair, right? You dodged a bullet.

But computers depreciate in value like few other things. The value of that computer you bought two years and eleven months ago is today not even worth the price of the extended warranty you purchased on it.

There's a theory in the computing world called "Moore's Law." It states that the number of transistors that can be cheaply put on a circuit doubles every two years and the cost steadily declines. For you and me, this simply means computers are getting better and faster all the time, roughly every two years. So a three-year-old computer that breaks down is not worth what you paid for the warranty to repair or replace it. It's just an expensive doorstop.

Many credit cards will double the manufacturer's original warranty up to one additional year if you use them to make your purchase. That's the "Clark Smart" way to get an extended warranty for free!

# STAYING SAFE ONLINE

## Avoid the ten most common online passwords

With all the talk of high-level hacking, it's easy to forget that we are the ones who make ourselves most vulnerable on a very individual level. *PC Magazine* recently compiled a list of the ten most common passwords in the United States today. Do not use these on confidential e-mail accounts!

1. password
2. 123456
3. qwerty
4. abc123
5. letmein
6. monkey
7. myspace1
8. password1
9. link182
10. (your first name)

These are the first passwords that a criminal will try when attempting to hack your account. Other types of passwords you want to avoid are birthday dates and the names of your children or spouse.

I've had some particularly creative passwords over the years. In the past, I've used an employee ID number from a company I worked at in the 1970s. Then I came up with an even better idea, which I can't divulge for obvious security reasons!

The key is to create a password that is unrelated to anything someone might be able to find out about you if they were digging into your background. Tricky alphanumeric passwords—ones that include letters, numbers and symbols—usually work best.

## Know what personal info not to post to social media sites

The growth of social networks like Facebook and Twitter has been amazing—and they're only poised to get more popular. While these services offer a great way to reconnect and keep in touch with old friends, I have to recommend the utmost caution about what you post in your profile.

A new Experian study has found that more than half of adults age forty-five and over post enough info on their Facebook page to open themselves to identity theft. Meanwhile, more than a third of people of any age haven't put any privacy settings in place on their Facebook accounts.

Some privacy experts are now suggesting you lie about your city and gender as a way to protect yourself. But that defeats the purpose of having Facebook as a safe venue where you can trust sharing info with your contacts.

Here's a quick rundown of information you *shouldn't* post on Facebook: full home address, place of birth, phone numbers, and educational background.

While I don't want to scare you away from the joys of feeling connected, I do want you to be smart about it and stay safe.

## Watch out for post-transaction marketing charges on Facebook

Are you addicted to those cute little games like YoVille and Mafia Wars on Facebook? You might incur unexpected charges on your credit card if you're not careful.

Let's say you're on Facebook connecting with your friends. While there, you accept an offer for a risk-free trial as part of an ad that might be embedded in a game. You're typically asked for a credit card or checking account number to participate in the supposedly free trial, but then your account is charged up to several hundred dollars.

Facebook has so far denied any responsibility for this post-transaction marketing. Zynga, meanwhile, allegedly made up to $80 million from these offers.

But it's not just social networking giants doing this kind of stuff. The *Los Angeles Times* reports RealtyTrac has been accused of working with a post-transaction marketer that charges people $45 each month for a subscription to a sister service that promises to make you "a real estate investment pro."

The takeaway here is simple: Be sure to check your credit card statements and bank accounts each month for unknown charges and dispute them.

## E-greetings might contain dangerous spyware

If you've been receiving phony e-greeting cards in your inbox, you risk getting spyware and other kinds of malware on your computer upon opening them.

I'm really upset about this because e-greeting cards should be a pleasant thing. Unfortunately, something that's so innocent has been corrupted.

The latest incarnation in this rip-off scheme works in the following way: Criminals send out bogus e-greeting cards, and if you open them, you download a program that steals e-mail addresses from your contacts list. Once the criminals have those e-mail addresses, they send out another fake e-greeting that appears to be coming from you, starting the cycle all over again.

The worst part is that when the initial e-greeting is opened, it usually unknowingly downloads a "keylogger" program to the user's computer. A keylogger is a malicious program that tracks every keystroke you made on the computer, including usernames and passwords for bank, brokerage, or mutual fund accounts.

Under the law, you are protected if money is stolen from your bank account but not from your brokerage or mutual fund account. Some brokers have issued their own policies that allow for customer protection. But the bottom line is that you must run antivirus and anti-spyware software on your computer.

I like Spybot Search & Destroy (available through Safer-Networking.org), Malware-Bytes.org, and SuperAntiSpyware.com, all of which offer free downloads (donations suggested but not required) that eliminate keyloggers and other spyware on your system once you're infected.

Of course, prevention is the best medicine. That's why you should run a good antivirus protection program, do periodic scans for spyware, and avoid clicking on suspicious e-mail links or websites.

I recommend free options like Avast! Antivirus Home Edition (available through Avast .com/Free-Antivirus-Download), AVG Free Antivirus (available through Free.AVG.com), or Microsoft Security Essentials (available through Microsoft.com/Security_Essentials).

Pick just one of these to help protect your computer from infection before the fact. There will be conflicts if you try to run more than one at a time.

## "Scareware" viruses can masquerade as antivirus warnings

We've all been so browbeaten into watching for viruses on our computers that it was only a matter of time before crooks wised up and started creating viruses that actually mimic common antivirus warnings!

That's the idea behind what's called "scareware"—bogus virus warnings that actually load a virus on your computer when you click on them.

You're surfing the Net and suddenly an official-looking screen pops up warning you that there is a problem on your computer, such as: "Your computer may be infected with harmful spyware programs. Immediate removal is required. To scan, click 'Yes.' "

You're not sure if it's real or not, so what do you do? Be careful, this might be scareware, and you'll be snared from the minute you click on the impostor pop-up window that supposedly alerts you to an existing virus.

If there's any doubt, you can close your browser immediately by pressing ALT+F4 (Mac users press Command/Apple+Q). This will prevent any scareware from loading.

My executive radio producer, Christa DiBiase, recently had her computer compromised by a pop-up that masqueraded as a virus warning from Norton Antivirus. It even displayed a virus count, as many popular antivirus programs will do.

So if you see a pop-up window that seems to be from your antivirus program, don't click on it. Instead, go directly to the antivirus or spyware program on your desktop and run it from there so it can find any security threats.

I mentioned several free spyware removal options in an earlier tip. I also recommend having multiple browsers on your computer in addition to the ever popular Mozilla Firefox—such as Google Chrome, Avant Browser, and Opera—all of which are free. The idea is that you can still navigate around the Web even if scareware hits your usual browser.

## Never reply to an e-mail from your bank asking for personal info

Scammers got very sophisticated in their phishing attempts following the numerous bank failures in our nation at the end of the last decade. I received a phishing attempt that looked very legitimate after Wachovia collapsed in 2008.

Within minutes of the original plan for Citibank to take over Wachovia, the scammers were blasting out e-mails. Each message said that in order to access your Wachovia account, you'd have to fill out an online form asking for all kinds of personal info. Unfortunately, many people fell for it because they were dumbfounded by the news about Wachovia, which was later bought by Wells Fargo.

Around that time, I also read a *Los Angeles Times* report stating that British researchers had found that sophisticated phishing scams such as this one have a 90 percent success rate. That's really scary!

You should *never* reply to any supposedly legitimate e-mail from a financial institution asking for personal info. Nor should you ever click on a hyperlink in an e-mail that supposedly takes you to your bank or brokerage house's website.

If you are in doubt, close out the e-mail in question, open a new browser window, and type the URL directly to verify the info contained in the e-mail.

If you think you might have already given up sensitive info, then you should immediately contact your financial institution and tell them to restrict access to your account. You'll also need to change all your passwords.

## Social networking work-at-home offers are likely to be rip-offs

As social networking gains in popularity, so too does the prevalence of scammers pushing supposedly amazing work-at-home opportunities using hot new websites.

One company called Easy Tweet Profits claimed you could make up to $873 a day online using Twitter. They even claimed one person earned $400,000 annually using their method of tweeting your way to success. The catch? By signing up for their program, you agree to be charged nearly $50 each month! They're the only ones getting rich.

There are a whole host of other companies with similar names (usually involving "make money" or "make profits") that suggest social networking can be a cash cow. But their game is all the same.

Whether you are talking about something you see on Facebook, Twitter, MySpace, Craigslist, eBay, or whatever's the next hot thing, you've got to be wary.

Speaking of eBay, beware of anyone who promises to show you how to get instant credibility as a power seller and have the opportunity to make a fortune selling online.

The once popular e-commerce site's transactions are way down and the company is going through a midlife financial crisis. One big problem has been the credibility factor of sellers and buyers alike. There's no insta-business solution when it comes to eBay. As a seller, you sustain yourself over time only by specializing in a niche market.

## "Vishing" and "smishing" are the new phishing

It seems like everyone's gotten hip to crooks using bogus e-mails that masquerade as official communications from a bank or a brokerage house. We all know these e-mails are really intended to try to trick you into divulging sensitive account information. Phishing is so 1990s!

Well, leave it to the scammers to up the ante and develop a sophisticated ruse where they use the triple threat of e-mail, phone calls, and text messages to trick you into yielding your info. The latter two attempts are being called "vishing" (voice mail) and "smishing" (text) because they follow on the heels of the traditional phishing (e-mail) attempt.

As always, this trio of messages will look and sound completely legitimate. They may prompt you to call a seemingly legit toll-free number and talk to an "investigator," or direct you to a website that looks real, with logos from your bank, credit union, or brokerage house.

The truly scary thing is that the criminals already have access to all your contact info and just need your private usernames and passwords to empty out your account.

What should you do if you think you're on the receiving end of this trifecta? Certainly you don't want to divulge your PIN number or other sensitive information.

After you close out the suspect e-mail, open a new browser window and go to your bank's website. You can find their real contact info there and call them to verify the vishing, smishing, and phishing. Never respond to what you see in an e-mail, even if it looks legit.

If you think you might have already fallen prey, contact your bank and tell them to check into it before the suspected crime progresses any further.

## Spear phishing and whaling pose a threat to businesses

Spear phishing is the latest, hottest criminal effort to crack the computer systems of wealthy individuals and businesses, including large corporations. As the name implies, it's a phishing attempt that's highly targeted to a specific person in a company.

Spear phishers will usually find a third-tier executive in a company's organization and send a direct personal e-mail to the recipient, pretending to be an official bank communication.

The *San Francisco Chronicle* reports that spear phishing is becoming more and more sophisticated all the time. In one variation, the criminals will use a subject line that's directly related to a new product or specific issue at that company and *bam!*—the executive loads malicious software on the computer when they open the e-mail.

Business types are also at risk of what's called "whaling." While commonplace phishing targets the general public, whaling targets only the big fish in corporate America or wealthy independent business owners—hence the name.

According to a CNET.com report, top corporate executives and business owners were getting e-mails alerting them to a bogus U.S. District Court subpoena. When they clicked on the link in the e-mail (never a good idea!), they were taken to what looked like a real subpoena.

But it wasn't, and it loaded a keylogger virus onto their computers. A keylogger captures all your account numbers and passwords, and it even alerts the criminals when you log on to your bank or brokerage account. The criminals can then sign in, change your password, and steal your money.

There's actually a low-tech way to assess the danger of a link if you're thinking about clicking on it in an e-mail or on a webpage, which, again, is never advisable in the first place. Simply run your mouse over the link and look at the bottom of your Web browser to see what it says.

If you're about to click on a link that purports to be "ClarkHoward.com" but points to "StealYourIdentity.com/ImGonnaGetcha," well, you better not do it!

You should also be wary of seeing an "at" sign (@) anywhere in the URL. It could be a dangerous redirect. To avoid this, try right-clicking on the URL in an e-mail or on a website and selecting "copy." You can then paste it into a word processing document and vet it carefully for the @ character without ever having to click on it.

# Consumer Issues

The Great Recession made us hyper-vigilant as consumers. In this new economy, people have put their spending on a crash diet. But we're still being plagued by the same old problems like "customer no-service" from uncaring companies, big banks that take tax dollars and then fee you to death, or bill collectors who just won't leave you alone—even if the debt isn't yours.

In this chapter, I'll show you how to hold the collectors at bay, stretch your purchasing power at dollar stores and hard discounters, and use the Internet to both score deals and bring misbehaving banks and corporations to heel. Being an empowered consumer who packs a real punch in the wallet begins here.

## "CLARK SMART" CONSUMERISM

### Be a "freegan"

I've been called a lot of things over the years, from "thrifty" to "frugal" to "cheap"—the latter being my personal favorite. But when I read about the "freegan" movement, I began thinking that I might actually be one of the last of the big time spenders!

Freegans are people who live off society's cast-offs and get all their possessions for nothing. They take what's considered trash and turn it into treasure, not unlike *Sesame Street*'s

Oscar the Grouch! Some folks do it to further a political agenda and some do it just for the free discarded furniture, stereos, TVs, food(!), and more.

*The New York Times* recently ran an article about freegans showing up at New York University residence halls when it was time for students to move out at the end of the school year. Some of the goods the freegans found in dumpsters included artwork, iPods, and desk lamps. Wow!

Now, don't get me wrong; some of the more extreme dumpster-diving practices like getting discarded food from behind a supermarket or out of the garbage ("urban foraging" in freegan lingo) really gross me out. But you could save a bundle by trying out some of the more sanitary approaches to this lifestyle.

As for me, I'll fess up to having dumpster-dived only once in my life, when my wife threw away a box from something I'd purchased. I dove right into the trash when I needed the UPC code in order to get a $100 rebate!

Visit Trashwiki.org for general info on freegans and DumpsterDiversParadise.com for a message board dedicated to this lifestyle.

Meanwhile, you can be a virtual freegan by going to FreeCycle.org or Yoink.com, where you can arrange to gift or receive free stuff from the comfort of your own computer.

## Shop local "one-deal-a-day" sites

I bought my two youngest children the chance to go on a helicopter ride for a mere $39 each. If you know anything about helicopters, you know the cost of putting one in the air is enormously expensive—certainly much greater than $39.

I was alerted to this great deal by Groupon.com. The function of Groupon is implied in its name, which is a marriage of the words "group" and "coupon."

Once you join this free website, you and every other member essentially leverage group-buying power to get one deal per day for extra cheap in select metro areas across the country. Each daily deal must attract a certain minimum number of buyers—set by the business offering the deal—or else it gets canceled.

Groupon is available in Atlanta, Chicago, Dallas, Los Angeles, New York, San Francisco, Seattle, Washington, D.C., and other large cities. Many of the daily deals are half-price offers for services, restaurants, and activities.

Unlike other deal-a-day sites such as Woot, you have to specifically live in or have access to a metro area to take advantage of Groupon deals. It's also different from Woot because the voucher you receive for your money can be redeemed only at a later date—not the day of the purchase. It would be too disruptive to the restaurants and other clients who advertise their businesses on Groupon if everyone rushed in to redeem their voucher on the same day.

The success of Groupon has spawned competitors like MyDailyThread.com and Living Social.com. Each service targets certain large cities, with an eye toward rolling out into more markets. If they're not in your area yet, set up an e-mail notification so you'll know when they are.

Groupon has gone a step beyond by making highly targeted offers to people in each city. You fill out a questionnaire online and then they're able to feed deals to you based on your responses.

As long as you don't spend money on things you wouldn't normally, this can be a really fun way to save! The only risk with these kinds of sites is the possibility that a business goes bust before you can use your voucher.

One other recent entrant into the "deal a day" field that I like is called ScoutMob.com. This one doesn't require you to buy a deal ahead of time and then find a time to redeem it as the others do. With ScoutMob, you simply get a text message with a 50-percent-off coupon, for example, and then save it until you decide you want to redeem it with the issuing merchant. That keeps you from possibly losing money for a deal you spring on but never get around to redeeming.

## New e-commerce site Glyde promises eBay for dummies

Get ready for eBay for dummies, courtesy of a new e-commerce site that's in beta called Glyde.com.

Launched by a former eBay insider, Glyde promises to take all the hassle out of buying and selling online. Sellers can list an item—a CD, DVD, or video game, for example—by typing in its title and making a notation about the condition.

If it has a UPC code, Glyde will upload a picture of the item for you and even suggest a market value, which can be changed any way you see fit. No mess, no fuss.

If there's an interested buyer, Glyde mails you a preaddressed, prestamped bubble-wrapped mailer and you simply drop your item in the mail within twenty-four hours. You can then request a check in the mail from Glyde once the buyer is happy, or donate all or part of your money to select charities.

The service takes 10 percent for facilitating a transaction. You as the seller are also responsible for an additional $1.25 for the price of the mailer.

Think of Glyde as Netflix meets eBay. It takes the complexity out of the whole process. As Glyde creator Simon Rothman told *The New York Times*: "We want the middle-aged Midwestern soccer mom to easily be able to buy and sell her stuff. It's a pretty straightforward ambition."

# ENTERTAINMENT

## Get $1 DVD rentals

We're in an era in which consumers won't spend on entertainment without really thinking about it. Some of the clear winners that have emerged in the quest for cheap entertainment during the recession include Redbox and Blockbuster Express. Both services offer automated kiosks—usually found in stores such as Walmart, fast-food restaurants such as McDonald's, and a variety of grocery chains—where you can rent new movies for $1.

Contrast that with the average of $14 for two discount movie tickets at a theater. Add in some refreshments at the movies and your bill could easily be $30! Which would *you* rather pay: $30 or $1?

Redbox allows you to reserve your movie online and then go pick it up at one of its 25,000 locations. When you're done, you can return the DVD to any Redbox kiosk nationwide. Now the company is experimenting with Blu-ray DVD rentals for $1 at select locations. Hey, at this price, you might even decide to dump pay-movie channels like HBO and Showtime!

The popularity of the $1 DVD rental kiosks has really hurt the traditional DVD rental stores. In fact, both Blockbuster and Hollywood Video have had to file for bankruptcy. The marketplace has decided that a DVD should rent for $1 a night, and the traditional rental stores are quickly becoming fossils.

The $1 rental kiosks branded as Blockbuster Express (BE) at grocery and convenience stores aren't owned by Blockbuster per se but by a company called NCR. Again, you can reserve your movie online before picking it up and return it to any of the 10,000 BE locations. BE is even edging out the dominant Redbox by having select kiosks download movies in digital form to SD cards.

The major Hollywood studios have had difficulty adjusting to this new, cheaper price point in entertainment. They hate the $1 DVD rental kiosks because they're demolishing studio profit margins. Why would anyone pay $15 for a new release in a store when you can rent it fifteen times over for the same price?

Visit Redbox.com or BlockbusterExpress.com to find a kiosk near you.

## Get cheap sporting and concert tickets online at auction

Don't blow all your cash on expensive tickets for concerts or sporting events. There's a new website that uses predictive analysis to let you know when prices will be at their lowest.

Too often, fans will overpay for an event because they simply must see that concert or that sports team. But imagine if someone could crunch the numbers for you to let you know the peak moment to buy. That's exactly what SeatGeek.com promises to do.

SeatGeek claims to use an algorithm that is more than 85 percent accurate. Their goal is to let you know whether prices are likely to be going up or down and if you should buy now or wait. If you choose to wait, you can sign up for e-mail alerts to let you know when prices take that plunge you were hoping they would.

The site displays real-time seat availability on a venue map for all tickets currently available for purchase. And if you decide it's the right time, you can buy the desired tickets right there on the site.

Keep in mind that this service will not work for every venue, every event, and every team or artist.

Several years ago, Madonna decided to allow the marketplace to set the price for tickets to her Sticky and Sweet tour. She teamed up with StubHub.com to allow fan-to-fan resale for those who couldn't otherwise get tickets. Sellers on StubHub were able to charge whatever price the market would bear. Zigabid.com is another site that is built on similar market principles.

Don't forget about Craigslist.org for tickets, either. Just beware of buying counterfeit ducats. If you use Craigslist, meet at the venue and verify the tickets at the box office before handing over your money to the seller.

Sometimes I miss the old days before the Internet. Whenever I used to want cheap tickets, I would go to a venue's season ticket holder parking lot and talk to people on the way in. The season ticket holders were usually corporate types who wanted to sell me their extra tickets for face value. But I would usually start out by offering $5 on a $50 ticket and let them haggle me up to $10.

The price would really drop if you waited until after the event started. A few years ago, I was at my thirty-fifth high school reunion, where a former classmate reminded me about how I bought tickets to a Notre Dame game for a scant $5!

### Get public domain books for free on e-reader devices

Have a bookworm on your shopping list? E-readers like Apple's iPad, Amazon's Kindle, and Barnes & Noble's Nook are all reshaping the book business. And while tiny netbook computers have been the hot holiday item of the past few years, I think e-readers are going to be what's popular for the next couple of Christmases.

With the book readers settling at a street price of around $100, the difference from one to another will be the features, and it will take a lot to convince you to pay more.

E-readers allow you to digitally download books and take them with you on the go. You can store up to 1,500 full books on these devices at once, which means you'll never be at a loss for something to read!

A big benefit to e-readers is that they will make huge numbers of public domain books— including many classics—available digitally for free. The book business is poised for the kind of shift that the music industry underwent with the advent of the MP3 and the iPod— minus the Internet piracy, I hope!

### Get thousands of free stations with an Internet radio

A few years ago, I bought an Internet clock radio for my wife Lane's birthday . . . and she was underwhelmed to say the least. At first glance, the gadget I bought her looked like a very boring and traditional clock radio. But when she plugged it in, she was getting 11,000 stations for free!

That included virtually any commercial station in the United States and all the Internet-only broadcasters. She got every format of music, talk, sports, and so much more, from the most obscure to the most mainstream with hundreds of choices in each category.

The one I bought was called the Aluratek Internet radio alarm clock with built-in Wi-Fi, and I paid $99 for it on Amazon. But there are a lot out there in the marketplace now for under $100.

It's no wonder satellite giant Sirius XM—a paid subscription service—is suffering. Internet radio is the future of radio. Soon, Internet radios will be in cars and offer the same kind of access that Sirius XM does now but for free. (You may pay a connection fee for the Wi-Fi, but the programming itself will be free.)

Internet radios have one substantial advantage over simply listening to a free radio stream on your computer: You don't have to be tech-savvy or computer-minded to use an Internet radio. It works just like a traditional radio if you have Wi-Fi at your home.

## Get free streaming music online

One thing you never want me to do is sing for you. Years ago, I appeared on an FM morning show's version of *American Idol* and was asked to sing a Britney Spears song. My rendition was so awful that I actually wound up making it to the final rounds of the mock competition.

Needless to say, I didn't win! But when it comes to helping you get connected with free music online, well, I'm your guy.

It's been so difficult to get people to pay for music after they've become accustomed to stealing it online. But a lot of promising initiatives have been launched in the last few years.

One of the early entrants was Pandora.com, which has long offered a free legal alternative to stealing music. The website uses artificial intelligence to play an endless stream of music suited to your personal tastes. You just enter a song or an artist and Pandora creates an Internet radio station for you. There's no downloading of music, however.

Another option comes from Grooveshark.com, a service introduced to me by one of my producers, Kimberly Drobes. Unlike Pandora, Grooveshark also gives you the option to download free music via a credit system.

For every song you upload, Grooveshark gives you credits that can be used to "pay" for downloading songs that others might have available. The rarer the track you upload, the more credits you'll receive. You get to own everything you download. Grooveshark handles all the compensation for artists, labels, and uploaders.

If that business model sounds a little suspect to you, consider this: EMI Records sued Grooveshark in 2009 but then reached a licensing deal out of court in a matter of months. As I write this, Universal Music is now suing over licensing issues. We'll see what happens, but I hope a licensing deal can be struck just as it was with EMI.

For those who just want to listen to music online and not own it, there's what's called Grooveshark Lite. This jukebox-style option allows you to stream music on your computer for free, similar to Pandora.

The main limitation to both Grooveshark and Pandora is that you can't download to an MP3 player. Pandora is available on the iPhone, the Android platforms, BlackBerrys, and probably a phone near you soon. As technology advances and new devices become more affordable, anything is possible.

# GROCERIES

## Save on your grocery bill at a hard discounter

I love traveling to Europe but am often taken aback by the high cost of food. My solution? Shopping at any of the ultra-cheap grocery chains that in industry lingo are called "hard discounters."

Hard discounters—whether in Europe or the United States—are infamous for their limited selection, emphasis on store brands, and dirt-cheap prices. They typically offer a very polarizing shopping experience that is loved by some and hated by others who are more comfortable in traditional supermarkets.

Germany's leading hard discounter, ALDI, has been making great inroads in the United States with about 1,080 stores in thirty-one states and growing. Save-A-Lot is another hard discounter that has its roots in the United States. Visit ALDI.com and Save-A-Lot.com to find a store near you.

*The Wall Street Journal* reports that Americans spend only 1 percent of their grocery dollars in hard discounters. Europeans, however, spend a full 11 percent. Europeans also choose store brands for one out of every four items they buy.

Here at home, however, we're so influenced by advertising that many people won't touch a store brand. Yet the store-brand food at ALDI and Save-A-Lot is just as tasty as that of a name brand but costs you up to 40 percent less than a traditional supermarket's prices.

When I shop at ALDI, I'll try their brand one time in each category. Sometimes it works, sometimes it doesn't. Their version of Oreos failed a Howard family test. But when it does work, we save that typical 40 percent.

As I mentioned earlier, beware that the shopping experience might not be for everyone. ALDI stores, for example, are about the size of a neighborhood chain drugstore; they have limited hours; there are no grocery bags; many take only cash, while others might accept select debit cards—but no credit cards; and you can usually count on long lines, small aisles, and limited selection.

I think the small selection can actually work to your benefit—there's no need to compare five brands of the same item because you have only one or two choices. What a time-saver!

*I buy my produce and fruits by bulk from a group of local produce warehouses. There are 5 families—all neighbors sharing the bounty. We are enjoying locally grown, inexpensive and fresh produce every day for a fraction of the cost of supermarket produce. All fruits and vegetables come in at least 50-pound boxes or cases and we split them. For example, we pay only 25 cents a pound for the biggest, sweetest Fuji apples. Also, the warehouses are right next to my son's school, so there's no extra gas for me to pay for, either. Check out your own local produce warehouses and form your own neighborhood co-op. Boycott the huge supermarket chains forever!*

*May T., CA*

## Buy nonperishable groceries only once a month

If you're watching your budget, try to limit the amount of time you're in a store—even for groceries. Go to a strict shopping-list system to avoid impulse purchases and buy your nonperishables only once a month. When it comes to perishables, you should get them only on an as-needed basis.

You can save by *not* being in the grocery aisle. Also, try Amazon.com or Alice.com as a place to buy your nonperishables. I haven't been thrilled by the prices at the latter, but you might find a deal.

I once interviewed a couple for a TV story who agreed to go to the supermarket for perishables only once every other week and to get nonperishable food items only once every six weeks. They paid off a mountain of debt in a very short time using this method.

## Get coupons on your cell phone

Okay, El Cheapo Man has a confession to make—I'm not that great with couponing. I really don't like going through the Sunday fliers and clipping coupons. I'd rather just go to a hard discounter like ALDI (see page 70) and buy groceries at great savings without the extra hassle!

Even when I do clip coupons, I'm such a flake that I'm more apt to lose them than use them. I once had a coupon to get the oil changed on my car, but it took me two days to find the coupon before I could use it!

On the other hand, my TV producer is so obsessed with coupon clipping that she has a big notebook sorted by categories like breakfast, lunch, and dinner. When she's in the breakfast aisle at the grocery store, she simply looks in her notebook and there's a battery of savings at her fingertips. That's so not me!

That's why I'm pleased with free services like Cellfire.com that allow you to get coupons sent directly to your smartphone, which is much more my style. The coupons can be scanned at the register straight from your phone, or else the cashier can type in the bar code. This definitely helps address the flake factor of losing those loose clippings. While Cellfire.com itself is free, your wireless carrier might charge a fee when you use the service. See the company's terms of service for more information.

If you want to take one step further into the realm of e-couponing, one new free smartphone app called Shopkick.com has partnered with Simon Malls, Best Buy, Macy's, and others to feed real-time deals to customers on their smartphones as they wander around participating stores.

It was enough to remind my executive radio producer, Christa DiBiase, of what we saw in 2002's *Minority Report*. The prescience of this Tom Cruise flick is eerie. In the film, Cruise is implanted with a new pair of eyes obtained on the black market that effectively change his identity in a world where everything is done by retinal scan. As Cruise walks into a Gap store, he's addressed with a "Hello, Mr. Yakamoto" by a saleswoman's hologram . . . because that's the name of the person whose eyes he got in the retinal transplant!

Putting the scare factor aside, if you're willing to trade some privacy for savings like I am, there are great deals to be had.

# RESOLVING DISPUTES

## Use guerrilla tactics when you have a company beef

There's no one silver bullet for dealing with customer no-service. Most of modern corporate America has decided to put customers with complaints on mute and that's really unfortunate for both customer and company alike.

Sometimes I tell people it's not even worth it to waste their time calling a company's general customer service number to complain because you can't get a live person on the other end of the line! If you still prefer that approach, there are two sister websites called GetHuman.com and Get2Human.com that tell you how to get a live person on the phone at a variety of big companies. Try searching the company you need to contact at both sites.

Often, however, you're better off going guerrilla. That means going to a company's website and identifying "C list" executives who are three rungs below the top brass. Look under the investor relations part of their website, or read press releases and other financial filings to find the names you need. Then call the company headquarters and ask for those individuals by name. You'll usually be able to speak to them or someone on their team who can resolve your problem. If your timing is right, December can be a great month to do this. The "gatekeeper" corporate secretary types are away and the real decision makers are more likely to answer their own phones.

I want to remind you that most businesses still really do want to serve their customers. It's not like they wake up in the morning and think, "Hmm. What new way can I use to rip off customers today?" But as companies get bigger, they tend to get dumber and lose the ability to connect. You've got to make them reconnect.

## Take your gripes online with the power of the Internet

If you're having trouble dealing with a noncompliant company or getting the customer no-service runaround from a major corporation, I have a new weapon to add to your arsenal: Try taking your gripes online with the power of the Internet.

It's become very important to companies to stage-manage their online image. If they're not doing it, a story can get away from them. The classic example of this has become the popular United Breaks Guitars viral campaign. If you haven't seen it yet, it's a humorous, low-budget YouTube video for an original song created by a customer to protest how United Airlines broke his guitar on a flight and refused to pay for it.

This clever man was able to use the online orbit to bring a major airline to heel, in a classic case of a David felling a massive corporate Goliath. United eventually came back with its tail between its legs and offered compensation. But the disgruntled musician refused and told United to donate the money to a charity of his choice.

In the aftermath of the fight, 10 million people learned about United's rotten customer no-service. Just do an Internet search for "United Breaks Guitars" and you'll see what I mean.

In a similar way, *USA Today* recently spotlighted a couple whose honeymoon was botched after Expedia told them they didn't need visas to enter Russia. Expedia denied that one of its representatives gave out such advice and at first wanted to pony up a mere $100 hotel credit for its mistake.

That's when the couple started blogging while stranded in Frankfurt, Germany, because of the visa issue. The couple's friends made their compelling story viral via Twitter and Facebook. Soon enough, everybody around the world knew all about the honeymooners.

That's when the outrage grew so loud that Expedia couldn't ignore it any longer. The company suddenly produced a record of the conversation and fessed up to its wrongdoing. The online travel agency eventually offered a full refund and threw in a $3,000 credit for future travel!

Of course, not everyone who Tweets or blogs or makes a gripe video will get results. But it can be a great strategy if you do it with humor or have a compelling story like the honeymooners or the guy with the broken guitar. One word of advice: Don't rant like a madman. Do it with humor and satire to make your point. If it goes viral, not only will you get your problem resolved, but you'll expose to all how much the company you've been dealing with stinks.

### Get your right to return TV infomercial products for a refund in writing

I probably appeared to be the most clueless man in America when someone mentioned the Snuggie to me and I had no idea what he was talking about. How could I have missed out on this pop culture phenomenon?

I finally saw an ad on TV for the Snuggie and later saw Snuggies for sale in a store. And just like that I got hip to the marketing allure of this wearable blanket.

But shortly after that, *Consumer Reports* took a closer look at the Snuggie . . . and the results were anything but warm and fuzzy. The magazine found that Snuggies don't hold up well to repeated washings, among other complaints.

Faring better in the *Consumer Reports* investigation of TV infomercial products was the magicJack, a Voice over Internet Protocol (VoIP) device that I routinely use when traveling. The magicJack lets you use your high-speed Internet as your connection to make and receive unlimited calls at a rock-bottom price: $40 for the first year of service and $20 annually for every year after that.

Well, the magazine found magicJack delivered a calling experience that is second only to a regular corded phone. I think that's high praise considering *Consumer Reports* won't accept lower quality for a lower price like I will! My audience, however, has given magicJack mixed reviews in the feedback they've shared with me.

One of the hot TV infomercial items a few years back was the Awesome Auger, a gardening tool designed to eliminate the backbreaking labor of digging holes in your garden.

While *Consumer Reports* didn't review this one, a Cincinnati TV station did. Unfortunately, the reporter said that the only thing "awesome" about the product was the extra charge you might find on your bill once you ordered it. The Awesome Auger was advertised at $19.99, but the "shipping and handling" charges totaled $140! The reporter went on to list all the complaints the Better Business Bureau had received on the product.

When you see something advertised on a commercial or an infomercial, the sales pitch is designed to create a sense of urgency before you come to your senses. ("But wait! There's more!") Know that you can never be sure what you're going to get. If you do buy something, make sure that you have—in writing—your right to return the product for a refund. Pay only by credit card so you can dispute the charge within sixty days if necessary.

# RETAIL

## Know what's a deal and what's not at the dollar store and warehouse clubs

During the Great Recession, dollar stores and other discounters were king. Everyone was looking for ways to cut their budget, and, hey, who could pass up the chance to pick up toiletries and household goods for a buck?

Well, *Consumer Reports* took a close look at dollar stores in their *Money Adviser* publication and revealed what's a deal and what's not.

Cotton rounds, gift wrap, birthday candles, paper bags, composition notebooks, plastic cups, security envelopes, napkins, foam plates, and tissue paper are all named as being among the best deals.

However, *Money Adviser* warns against buying jewelry (too much lead content); electrical products (possibly fake UL labels); medication (expired products); and vitamins (not from reputable sellers) at the dollar stores.

Now, I routinely buy medication like ibuprofen at dollar stores and have not found it to be past its expiration date. Sure, I could get a better deal on ibuprofen in bulk at a warehouse club. But unless you're in constant pain, who can use all those 12 million pills before they expire?

One word about how to spot discounts at the major warehouse club chains. At Sam's Club, look for anything that ends in a penny—such as $24.41—or anything marked with a "C" for clearance. At Costco, look for anything that ends in 97 cents. BJ's Wholesale, meanwhile, will clearly tell you on the label when they mark down.

My friends and fellow consumer advocates Ken and Daria Dolan recently identified some product categories they believe are *not* deals at warehouse clubs. These include produce and jewelry.

I completely disagree with them on the latter because the markup on any item at Costco, for example, can be no more than 14 percent. But I have to go with them on the former. If your produce goes bad before you can finish it, then it's no deal indeed.

## Buy gently used clothing at secondhand stores

Some sectors of the economy actually benefited from people's wallets getting pinched during the recession. Thrift stores are one perfect example. That includes giants such as Goodwill and the Salvation Army, along with smaller boutique-style shops like Plato's Closet.

I'm fond of picking up dress clothes at secondhand shops and have bought a few pieces of used formal menswear for between $1 and $7 apiece. They're usually in great shape because few men dress up for work anymore. Instead, today's standard office outfit usually includes khaki pants and a golf shirt.

On the other hand, I typically won't buy casual men's clothing at a thrift shop because guys tend to wear what they really like until it's threadbare!

One major impediment that some people have to buying used clothing is the pride issue. If you think it's beneath you to buy used, that's fine; there are others who love snatching up the savings of 75 percent to 90 percent!

Finally, it's always advisable to have your purchases professionally laundered or dry-cleaned for hygiene reasons, even though many secondhand stores say they already do it for you.

## Take advantage of automatic price-protection policies

In the Travel chapter, I'll tell you about a service called Yapta.com that will track airfares online and help you get a refund if the fares drop after you've purchased your ticket. Fortunately, there are a couple of free websites that take the basic idea of Yapta and apply it to consumer goods.

Many stores and some online retailers offer a price-protection policy. So if you buy something and the price drops within thirty days, the retailer might give you a refund. But who's really combing circulars and online ads *after* you've made your purchase? Enter the magic of the Internet.

PriceProtectr.com is a free website that does all the work for you. You simply enter the URL of what you bought and they'll begin tracking the price and send you an e-mail if it drops. The e-mail has specific instructions on how to request your refund, but it's up to you to pursue the money.

It can even be used for purchases made in traditional brick-and-mortar stores, so long as the item you buy has an associated URL on the store's website.

PriceProtectr.com claims to have so far saved consumers more than $3 million. Go out and get your chunk of change back!

## Buy from a well-regarded online retailer

If you've ever shopped online, you know the Big Three online merchandising sites are Amazon.com, eBay.com, and Walmart.com. *The Wall Street Journal* periodically tries out all three to determine who is tops in the world of e-commerce.

In their testing, they found Amazon delivered the best overall shopping experience—though not necessarily always the lowest price. eBay came in second with cheaper prices, especially on used or reconditioned goods. Walmart.com, meanwhile, lagged way behind, with a far inferior user experience.

I buy on eBay several times a year. The key criterion I look for is a seller rating of 99 percent or above. I don't even consider someone who has an approval rating below 99 percent. Because eBay doesn't ultimately stand behind its sales, the best way to avoid potential problems is to see what your peers have to say about a particular seller.

I had an experience where I ordered a charger for a new cell phone. And I thought I was ordering the right one. Including shipping it cost $4, which is funny considering how much you'd pay in a cell phone store. When it came in the mail, I realized I had gotten the wrong one. It was my fault.

Well, the seller has a policy that it wants everybody to be happy. Even if you make the mistake, the seller will replace it for free with the right stuff. I just couldn't do it. I could not take advantage of somebody who has such a generous policy in how they treat customers. So I lost $4.

But that shows you how high the stakes are right now in the world of making sure that people have a good buying experience online.

Online shopping is morphing, and you can even find competition if you're looking for ultra-fancy luxury items. There are a slew of members-only websites—iDeeli.com, BeyondtheRack.com, EditorsCloset.com, Gilt.com, HauteLook.com, RueLaLa.com, and Totsy .com—that promise up to 70 or 80 percent off exclusive boutique-style clothing.

The neat thing is these sites offer free membership. In some instances you might have to be referred by an existing member. It's not my cup of tea, but I know some people love this kind of stuff.

## Open your electronics purchases before leaving the store

During a recent Christmas selling season, Nintendo DS rocked one consumer in a very unexpected way, according to something I read in *The Dallas Morning News*.

The paper's technology blog featured a story about a woman who bought the extremely popular video game system from Walmart as a gift for her sixteen-year-old son. But when the young man opened the box, he discovered that it contained nothing but rocks and scraps of Chinese newspaper.

This kind of thing happens a lot in the electronics business—either from internal theft or at the hands of devious customers. People will buy an item, bring it home, open the box, put in an equivalent weight of rocks or other material, and shrink-wrap it back together. Then they'll return the box to the store as an "unopened" item.

Most retailers don't take responsibility in cases like these. Walmart certainly didn't at first. It took a reporter's calling the store to make them check their records. It turned out the particular unit in question had already been bought and returned once, so Walmart was able to make the customer whole with another unit.

Not everyone can have a newspaper reporter as their advocate. So be sure you have the merchandise you paid for before you actually leave the store!

# SEASONAL

## Buy seasonal clothes the day after the season begins

The calendar is your best ally when you want to beat the clothing retailers at their own game. Retailers work one season ahead all year round when it comes to clothing. So they put spring clothes on the racks during winter, summer clothes out during spring, and so on. If you buy according to their cycle, you're probably going to overpay.

But if you'll just watch the calendar and wait until the day each new season starts, you'll get clothing you can wear today at a deeply discounted price. For example, light jackets and spring dresses usually go on discount beginning March 20 or 21—whenever the first day of spring comes around on the calendar. The retailers are already on to summer fashions at that point.

## Black Friday websites scoop the holiday deals early

A decade ago, nobody outside the retail world was really familiar with Black Friday. Then suddenly it became *the* thing to do to camp out on the night of Thanksgiving and hang out until stores open Friday with their door-buster deals at 4:00, 5:00, or 6:00 a.m.

Talk about inefficiency. The crowds that waited so long would thin out by 9:00 a.m. and stores were like ghost towns the rest of the day. And retailers probably didn't make any money on the stuff they were selling for deep discounts anyway!

Then there have been the actual physical dangers of having large crowds of people mill around and dash like mad to snatch up deals. During Black Friday 2008, a Walmart employee was actually trampled to death by a mob of shoppers in New York.

Fortunately, you can now monitor the best deals out there on any number of websites dedicated to Black Friday deals. BlackFriday.info, GottaDeal.com, and BFAds.net are some of the ones I've checked in the past. They begin posting the Black Friday deals that leak out about a month before the actual day.

One of my best deals came when I learned about a laptop at Best Buy for $249 on November 11. It was part of a one-day sale that the electronics retailer was having to kick off a recent holiday shopping season.

For the past few years, retailers have been worried about shoppers feeling pinched in the wallet and dialing back on spending. That's led them to really make the idea of Black Friday something that starts early and lasts late. So there's no longer the same need to rush out on that exact day for the best deals.

Another way to beat the crowds is to skip Black Friday altogether and wait for what's called "Cyber Monday." That's the Monday following Black Friday, when online retailers offer promotional pricing on their products. When it comes to tracking the best deals on the Web, DealNews.com is my "go-to" website. DealNews ranks deals by "hotness" level to let you know when a real winner comes along. You order from the comfort of your own home and save big in the process. Now that's the "Clark Smart" way to beat the crowds!


## Vet charities before donating to them

Whenever the holidays approach, we're susceptible to being taken advantage of by our generosity. Anytime a solicitor calls seeking funds, your standard answer should be, "I don't give money over the phone. If you'd like, you can send me some literature on your organization so I can make an informed decision."

If you say that to scammers, you'll probably hear Mr. Buzz—the dial tone—because they'll be on to the next caller. One area that's been full of rip-offs has to do with phony solicitors seeking money for fire departments, police departments, and the military.

I recently heard about one group raising money for soldiers. But it turned out that only one-third of 1 percent of the money was actually going to soldiers. That means 99.7 percent was being stolen from people like you with false promises!

The state of California recently cracked down on more than a dozen bogus telemarketing firms working in this area that were pocketing the money themselves.

The seventeen telemarketing organizations targeted by the Golden State had completely legit-sounding names, such as the Disabled Firefighters Fund and the American Veterans Relief Foundation.

One of these operations called itself the California Organization of Police and Sheriffs. They had collected $30 million from people across the country. The money was intended to buy bulletproof vests for police and provide funds to surviving families of slain cops, among other things. So how much actually went for those two purposes? Zero dollars, according to the state's attorney general. It was essentially stolen under false pretenses.

Here's my rule of thumb when it comes to donating: You should have firsthand knowledge of any group you're considering funding. Give your money to organizations you know you can trust and believe in. The best organizations for this are ones you're involved in yourself.

You can also use websites like Give.org (a service of the Better Business Bureau), CharityWatch.org (a service of the American Institute of Philanthropy), and CharityNavigator .com to vet charities. Finally, established charities register with the Internal Revenue Service. You can search for specific nonprofit organizations at IRS.gov. Report any suspected instances of fraud to the nearest Better Business Bureau and the attorney general's office in your state.

## Don't buy gift cards

Gift cards are a holiday season favorite for a lot of people. But they are vastly inferior to cash.

Why would anyone want to take real U.S. money and turn it into fake money that's good only at a certain retailer or restaurant? And what happens if that restaurant or retailer goes bust? Consumers have been burned too often when there's no one around to make good on unredeemed gift cards.

That's part of the reason why gift cards are loved so much and pushed so hard by retailers. Gift cards offer the lure of "breakage," which is the amount of money an issuing business makes from cards that go totally unredeemed or are used only in part.

Recently, the Federal Reserve issued new rules on gift cards that have made these much-maligned holiday favorites slightly more consumer friendly.

The new rules pertain mainly to dormancy fees, service fees, and inactivity fees. Under the new terms, you'd have to forget about a card for an entire year before any inactivity or balance inquiry fees or other fees go into effect. Best of all, the fees must be clearly disclosed—not printed in mice-type by some lawyers spewing out legal hieroglyphics. In addition, all gift cards issued from August 2010 forward are valid for a full five years from the date of issue. Only after five years do any unused funds go back to the merchant who issued the gift card.

One thing the new rules did not do, however, is put in place a bonding or reserve requirement on gift cards that would safeguard the money in the event a gift card issuer goes out of business. So I still think giving a nice note with cash is preferable to giving a gift card.

There's only one exception to my "no gift cards" rule, and that has to do with cards for which you get goods or services in excess of what you pay. Then it's worth the risk that the issuing merchant might go bust. For example, you might pay $100 for a gift card at a restaurant and get a $120 food credit in return. That's great, but even then you want to be sure to use that gift card as soon as possible.

If you're on the receiving end of a gift card, treat it like a hot potato. Both holiday clearance sales and white sales in January offer great ways to use up gift cards you might receive during the Christmas season. Last January I bought new giant bath towels for $2.50 each and washcloths for 25 cents each at a white sale. Wow!

## Buy an artificial Christmas tree

One of the best bargains of the Christmas season is an artificial tree. Many people prefer a real tree for sentimental reasons and because they like the smell of it. But over time, artificial trees will save you a lot of money.

Sure, real trees are less expensive as a onetime purchase. But an artificial tree can deliver payback in just two seasons and you will have it for years to come. The best day to buy an artificial tree is December 26, when the price has been marked down, of course!

One word about what you put under that tree. If you've had a rough year financially, you shouldn't let guilt drive you to buy loads of presents for your children. When I was growing up, most children would receive just one gift. The notion of giving piles and piles of gifts and toys is a very modern one.

A few years ago, my youngest child, Grant, who was then two years old, was given too many presents. He wound up being more interested in playing with some Tupperware we had lying around because it really stimulated his imagination and motor skills. He didn't need an official toy to engage in play!

Remember, your kids don't love you based on what material goods you give them; they love you based on how much of your heart you share.

### A CLARK FAVORITE
*Buy roses for Valentine's Day at grocery stores and hand deliver*

Every year on February 14, I see those guys who haven't planned ahead for Valentine's Day making a mad dash for last-minute purchases at the end of the business day. I just know they're getting fleeced on whatever they're buying for their sweethearts.

If you are into romance *and* saving money, you've got to plan ahead. I often buy flowers for my wife from the warehouse clubs throughout the year, so there's no mandate in my house for flowers on Valentine's Day. But I buy them anyway in advance of the big day just to show that I'm thinking of her before the fact.

When it comes to the price of roses, even Costco marks them up around Valentine's Day. Normally you can get two dozen for $15 there. But during peak season, the warehouse club sells one dozen for $15.

Supermarkets are a great place to buy roses. The chain stores that have floral departments will often have multiple staffers on hand to accommodate people dashing in for last-minute bouquets. Another great place to go is a nursery. It's a very quiet time of the year for nurseries, and they usually sell flowers very affordably.

Delivery costs are another area that can really eat up your wallet. They can be as much as five times the cost of buying the roses yourself at a warehouse club! That's why I suggest picking up some roses and delivering them yourself to your sweetie's workplace. You'll save big and score a lot of brownie points in the process.

Holidays are mostly market-driven these days; you shouldn't feel like you have to spend a fortune on flowers or jewelry. Many times the woman you love would be more interested in your thinking up something romantic than blowing a wad of cash.

Handwriting a declaration of love is likely to be appreciated, even if you get the card at a dollar store. You should also consider eating out the night before Valentine's Day to avoid the crowds.

Around Valentine's Day, local dating services that use commissioned salespeople are heavily advertised. The Better Business Bureau often gets a lot of complaints about online dating sites, but no more so than soon before Valentine's Day.

The complaints include lies about the pool of dating candidates available; high-pressure sales tactics; and bad customer service. In my TV work, the station once sent hidden cameras to expose what potential clients face at dating services. One very tough woman who went in undercover came out in tears because of the ordeal.

Online dating services have proven to be very popular, but they typically cost money to join. OKCupid.com and PlentyOfFish.com are two of the newer players in the market offering free online dating services that I've heard praised by my listeners.

*I won't buy a thing without getting a deal on it. I'm single because Match.com does not offer discounts, and no one likes it when I whip out a 2-for-1 coupon at Chili's. I don't know why they don't like being picked up in my 8-year-old fully paid for Suzuki Aero . . . with my ideas of taking a walk as romance. If it wasn't for my absolute joy and pleasure in being so economical, I would have no love . . . but I love myself! Where is my lady version of Clark Howard . . . minus the glasses?! :)*

*Tony R., CA*

# Education and Jobs

Small business is the lifeblood of American capitalism and entrepreneurs have been the secret weapon of our country's prosperity. With the surge in unemployment because of the Great Recession, more formerly salaried workers are becoming entrepreneurs.

In this chapter, I'll show you how to start a business and help it thrive, and how to save money for college—whether school is eighteen years down the road or starting next semester. I'll also tell you how to find work at home that's legitimate. There are too many scams out there. Be careful!

## STUDENT LIFE

### Avoid bad 529 plans

What's the best way to save money for your child's education? I like 529 plans, which allow you to save money tax-free that's spent tax-free down the road on a child's college expenses.

But 529 plans can be unnecessarily confusing; each one is sponsored by a state and any state can lend its name to multiple plans. So how can you know which plans in a given state are good and which to avoid?

I've compiled a list that's available at ClarkHoward.com. Just search keyword "529 guide" to see my picks. I've singled out three particular plans in three states that make my dean's list (the highest distinction) and others in more than thirty states that are on my honor roll. You can apply directly to the plan of your choice right from the links on my website. Best of all, my picks are all sold commission-free.

Before you view my list online, I want you to understand that you don't need to put your money into a plan that your state sponsors; you can pick a plan from anywhere in the nation.

However, you may get state tax benefits (if applicable) for contributing to one of your own state's plans. If that's the case, a recommended plan in your state that's on my honor roll generally trumps any of the ones on my dean's list (for a nonresident). Of course, if you live in a state that doesn't have an income tax, it doesn't really matter; you can then just stick with any of my dean's list picks.

When you set up a 529 account, be sure that it's in your name and that you put your child down as the beneficiary. If your child doesn't go to college, the money can later be transferred to another beneficiary and spent tax-free on that person's college, or you can withdraw the 529 money and use it for anything—after paying tax on the earnings plus a 10 percent penalty.

A 529 is really just a shell and you need to fill it with individual investment picks. I like age-based portfolios best. The risk level is automatically adjusted every two years or so by the plan administrator, allowing you to take a "set it and forget it" approach.

Think about it like this: You need a different investment mix when your kids are five versus when they're fifteen. Typically, you want to be more heavily invested in stocks during their early years and pick safer options, like stable-value funds, as college approaches. Again, all of this is handled automatically by the fund manager of your age-based portfolio.

Another unique feature of 529 plans is their flexibility. You can put in as little as $15 each month. Or a rich grandparent can pop in as much as $65,000 at once without being eaten alive on taxes. Better still, the grandparents can retain control of the money in case a grandchild decides to major in Harleys rather than attend Harvard!

One final caveat: I always tell people that you shouldn't save a penny for college unless you are already saving the maximum you can for your own retirement. College can be paid for with grants, loans, scholarships, and work. Retirement happens only if you have saved the dough.

## Avoid private student loans

The private student-loan industry is one that really sickens me. Back in 2005, the industry bought off enough politicians to gain the right to do anything short of causing you bodily harm in their efforts to collect delinquent loan payments.

If you're in default, a private lender is allowed to seize your wages and empty your account without proving you owe the money. And private student loans typically can't even be dismissed in bankruptcy.

Simply put, private loans are the worst kind of student loan debt to have.

That's why I advise people who have both federal and private student loans to pay only the minimums on the federal loans and throw every dollar possible at the private ones. The sooner you get the private loans out of your life, the better.

Today's average student graduates with debt of over $23,000, according to the most recent figures I saw in *The Wall Street Journal*. Here's my rule of thumb regarding borrowing for undergraduate studies: Your entire loan burden for four years should be equal to or less than your expected earnings during your first year of employment after school.

If you're contemplating taking on debt to pay for school—especially if that means taking out private student loans—the alternative is two or even four affordable years of college at a community school. (See "Attend a Community College for the First Two Years" on page 88 for more details.)

## Try peer-to-peer lending specifically for the student loan market

The credit crunch leading up to the Great Recession hit all sectors of the economy, including student loans. The tightening of lending made it particularly hard to get a private, nongovernmental educational loan. (Not necessarily a bad thing, as I noted above!)

Previously, the best I could do was suggest that students who needed additional funds petition the financial aid office if they were at a private college or talk to deans and department heads if they attended a state school.

But now I have two new options to share with you. GreenNote.com and People2Capital .com both specialize in peer-to-peer (P2P) lending specifically for the educational market. Students can borrow from friends, family, and strangers alike after creating online profiles that detail who they are and what education goals they have.

Many of the same hazards and opportunities of the traditional P2P world apply here for lenders and borrowers alike. See page 173 for a more detailed discussion of what I mean.

## A CLARK FAVORITE
### *Attend a community college for the first two years*

Let's face it: The cost of college has become prohibitive for many Americans. Even the state schools have run up their tuitions as they face state budget crunches. So how about going to a two-year community college? They can be a great way to start your education on the cheap.

According to numbers I've seen, the cost of a community college is one-tenth to one-twentieth that of a private college on average. Of course, that varies widely from school to school.

Let's say you decide to do your first two years at a community college, and then transfer to a "name" school to complete your degree. People often worry about the lack of prestige associated with the community college. However, most employers look only at the name of the traditional college that issues your degree *after* you've put in your time at a community school.

In fact, I believe an employer might even prefer someone who worked their way through a community college and had to struggle financially. Doesn't that make for a more compelling candidate than somebody who cruised through a four-year college on the silver-spoon plan?

Historically, community colleges offered only two-year associate degrees. But seventeen states now allow their community colleges to offer four-year bachelor's degrees, according to the Community College Baccalaureate Association. Florida leads the way with more than a dozen community colleges offering bachelor's degrees.

So if you're contemplating borrowing yourself into oblivion to pay for school, perhaps the alternative is an affordable start at a community school.

*When I was a high school senior, I was unsure of what my future would hold. With limited guidance and even scarcer financial resources, I began working part-time for a major pharmaceutical company as an entry-level administrative assistant during my senior year in high school.*

*After graduation, I decided to attend a local community college. The experience was rewarding both in terms of cost and academic opportunities. Making an entry-level salary, I was able to afford the classes, books and fees on my part-time income. I took classes for two years, left without any student loans or debt, and transferred my credits towards a private on-line university bachelor's program that allowed me the flexibility to complete my degree in Business Administration as a single mother.*

*The community college charged $100 per credit hour, while the online university charged $372—more than three times the cost! I was also able to transfer my credits from the community college and complete my bachelor's in two and a half years at a significantly lower cost than had I attended the online school all four years.*

*Lillian D., NJ*

## Finish your degree in three years

When we think of college, we typically think of a traditional four-year experience or even longer. But by cramming an education into three years, you can actually save a bundle by eliminating the cost of housing, meals, and transportation for a fourth year.

That move alone will typically reduce the final cost roughly by a quarter. This is exactly what I did when I worked during the day through undergrad school and took classes at night over three years.

More schools are now experimenting with this idea. As just one example, *The New York Times* reported Hartwick College in upstate New York was offering a three-year undergrad degree. It involves a modified schedule where you go to school for a fall term, followed by a January term (sometimes called a "minimester") and then a spring semester. This kind of scheduling saves you $40,000 at Hartwick over the course of your education.

State schools can also boost their bottom line by adopting three-year degree programs. After all, the state schools are already bursting with new students who have enrolled in pursuit of a cheap education. So a full-year calendar increases the capacity of a state school by 33 percent without the expense of having to build any new facilities. Now that's stretching taxpayer dollars!

## Rent your textbooks online

I got my introduction to the high-price world of college textbooks when my eldest daughter was a freshman several years ago. At the time, I had to pay $135 for one book for one class! The average student spends $575 to use his or her books for about twelve to fifteen weeks—then they become yesterday's news at the end of the semester.

Fortunately, the Internet has come to the rescue by offering a number of websites like Chegg.com and CourseSmart.com that rent college textbooks. The latter even gives you digital access to textbooks on an iPhone or iPad.

Several years ago, I talked on my radio show about what a racket it is that professors get paid to revise their textbooks annually and push the updated editions in course syllabi. I heard from an angry science professor saying that the field of science evolves so rapidly that educators would be shortchanging their students if they didn't update.

That might be true at the graduate level but not at the undergraduate level. Most undergrads are just trying to decide what they want to do for a career. As part of that process, they're required to take a lot of different courses that may have nothing to do with their eventual field of study. So to make underclassmen buy an updated textbook every year is ridiculous.

That's why renting is such a smart option. In addition to Chegg and CourseSmart, other popular textbook rental sites include BookRenter.com, eCampus.com, and Skoobit.com.

Of course, you shouldn't forget about the old standby options of eBay and Craigslist. You might be able to score a real deal on some great books—both college textbooks and regular books—that you can buy to keep for extra cheap!

> *I took Clark's advice to look for books used online instead of new from bookstores. It's saved a ton on travel books. Best deal so far, I got Clark's first book on eBay for $.01! (turns out it was autographed too!) Despite the fact that it sold so low, I think Clark would be pleased that it went to someone who was being Clark Smart!*
>
> *Chris O., NC*

## See if you're eligible for student loan forgiveness

Every time I talk about special loan forgiveness for federal student loans, I get a wild surge of interest from my audience.

Under new rules, public service employees can enjoy full loan forgiveness after ten years of making on-time monthly payments on their federal loans. This is available to teachers, government workers, members of our armed forces, and those involved in emergency management, public safety, law enforcement, and public health, among others.

Visit the U.S. Department of Education's website at ED.gov and go to the "How Do I Find . . ." module in the upper right corner, then click the "More" button. From there you'll see a link for "student loan forgiveness" in the college section that has full details of the program as it pertains to teachers.

The folks at Money-Zine.com have put together a compilation of more wide-reaching forgiveness options, including some for Peace Corps volunteers and members of Ameri-Corps, as well as others. Search keyword "student loan forgiveness" at their site to see it.

As I said earlier, these forgiveness options are for federal student loans only. If you have private loans, you're out of luck!

# CAREER CENTER

## Don't fall for rip-off work-at-home ads

Many people want to do part-time work at home, especially when they have a newborn. But most work-at-home offers are scams. One stat that I've seen says that for every legitimate offer you might see, you're going to come across forty-two scams.

So you've got to be careful if you're looking to work at home. Be sure to avoid the ads in the back of women's magazines about envelope stuffing, doing medical office paperwork, and the like.

One area that has proven legitimate over time is becoming a call center worker from your home. JetBlue was one of the pioneers in the home-based call center industry. Now companies like 1-800-Flowers and J. Crew are also getting in on the action.

I have a list on my website of work-at-home jobs—many of them phone-based—that I believe to be legitimate. You can search "work from home" to see it. It's routinely one of the most popular searches on ClarkHoward.com.

Recently, *SmartMoney* magazine compiled a list of five work-at-home scams to avoid. If you've listened to my show or watched me on TV, many of these might be familiar to you as "golden oldies." Others, though, are of a more recent vintage.

### 1. Assembly and craft work

This is perhaps the oldest on the list, as it dates back to the 1980s. Don't fall for the pitch that you'll be able to do assembly work in the comfort of your own home.

### 2. Medical billing

This one first popped up in the mid-1990s. The gist of it involves buying a software package that allows you to process medical paperwork from home. There's a small kernel of truth here—some longtime employees of doctor's offices do this kind of work remotely—but the way it's being sold is a falsehood.

### 3. Mystery shopping

Here's another relative oldie. There are some legitimate mystery shopping sites such as Volition.com, which serves as a clearinghouse for this kind of thing. But most others are a false lead. Never pay anything up front in order to do mystery shopping or get information about it, no matter who is offering you the supposed opportunity.

### 4. Rebate processing

Here's a more recent rip-off. Rebate processing is a high-volume, low-margin business that's done at big processing centers and usually handled internally. This kind of work is generally not farmed out. The only exception might be a handful of hires who live close to a processing center.

### 5. eBay PowerSellers

This is another newer scam that promises you instant credibility on eBay and the opportunity to make a fortune selling online. But eBay transactions are way down, and the company is going through a midlife financial crisis. One big problem is the credibility factor of sellers and buyers alike. In reality, there's no insta-biz solution when it comes to eBay. As a seller, you sustain yourself over time only by specializing in a niche market.

## Beware of fake government jobs and grants

At a time when jobs are still hard to come by, one employer seems to have continuous hiring needs all around the country. This should actually come as no surprise—it's the federal government.

As government grows larger, there is obviously a need for more employees. In addition, there are waves of older employees getting ready to retire. Most of them were originally hired during President Johnson's Great Society initiatives in the 1960s.

The high attrition rate has led to a lot of bogus websites into the business of luring you with promises about having the inside track on federal hiring, usually for a fee. Know this: There is only one legitimate site for federal government hiring and it's free—USAJOBS.gov.

Once you apply for a position, the federal screening process begins, and it can be very confusing to those in the private sector. I recommend networking with anyone you can find—a relative, a friend, or even an acquaintance at your house of worship—who is already in the system.

While we're on the topic of the government, I want to say a word about offers you might see that promise to connect you with info about government grant money that's supposedly just sitting there waiting for you to claim it—again, for a fee.

There is only one legitimate grants resource that I know of online. It's Grants.gov and it states very clearly on the home page that it does not offer personal financial assistance.

Now, that's not to say there isn't government assistance available to some. You'll see a link on the Grants.gov home page over to Benefits.gov, where you can read about assistance that's available. In general, you have to apply and then meet specific eligibility requirements. Sometimes the assistance does not come in monetary form. So basically there are a lot of hoops to jump through. It's not anywhere near as easy as those ads make it seem.

On another note, what about those supposed jobs with the United States Postal Service? While the USPS is independent from the government, it hasn't been immune from crooks who promise to loop you into a goldmine of jobs if you pay them for their insight.

Not only is the Postal Service *not* hiring, but it had 160,000 too many employees at the end of the last decade. Remember that the next time someone promises to get you a USPS job in exchange for your hard-earned money.

## Fix credit report errors or risk not getting a job

A bad credit reputation might keep you from getting a job in a tough market. The best estimate I've seen is that between 40 percent and 50 percent of employers are running credit checks on would-be employees. And we're *not* just talking about jobs in the financial sector, which is where this practice started—we're talking all industries nowadays.

However, a recent study from Eastern Kentucky University found that there's *no correlation* between credit score and job performance.

So employers are going into battle with the wrong weapon. They're listening to the human resources departments that tell them to get a credit score on all potential hires, even though it's a meaningless indicator. Silly, silly, silly.

The real problem here is that many credit reports have errors. Public Interest Research Group estimates that close to one-third of reports contain serious errors that can cost you a job offer or prevent you from getting new credit.

This is yet another reason why you should visit AnnualCreditReport.com to pull one of your three credit reports every four months. (See "Get Free Credit Reports at the One Legitimate Site" on page 179.) Every year, you can get a credit report from each of the three main credit bureaus—Equifax, Experian, and TransUnion.

Paying off any small nagging debts will immediately help your credit. But if you have legitimate errors, be sure to challenge them both with the individual credit bureau *and* the credit issuer. You'll want to file both disputes at the same time by send all supporting evidence via certified mail. Tell the credit issuer that you'll sue them for damages if the fix is not made in a timely manner.

## Get a job in a city where your money goes further

In a time when unemployment is high, people are assessing where they want to live and where they can make their money stretch. After all, Americans have always been a migratory people when the chance to follow opportunity arises.

Salary.com's Salary Value Index (SVI) surveys American cities to determine where your paycheck will stretch the furthest.

At the top of the list sits a suburb of Dallas called Plano. The No. 2 spot was nabbed by the Denver suburb of Aurora, Colorado. One shocker on the list for me was Seattle at No. 10. I've always considered the Emerald City a very costly place to live, but then again, salaries are high throughout the area.

The worst place to live when it comes to stretching a buck? New York City, followed by Washington, D.C., Los Angeles, Honolulu, and San Francisco.

Salary.com also offers a feature where you can plug in the proposed salary of a job offer in another city and see how the cost of living there compares with that of your current home.

## Obtain a patent on the cheap

I don't have much creativity and inventiveness in this brain of mine, so I'm always impressed by those who do.

Most inventions start with an "Aha!" when inventors realize they can create something that will benefit themselves and other people. Once you have your eureka moment, it's important to do something that's so cheap but will be so helpful down the road: Write your thoughts down on paper and mail them to yourself.

For the price of a first-class postage stamp, you've now established a time line that proves your claim to an idea if someone else forces you into an intellectual property dispute at any point.

Stay away from any organization with ads on TV telling you to contact them if you have an idea. They'll trick you into believing they love your idea . . . but need several thousand dollars to take the idea to the next level. Before you know it, you're scammed out of thousands and are no closer to bringing the idea alive. (More on that in the next tip.)

So where can you turn? Try visiting the United States Patent and Trademark Office's website at USPTO.gov. They do a pretty good job explaining the basics of patent and trademarks in something approximating English, not governmentese.

I also like a book called *Patent It Yourself* by David Pressman. A new copy runs a little more than $30 at Nolo.com, and you can find it used for less. David explains in simple English how the whole patenting process works. His book will help you decide whether you want to proceed down the self-help path or hire an intellectual property attorney. The latter option can be pretty pricey.

Getting a patent is not the most difficult part; the most difficult part is finding a market for your idea. Building a "looks like, feels like" prototype is very important if you ever hope to bring your idea to market. You need to have more than just an idea on paper.

Think of this whole process as a journey, not just a single pit stop.

## Avoid phony inventor sites and scams

It's such a shame that phony invention groups prey on enterprising, hardworking people who could enrich their own lives and the lives of so many others with a unique idea or product. There was even a law passed a decade ago—the American Inventor's Protection Act—to safeguard consumers against these fraudulent companies.

The scams usually work in three steps. At first, they send you a free information kit. Then, they hit you up for $500 to $700 to do some "preliminary research" into the viability of your idea. After a few weeks, you receive another, thicker package, with a letter saying your idea is a hit and the company needs more money to start a marketing campaign. Only this time, they hit you up for $5,000 to $10,000! Don't allow yourself to be taken.

How can you find legitimate groups instead? For general information, HowStuffWorks .com is a good starting point where you can do a keyword search for "patents." Another good resource is InventorEd.org, which is an informational site for inventors.

Then there is the International Federation of Inventors' Associations (IFIA) at Invention-IFIA.ch. The IFIA even has information specifically for women, who tend to experience some discrimination from men in the inventing world.

You can stay out of harm's way by being educated. And when you see those ads on late-night TV promising to take your invention and make you rich, you'd better steer clear.

## Consider self-publishing if you're an aspiring author

Over the years, I have had a lot of questions from people wanting to publish a book. Most didn't know where to turn after they'd been rejected by all the giant publishing houses. Or else they'd been contacted by fake publishing houses that were more interested in their money than in their book.

Then in the late 1990s, bookstore chains and other legitimate players got involved in the self-publishing business. That trend has grown and grown until today it's now possible to hire a self-publisher for around $500 and get your book out there. Lulu.com and Blurb.com are just two of the more respected elders in this new world of self-publishing that's booming thanks to the power of the Internet.

With these kinds of services, you can make any number of arrangements. At Lulu.com, for example, binding your first book can be as low as $4, plus 2 cents a page. Blurb.com has several more features and the costs are a bit higher. But these are legitimate alternatives to the mega-publishers.

Other sites you might want to check out include 1stBook-publishing.com, Xlibris.com, and iUniverse.com.

Remember, these do-it-yourself services are ideal if you're publishing in small batches, such as a family history for a limited number of relatives. Don't expect to strike it rich from your self-published book. That takes a lot of market research, a well-conceived marketing plan, and some deep pockets.

Financial enrichment is the wrong reason to self-publish a book. Do it instead for the love of writing and telling a story. And if you do benefit financially, then you'll be surprised and pleased!

# ENTREPRENEURS AND SMALL BUSINESS

### Get free help launching a small business

Call me crazy, but I've long believed that the best time to start a business is during an economic downturn.

Space, equipment, and staff all come cheap during down times. To give you one example, aspiring restaurateurs have found that they can afford to rent a space with kitchen equipment abandoned by previous tenants during the Great Recession.

Whenever someone asks me for advice about how to secure funding and launch a small business, I refer them to the Service Corps of Retired Executives (SCORE).

SCORE is a group of grizzled "been there, done that" businesspeople who believe so much in capitalism and entrepreneurship that they make themselves available for free guidance when you want to launch a business.

Once you have a written business plan, they'll shoot it full of holes and then help you put it back together until it's airtight. Many SCORE people are also experts at securing funding through the Small Business Administration, particularly micro-loans of up to $35,000.

Visit SCORE.org to get hooked up with a representative in your area.

## Use a "kitchen cabinet" to help your small business succeed

A "kitchen cabinet" is indispensable for anyone who owns their own business or wants to start one. Much like the president's Cabinet, a kitchen cabinet is an informal group of advisers who help guide you and develop new strategies to improve your business.

If you don't have a group of trusted heads readily at your disposal, I recommend seeking out assistance from SCORE, as described in the last tip.

*The Wall Street Journal* also reports that there's a group called Athena International, which specifically helps women small-business owners with free mentoring. This particular group operates in many states through local chambers of commerce. Visit AthenaInternational.org to see if there's a chapter near you.

Finally, small-business development centers that are affiliated with universities in your community might also be of help. Check with the university nearest you to see if there's one available.

There's so much emphasis on assisting the entrepreneur who is just starting out. But often you need the most help about twelve to eighteen months after starting your business. That's the most important time to draw on the experience of your informal kitchen cabinet.


## Start a business and work out of your house

An economic downturn is *the* best time to start a new business. Space, labor, and equipment all come cheap.

In addition, we have something going for us here in America that makes our country one of the best places to start a business: We have the biggest houses on average of just about anybody in the world. Use those underutilized rooms to launch your business! The rent will be free!

*The Wall Street Journal* reports that more than half of all U.S. small businesses are based in the home rather than in traditional commercial, industrial, or retail space. That's almost 7 million small businesses being run out of homes across the country.

The average home business employs two people—the entrepreneur, plus one other. And amazingly, more than one in three home businesses generate a six-figure income.

One word of caution: Check on local city ordinances to make sure you don't run afoul of antiquated zoning policies.

But the benefits of in-home entrepreneurship are clear. No commute, no rent, and you might get a tax benefit by writing off a portion of your home for the business, including utilities. Best of all, the reduction of overhead cost improves your odds of success as a start-up.

So, is there an entrepreneur in *you* who could use that spare room at home?

## Work in a field first before considering franchise ownership

I have a longtime bias in favor of entrepreneurs and often call them the "secret weapon of our prosperity" in America. They're the ones who really create jobs in our country.

The lure of franchising is powerful during a down economy. Who wouldn't want to be their own boss and call the shots? But before you get involved in a franchise, you should first work in the industry that you're considering entering. Sweep the floor or empty the trash cans if you must. Just get in there and learn the ropes—and don't tell your boss that you'll be an eventual competitor!

Franchise ownership can be a dicey proposition, with some chains having great success rates and others having abysmal failure rates. Banks will often consult with an industry publication called the Coleman Report to determine if they'll lend to you as an aspiring franchisee.

Between 2000 and 2009, there were ten franchises that had a zero percent failure rate, according to the Coleman Report: Comfort Inn, Comfort Suites, Christian Brothers Automotive, Sleep Inn, Motel 6, Kiddie Academy, Taco Bell, Baymont Inn & Suites, Chicken Express, and Red Roof Inn.

On the flip side, ten franchises had some of the highest failure rates during the same period: Wings n Things (82 percent), Noble Roman's Pizza (76 percent), Super Suppers (69 percent), Golf Etc. (59 percent), New York NY Fresh Deli (57 percent), Velocity Sports Performance (53 percent), My Gym (51 percent), Image Sun (50 percent), Steak Escape (50 percent), and Wireless Toyz (47 percent).

Be careful out there and do your research first!

## Cyber-thieves are targeting small businesses

If you own your own business, you are at risk of being bankrupted by sophisticated criminal operations that have become experts at exploiting the antiquated technology used by the banking industry.

The nation's banks are still doing wires and Automated Clearing House (ACH) transfers to move money around. Both of these procedures *predate* computers in the financial industry. The criminals know how to have money wired out, and you're generally liable for any losses under current rules—even though it's the banks that are forty years behind the times with their technology!

The FBI, the FDIC, and the Federal Reserve have all issued warnings about this danger and have suggested an easy way to protect your business: Use a dedicated computer that's only for financial transactions, including payroll and bill paying. No surfing the Web on your dedicated computer. No e-mailing. No visiting Facebook, MySpace, or Twitter.

This will reduce but not eliminate the risk of a security breach. High-net-worth individuals might also want to consider using a dedicated computer for all financial transactions.

Computers have become so affordable that it's possible to get a fully functional laptop for around $279. Compare that cost with the cost of possibly having your account emptied out!

As a side benefit, taking this step will likely save your business even if your business account does get hacked. That's because you can demonstrate that you've taken what's called "due care" under the Uniform Commercial Code to secure your account.

One final suggestion: Contact your bank and request double or dual authentication on any wires. That means a wire won't automatically take place when someone requests it. The bank must take the additional step of getting a second go-ahead from someone at your business—preferably you—before completing it.

## Avoid business credit cards and use a personal card instead

What's the difference between small-business credit cards and personal credit cards? One can decimate the revenue of small businesses, while the other offers a great work-around and protections for entrepreneurs.

Politicians pay a lot of lip service to small business, but they really stab this economic engine in the back with their actions; everything they do is for the big guys who line their pockets. An example of this is a loophole in the Credit Card Accountability Responsibility and Disclosure (CARD) Act that offers some great protections for individuals but leaves small businesses high and dry.

Perhaps you've heard that the interest rate can't be raised on existing balances under the much ballyhooed new rules? Well, that rule applies only to personal credit cards. Small businesses have been exempted from this protection and others, leaving them exposed to retroactive rate increases, shorter billing cycles, and more.

In fact, small-business credit card interest rates went up six times faster than interest rates on consumer cards in 2010, according to BillShrink.com.

But wait, there's more! There's also a second level of liability specific to small-business cards. When you use one of these cards, the lender can do what's called "piercing the corporate veil." In plain English, that means if your business can't pay the bill, the bank comes after you personally.

And what happens when you lose a business card or it gets stolen? The liability of a small business can be *unlimited* under current law. Contrast that to the fact that an individual's liability on a stolen or lost personal card is capped at a maximum of $50.

No matter how you slice it, business cards absolutely stink for small businesses! So I have a simple work-around strategy: Use personal credit cards for your business. You can *pay* the bill out of your business funds but don't actually *use* any business cards. This is a surefire way to protect yourself.

# Health and Health Care

Health care spending accounts for 17 cents out of every dollar in our economy and it's not slowing down anytime soon. We have an unfortunate system where there's almost no transparency in pricing, so the one thing you usually can't find out is what a doctor will charge for a given service.

But the promise of consumer-driven health care is coming. In this chapter, I'll show you how to get the most for your money—whether it's negotiating a bill, getting coverage when you have a preexisting condition, or finding the cheapest prices on expensive prescription medications.

## SAVE MONEY ON PRESCRIPTIONS

### Get free or discounted prescription drugs

Did you know that one in three prescriptions sits unfilled? People will go to their doctor, get the script, and even drop it off at the pharmacy. But when they're told what the final cost will be, they let it just sit. Meanwhile, their condition can get worse, especially if they have a chronic illness.

A couple of years ago, my allergist wrote me a prescription for a sinus infection that contained ten pills at a total cost of $110. That was $11 a pill. After the pharmacist told me the total cost, I nearly needed to visit the emergency room because I fell down and hit my head!

When I saw my allergist again, I asked her about the expensive script. She explained that doctors have no idea what medications actually cost.

So what can you do to protect yourself from the high costs of medication? Shop retailers like Walmart and Target, which offer a wide range of generic drugs for $4 per month or $10 for a three-month supply. A popular southeastern grocer, Publix, and a northeastern super-market chain, Wegmans, even offer fourteen-day supplies of select antibiotics for free!

When you're at any of these stores, I suggest you grab a brochure detailing the discounted drugs (or print it out online). Then take it with you when you go to the doctor and ask if any-thing on the $4 list will work for your ailment. There might be a good reason why a $4 pre-scription won't work for you. But if it will, why spend more?

*My sister is a pharmacist and she taught me about prescription co-pay assistance cards that are available directly from the pharmaceutical companies.*

*I was seeing four specialists who all loved to pull out their prescription pads. But with these discount cards, my co-pay on my monthly meds went from $260 a month to $2.57.*

*When a generic drug isn't available, check the medicine's website for a co-pay coupon or ask your doctor because the drug reps usually give them to them. You can sign up online or by calling. It's free, and you just show the card to the pharmacy.*

*I started by going to the website for each of my brand name prescriptions. With one, I completed an online form, and a savings card popped up for me to print.*

*Whenever I'm given a new prescription, I ask the doctor if they have a savings card for the drug. If they don't, a quick Internet search tells me if (1) a generic is available, (2) if a savings card is available for the brand name drug, and (3) the approximate cost of the drug. If my final out-of-pocket cost is too much, I ask my doctor for a different prescription. The discount cards work with insurance and are usually available regardless of income. Other programs are available if you lose your job, insurance, or have low income.*

*Sarah E.H., TX*

## Cut pills in half and disregard expiration dates

If you know that expiration dates on drugs are really just conservative estimates of their shelf lives, you'll save a lot of money in the drug market. Some twenty-five years ago, the military and the U.S. Food and Drug Administration (FDA) conducted an experiment and found that many expired drugs were still effective. The savings to the military as a result of not having to destroy and replace expired drug stocks was immense.

For example, the FDA found that Valium, Dilantin, and the antibiotics tetracycline and penicillin were all potent a full two years past their stated expiration date.

*The Wall Street Journal*, meanwhile, once reported that Bayer aspirin can be used effectively for four years, despite the manufacturer's printing a two- or three-year expiration date on the bottles. Of course, I'd prefer that you buy a generic brand of aspirin to begin with instead of a name brand, but you get the idea!

According to what I've read, some medications used up to five years after their expiration dates retain 90 percent of their potency. Consult with your doctor if you're in question. I want you to save money in the drug market and do it safely.

Another suggestion I have is to ask your doctor if your medication is cheaper in a higher-milligram dose and have them write the prescription accordingly. Then cut the tablet as needed for your proper dose.

For example, pill prescriptions that are 10 mg or 20 mg generally cost the same amount. So if you have a 10 mg prescription, you can instantly cut your drug costs if you purchase the 20 mg pills and chop them in half. It's like getting twice the bang for your buck. Some drugstores even have devices that will split the pill in half.

## Together Rx Access card offers 25 to 40 percent discount

Since the middle of the last decade, several pharmaceutical companies have been offering a prescription savings program called the Together Rx Access card. You get a card that can save you between 25 and 40 percent if you have no other prescription-related discounts.

To be eligible, you must be under sixty-five and receive no prescription drug coverage from the government or an employer. Some income limitations do apply. If you're single, you must make less than $45,000. If there are two people in your family, it moves up to $60,000. Add $15,000 for each additional household member up to eight people. As a side note, Arkansas and Hawaii are the only states with slightly higher income limitations.

Simply visit TogetherRxAccess.com to enroll or call 1-800-444-4106 for more information.

If you're eligible, don't assume the price is always the best in the marketplace. I also want you to check at whichever of the three warehouse clubs—Costco, BJ's, and Sam's Club—is convenient for you. You don't have to have a membership to get prescriptions from these places. And remember that you can get many common prescriptions for $4 or even free from retailers and supermarket chains. (See "Get Free or Discounted Prescription Drugs" on page 103.)

# GET THE MOST FOR YOUR HEALTH CARE DOLLAR

### Negotiate the price for nonemergency medical care

We often hear about people who are uninsured, but we don't hear about people who are *underinsured*. A lot of people have coverage, but it may be only minimal for some procedures. Figuring out what's covered and what's not is like reading hieroglyphics.

*SmartMoney* magazine says consumers can really benefit by negotiating up front for nonemergency care. The classic example of this is an uninsured pregnancy. The list price can be as much as 900 percent (!) above what an insurance company can negotiate. The key is to negotiate beforehand; after the fact, you'll have no recourse.

Consumers need to know that the price difference from hospital to hospital is all over the map. So my advice is negotiate, negotiate, negotiate. About two-thirds of people who haggle *do* get a lower price.

Whenever I give this advice on air, a lot of medical professionals get hot under the collar. They often allege that I'm turning medicine into Walmart. But they need to understand that health care is the only thing we buy that we don't know the cost of until *after* service is rendered. Doctors also need to know that a customer with a cash payment represents more money in their pocket than a negotiated insurance claim.

### Use a nurse-in-a-box retail clinic instead of the ER

One of the most expensive places to get medical care is in the hospital emergency room. There's a much better alternative if you need medical care when your doctor's office isn't open.

"Nurse-in-a-box" facilities, which are typically located in drugstores, discount stores, or supermarkets, offer the services of a nurse practitioner who administers basic medical care. They can be a great, cheap alternative to waiting forever in the emergency room. Customers love these kinds of "store within a store" operations because they're open seven days a week for extended hours.

But what's the quality of care you receive at a nurse-in-a-box facility? It's actually very good. The September 2009 issue of the *Annals of Internal Medicine* published a study that examined the cost and quality of the care that people who had three common illnesses—otitis media (middle-ear infection), pharyngitis (sore throat), and urinary tract infection—received at a doctor's office, at an urgent-care center, and in an emergency room at a hospital.

The study was done by a team of PhDs and MDs from the University of Pittsburgh working in conjunction with two health-related research foundations, and the results didn't surprise me.

"Overall costs of care for episodes initiated at retail clinics were substantially lower than those of matched episodes initiated at physician offices, urgent care centers and emergency departments. ($110 versus $166, $156, and $570, respectively)," the journal reports.

And then there's this conclusion from the study's authors: "Retail clinics provide less costly treatment than physician offices or urgent care centers for three common illnesses, with no apparent adverse effect on quality of care or delivery of preventive care."

That last phrase—"with no apparent adverse effect on quality of care or delivery of preventive care"—tells me everything I need to know!

*My daughter is away at college earning a degree in drama, and if you don't know anything about drama majors, let me just say, they tend to be a little . . . well, dramatic. So when she called on a Friday to say she fell and hurt her foot, I gave her the parental pep talk and told her she'd be fine.*

*Then she called on Saturday. Her foot is killing her but she's too busy with rehearsals to go to the local urgent care center.*

*Finally, on Sunday night, after the urgent care center closed, she said she thought she should go to the emergency room.*

*An emergency room on a Sunday night? After a weekend of rehearsals? I had visions of huge hospital bills. Knowing my daughter's flair for drama (and most importantly knowing that at the urgent care center I'd only be out a co-pay of $35) I told her to hang on one more day. Emergency rooms are for people with broken bones, not bruised feet.*

*So she waited. Then she called on Monday. She has a broken foot. She also has a story*
*she'll never let me forget about her cheapskate mother. Yes, I'm a little embarrassed, but*
*when I think about the cost of an emergency room visit (easily $1,000) I figure I will*
*happily pay the price of one more "cheap mom" story!*

*Patti D., KS*

## Read user reviews of doctors online

We hear a lot about "consumer-driven health care" these days. But what does that really mean? One facet involves consumers helping each other out by putting up user-generated reviews of doctors or medical facilities that allow you to make an educated decision about your health care.

RateMDs.com is one of the most popular sites for doctor reviews. It allows customers to rate doctors based on the friendliness of their staff, punctuality of appointment time, helpfulness, and knowledge. I think it's especially important to vet a potential doctor whenever you get a referral to a specialist. That's where a site like RateMDs can come in handy.

Because there's almost no transparency in medicine today, the one thing you usually can't find out online is what a doctor will charge for a given service. That's why I prefer nurse-in-a-box facilities, where all the prices are clearly disclosed. But I digress.

Some doctors who have a bad bedside manner are getting their feelings hurt because patients are acting like any normal consumer and rating them in cyberspace. Recently, a San Francisco man who posted a negative review of a chiropractor on Yelp.com was sued after claiming the doc cheats insurance companies. That case was quietly settled out of court just days later, according to the *San Francisco Chronicle*. It's important to note that Yelp is a user-review site that's not specifically geared toward the medical field.

So far we haven't seen enough litigation to create any chilling effect on user-generated reviews of doctors online. If you're reviewing a doctor online, remember to stick to the truth and not jump to crazy conclusions.

## Take advantage of health care advocates

Navigating the health care maze can be an exhausting process if you or your family members are sick. Employers are starting to understand this and make health care advocates available to their employees as a free benefit.

Health care advocates are usually former medical professionals who help people get what they need from the medical system. Right now about three thousand employers offer health care advocate access. But very few workers even know they're entitled to such a benefit. Check with your insurer to see if one is available to you.

I think of the health care advocacy phenomenon like I do expeditors. When you live in a city, sometimes you can hire an expeditor who knows the right people to contact to expedite any request. In the same way, health care advocates can assist you in getting to doctors and certain facilities that you might not be able to get to on your own.

Of course, it goes without saying that health care should not be this difficult. Yet that's the reality.

## Set up a health savings account

Health care in the United States is outrageously expensive, as you well know. The problem started in the 1960s when companies offered to provide health coverage in lieu of pay raises and other benefits. That's when people began not caring what health care cost because they weren't paying for it themselves. The whole thing has been upside down and backward ever since.

Well, fast-forward to today and there is a possible solution. As a key part of consumer-driven health care, health savings accounts (HSAs) allow people to squirrel away money tax-free in interest-bearing accounts for qualified current and future medical expenses.

HSAs work in conjunction with high-deductible health plans. A high-deductible health plan offers rock-bottom premiums, but you typically have to pay a minimum of the first $1,200 out of pocket for an individual or $2,400 for a family. You essentially act as your own insurer, paying minor expenses until you have met your deductible.

In practice, that means you are the one bankrolling a doctor's visit for the sniffles or an annual checkup. The money in your account that you don't use over time grows with interest and can be tapped for future health expenses or moved into an investment account for retirement. In that sense, it's different than a flexible-spending account because there's no "use it or lose it" deadline to beat every year.

If you see the doctor frequently, an HSA is probably not a good idea for you. But if you don't, you can end up with a big pile of cash that grows with interest if you remain fairly healthy.

Individuals looking for HSAs and companies looking to start HSA enrollment for their employees can get quotes and other info online at HSAFinder.com and HSAAdministrators. info. Be particularly wary of any bank that wants to charge exorbitant fees to open an HSA. I heard of one that wanted to charge an annual fee of $235!

There are some people who don't like HSAs, of course. They think all of the money is being funneled to the healthy and rich. But it's better than our current system. Of all the economic output in the United States, 17 cents of every dollar goes to health care. That's about 50 percent higher in than any other developed country. We are basically sapping our nation's economic growth with the enormous amount of money going to health care.

# DEALING WITH INSURANCE ISSUES

### Get price quotes from area doctors when battling your insurer

For more than twenty years, I've been receiving calls from people who are in dispute with their health insurers about "usual and customary" charges. This is a tactic used by insurers to shift costs away from themselves and onto consumers.

Say, for example, an out-of-network doctor bills your insurer $100 for a procedure. Typically the insurer might cover 80 percent and you would pay 20 percent after meeting a deductible. But using the guise of usual and customary charges, the insurer goes back to the doctor and says it's only reasonable for the doctor to have charged $50 for the procedure.

Well, the bill is still $100 despite what the insurer says. But now the insurer is paying only $40 (80 percent of $50) and you get stuck picking up the remaining $60 tab.

In a massive conflict of interest, insurers were using an internal database to calculate what level of reimbursement they would give out-of-network providers for usual and customary charges. At the end of the last decade, a settlement between the attorney general of New York and UnitedHealth Group Inc., which owned the database, changed all that.

When brought to task by the attorney general, UnitedHealth admitted no wrongdoing whatsoever. But under the terms of the settlement, UnitedHealth will pay $50 million to a nonprofit group to build, own, and operate a more transparent database.

If you're locked in an ongoing dispute with your insurer, I advise the following: Go to other doctors in your area and ask them what they charge for the procedure in question. This will give you a consensus to show your insurer that the charge should be closer to what your doctor says instead of what your insurer says—and that gives you leverage to negotiate.

Remember, though, that prevention is the best medicine. You can completely avoid the hassle of usual and customary charges by using in-network providers only. They've already set negotiated rates in place.

## Monitor your health credit report

Almost everyone knows that you have a credit report that monitors the health of your finances. But do you know you have a "health credit report" that insurers check when deciding whether or not to take you on as a new customer?

In the era of electronic medical records, Ingenix and Milliman are a couple of large organizations that make billions of dollars compiling information about prescriptions on an estimated 200 million Americans and selling that information to insurers. Ingenix even crunches a "pharmacy risk score" on you to tell insurers the risk level you pose as a potential customer.

Both of these companies obtain their information from pharmacy benefits managers (PBMs), which are third parties that administer prescriptions through free-market insurance, Medicare Part D, and the Federal Employees Health Benefits Program. PBMs are a very popular option because they offer cheaper prices when you get your drugs online or through the mail instead of at a retail pharmacy.

If you have privacy concerns, you can always be proactive about the whole thing and opt out of information sharing under the terms of the Health Insurance Portability and Accountability Act of 1996 (HIPAA). But some of us might already have active dossiers on file. Fortunately, you are allowed to see your health credit report once each year from both Ingenix and Milliman for free.

To obtain your Ingenix report, call MedPoint Compliance at 888-206-0335. To obtain your Milliman report, call 877-211-4816.

Another even broader credit report–style dossier is compiled by an organization called MIB Group. MIB tracks anyone who has applied for individually underwritten life, health, or disability income insurance during the past seven years. As with Ingenix and Milliman, you are allowed a free copy of your consumer file annually through MIB. Simply call 1-866-692-6901 to request yours.

Know what your insurer has on you!

## Get written insurance approval before radiological tests

If you're like most people, chances are you've had an MRI, CAT scan, or other radiological test at some point in your life. The use of such tests has surged by 50 percent in the last five years, partly because they're potentially lifesaving tests. But they're also overprescribed by doctors who are afraid of being hit with a malpractice suit for *not* running the tests. In doctorspeak, they're practicing "defensive medicine."

To complicate matters, the big insurers are now using radiology benefits managers (RBMs) to assess whether they want to cover the procedures or not. A *Wall Street Journal* reporter found case after case where an insurer would precertify a radiological test and then, after the fact, turn around and deny payment based on the recommendation of their RBMs.

So what can you do? Before you proceed with any radiological test, get approval in writing—even if preauthorization isn't necessary. Don't settle for approval over the phone; you must get it in black and white.

If you've already had a test done, and you're getting a referral to another doctor who is suggesting another test, take your films with you instead of undergoing a duplicate test.

## Challenge a hospital's tax-exempt status when denied charity care

Hospitals across America are doing covert "wallet biopsies" to deny lifesaving treatment for patients, according to *BusinessWeek*. This is even happening to patients who have insurance!

In a wallet biopsy, hospitals take a separately purchased health credit report, as I just mentioned, and factor in your income, insurance, and level of debt. The goal is to gain a profitability index score on you so they can determine how to handle your individual case.

If your index score is too low—meaning that your insurer is unlikely to pay and you're unlikely to meet your out-of-pocket expenses—they won't treat you, according to the patients *BusinessWeek* quoted that were in this situation. The article went on to say that hospital billing departments are looking at your credit score, available space on your credit cards, and what's in your 401(k) at work for a reason to deny you charitable care.

But there is a way to fight back. Many hospitals have nonprofit status, which means that they receive massive subsidies from taxpayers in return for the promise to provide charitable care. If you truly believe you qualify for charity care, have a family member go directly to the hospital's administrator and threaten to challenge its tax-exempt status with the IRS if it doesn't deliver.

## Hire a medical billing advocate

I've had two surgeries in the past few years. Both were pretty painful but not nearly as painful as the bills I received in the mail.

Not only were the bills outrageously expensive, they were impossible to understand. According to *Money* magazine, roughly eight in ten hospital bills have multiple errors. So almost always the bill will be wrong, and it won't be in your favor.

It's hard to blame hospitals for the mistakes because they are so difficult to run. Should you just roll over and pay the bills? No way!

My advice is to document everything that goes on in the hospital. Keep a log and ask a friend or relative to write down every medication you are taking and every procedure you have. Then when the time comes to get the bill, ask for it to be itemized. You can then compare everything you have written down to everything on the list. It's up to you to be on your toes in the hospital.

You can also hire claims assistance professionals or medical billing advocates to look over your bill and vet it for errors. They're available in more than half of all the states. Visit Claims.org (Alliance of Claims Assistance Professionals) or BillAdvocates.com (Medical Billing Advocates of America) to locate one near you, and expect to pay between $65 and $125 per hour for their services, depending on the geographic location.

While you might balk at that price, I recently spoke with Claims.org's co-president Katalin Goencz, who told me that a claims assistance professional (CAP) can usually tell if there is a mistake on a physician's bill in less than 15 minutes. About eighty percent of the CAPs in her organization will offer fifteen or thirty minutes of free consultation time to assess your situation and see if they can help you. So I strongly recommend that anyone who is uninsured and paying retail for expensive medical services go this route.

# DIET, FITNESS, AND HEALTH

## Be cautious of weakened organic food labeling standards

My wife loves buying organic food. She routinely shops at Whole Foods—a store that I jokingly like to call Whole Paycheck because it's so expensive. But are consumers really getting their money's worth when they pay extra for organic food?

*The Washington Post* has reported that food producers have been able to convince the U.S. Department of Agriculture to lessen its organic labeling standards over time. The result is that there are currently 245 products (up from just 77 in 2002) labeled as organic that contain nonorganic ingredients.

At the end of the last decade, organics were a $23 billion business and the fastest-growing segment of the food market. Customers like my wife are often willing to pay up to twice as much for that organic label.

However, the newspaper estimates that 90 percent of organic baby formula is not truly organic. Other organic products singled out by *The Washington Post* because they contain nonorganic ingredients include cheese, beer, and duck. In fact, Consumers Union—the publisher of *Consumer Reports*—claims that some supposedly organic foods even contain mercury and polychlorinated biphenyls (PCBs)!

If you insist on buying organic, you have to make sure the label reads "100% organic." Just seeing the word "organic" by itself is not enough. You should also look for an ingredient list, the name and address of the handler, and the name and seal of the organic certifier.

Try buying your store's in-house brand of organic food to dial back the price. Most retailers in the food business have private-label organic food available. You can also try shopping at Walmart. Yes, I know the monster mega-retailer is anathema to a lot of "green" shoppers. But the reality is that it offers better deals on organic food than other places and can help you save that other kind of green!

## Cook double portions at home and freeze them

Cooking can mean many different things to different people. To my mind, it simply means putting something in the microwave—preferably frozen—and changing the temperature of it! But at the peak of the recession, the *Los Angeles Times* reported that many recipe bloggers saw their page views more than double. These are the kinds of sites that were routinely being ignored during better economic times. Somehow it wasn't deemed worthy enough to know how to cook easy meals from ultra-cheap ingredients.

Christa DiBiase, the executive producer of my radio show, has long used sites like Recipe.com and Epicurious.com to figure out how to fix simple and nourishing meals for her family. But now there's a huge network of family cooks who share their money-saving ideas in a whole new generation of blogs dedicated to the art of budget food preparation.

Some of the ones I've seen are HopefulHousewife.com, TheFamilyHomestead.com, HillbillyHousewife.com, and AllRecipes.com.

In addition to the money you can save, cooking at home can also be a real time-saver if done correctly. My recommendation is to dedicate a few hours on a Saturday or Sunday to making double portions. You can have a home-cooked meal on the spot and freeze the leftovers for use later in the week when you're too busy to cook.

Even if you can't figure out how to make a masterpiece worthy of Julia Child, simply making food at home costs a fraction of what it costs to eat out. For those who can't cook, you can always be like me and buy your favorite frozen meals on sale.

## Food fraud a problem for some high-end products

Fancy food products such as sheep's milk cheese and sturgeon caviar that are sold at higher prices because of their content might not be the real deal, according to a *Washington Post* report I read about what's being called "food fraud."

Two New York City high school students, working in conjunction with scientists, tested sixty-six foods and found that eleven did not contain what the label promised. For example, some samples of sheep's milk cheese were made from cow's milk and some sturgeon caviar was sourced from the lowly Mississippi paddlefish!

In other examples of food fraud, manufacturers themselves have sometimes been scammed by suppliers. California winemaker E. & J. Gallo sold 18 million bottles of Red Bicyclette Pinot Noir (vintage 2006–2008) that were later discovered to have been made from cheaper Merlot and Syrah grapes in France. It's been dubbed the "Pinotgate" scam.

The FDA has long been charged with ensuring that food contains what it promises, but the organization can't keep up with the task in light of more pressing cases of dangerous food contamination. They've just trusted the marketplace not to lie.

My solution is either buy plain generic food that makes no promises about fancy ingredients or buy fresh and local so you can actually meet the grower or manufacturer. Until the industry comes up with a self-regulating body to ensure you get what you pay for, know that it may not be worth the extra money to pay for the label with the fancy promises.

## Be careful with supplements and herbal remedies

I am among the two-thirds of Americans who take a dietary supplement—as in vitamins, herbal products, or those miracle remedies you see on bad late-night TV. For me, it's two chewable vitamins every day. But my executive radio producer, Christa DiBiase, takes supplements, including magnesium and others.

The scary news is that a recent Dow Jones report suggested that people can experience kidney failure and liver failure because the contents of some dietary supplements are not regulated closely enough. Meanwhile, a survey from the National Institute of Diabetes and Digestive and Kidney Diseases found that roughly 10 percent of people with liver problems developed them from taking herbal remedies.

The claims made by herbal remedies are generally not verifiable. The U.S. Government Accountability Office has found there's a real problem here: Companies are not required to tell the Food and Drug Administration what ingredients they use; they're required to report only if someone is hospitalized or dies as a result of using their product—after the fact!

So now there's a big fight about whether or not the feds should have stricter standards for dietary supplements. The Center for Science in the Public Interest has been vocal in wanting manufacturers to verify what's in their products.

The closest thing to any kind of oversight is an accredited body called the United States Pharmacopeia (USP). If there's a particular product you're questioning the safety of, try visiting USP.org and searching for info about it there.

This stuff is the Wild West of medicine. You've got to be careful with what you put in your body—especially with the claims you see on late-night TV. I'm stunned by the number of ads I see for what I'll euphemistically call "evening activities." Know that you are being conned by the actors. The product might not harm you, but it will harm your wallet.

Finally, be sure to tell your doctor about any dietary supplements you take. That information will help him or her be aware of any possible drug interactions with traditional medications you might be taking.

## Don't buy bottled water

The master marketers at Coke and Pepsi did a phenomenal job of converting soda drinkers into drinkers of overpriced bottled waters like Dasani and Aquafina throughout much of the 1990s and the last decade. They convinced us we were doing something good for ourselves by buying and drinking bottled water.

But just read those labels closely and you'll see the water is sourced directly from municipal supplies before it's processed. In essence, it's glorified tap water!

The Great Recession did a lot to involuntarily quench America's thirst for bottled water. People who lost their jobs or had hours cut realized the folly of paying big bucks for the stuff when tap water is available for nearly free.

Meanwhile, the green movement has taught us that bottled water is actually harmful for the environment—because of the gas used to ship it to stores and the plastic that ends up in landfills. These have been factors in its sales decline.

Here's my favorite angle: Over the course of a year, bottled water can cost you more than one thousand times what tap water costs. Committed bottled-water drinkers can spend $1,400 in a year on the stuff according to one estimate I've seen. Tap water can run you about $1 annually, if even that much. Wouldn't you rather put that $1,400 back in your wallet?

Some people who want to give bottled water the boot say they're not comfortable with the taste of tap water. The compromise is to filter your tap water at home. You can get a cheap external filtration system for around $10 or $15 and a reusable bottle for well under $20.

## Test your tap water on the cheap

After years of my prodding, my executive radio producer, Christa DiBiase, finally made the switch from bottled water to tap water. So what made her cross over from the dark side? She got hold of something called the Watersafe All-In-One test kit, which is one of the recommended picks of *Consumer Reports* in this field. Visit DiscoverTesting.com for more information.

For about $20, she was able to test her family's tap water for bacteria, lead, pesticides, nitrates, chlorine, pH, and hardness. Well, the water passed with flying colors, and her brood has been drinking from the tap ever since.

Buying a home-testing kit is also a great way to avoid the marketing push from water-testing companies. A few years ago, Christa got a call from a company claiming she had missed her appointment to test the water quality at her home. At first she thought it was a scam marketer. But it turned out that her sweet but absentminded husband, Mike, had scheduled an appointment without telling her!

Mike is a marketer's dream. He doesn't like to say no and once even signed up for a credit card the family already had—just because someone asked him to! Christa later reminded Mike that she had bought the Watersafe All-In-One test kit several months before.

The complimentary water test the marketer was offering Christa likely would have involved a hard sell in the home. These companies practically convince you that if you love your children and want them to stay healthy, you *must* buy their product.

## Stay away from toning shoes

Are toning shoes the real deal? This popular new type of footwear is supposed to tone muscles, promote weight loss, and improve posture just by wearing these shoes and walking as you normally do throughout your day.

Toning shoes sell for $100 to $250 and appeal almost strictly to women. That's prompted Skechers, the leading toning-shoe company, to hire former football star Joe Montana to pitch them to men.

But the claims that you'll derive some kind of exercise-related benefit from wearing toning shoes are "utter nonsense," according to Barbara de Lateur, a professor of physical medicine and rehabilitation at Johns Hopkins University's School of Medicine in Baltimore, who was quoted in a *USA Today* article. In fact, people are suffering injuries as result of wearing these shoes.

The professor worries that toning shoes can destabilize how a person walks and that wearing this kind of footwear can give you strained Achilles tendons. The shoes might be especially problematic for seniors and equilibrium-challenged adults.

So steer clear of toning shoes, ladies (and gentlemen)! Save the money and don't believe the hype. If you've already bought a pair and love them, just read what has been posted online about the potential dangers. Then make an educated decision about whether you want to continue wearing them.

## Beware of at-home genetic testing

For years, the ability to identify genetic health risks for common diseases and discover your ancestral roots was out of the price range of most people. But that has changed in recent years.

I remember discussing on my radio show an early leader in the at-home genetic testing field called 23andMe.com in the early 2000s. At that time, their services started at around $1,000. Now, they offer their services starting at less than $400.

The costs just keep going lower and lower as more and more competitors enter the field. But should you spend your hard-earned money on at-home genetic testing?

Well, consider this. The Food and Drug Administration is looking to tighten the reins on companies that offer these kinds of services after 23andMe.com mailed the wrong test results to the wrong people. The *Financial Times* of London reported that nearly one hundred clients got incorrect test results because of sloppy record keeping on the company's part.

"The mistake left one client believing that her son was not her own, while another was led to understand that she was of African origin while the rest of her family is Caucasian," the newspaper noted.

In May 2010, a competing service called Pathway.com was supposed to begin selling over-the-counter testing kits starting at $250 through Walgreens stores across the country. But the FDA interceded and has suspended that effort for the time being.

In theory, genetic testing at home is supposed to help people. The idea is that disease management will be greatly improved when medical providers can offer guidelines for patients who know they're genetically predisposed to certain diseases.

However, some researchers are worried that if someone gets a report that indicates susceptibility to certain genetic illnesses, they'll go into full freak-out zone. As the head of one research center told *The Washington Post*: "Information is powerful, but misunderstood information can be powerfully bad."

Following the 23andMe.com debacle, the FDA contacted the company and four others in the field—Knome COMPLETE, deCODE Genetics, Illumina, Inc., and Navigenics—asking that they submit test results for approval before sending them to clients.

It will certainly be nice to have some oversight to avoid the kind of clerical errors that tripped up 23andMe.com. Yet I'm not naive enough to believe that you can put the genie of at-home genetic testing back in the bottle. This is one option in the marketplace that's not going away.

So if you're the kind of person who would worry yourself sick about a bad genetic report, then you should have the foresight to stay away from these services—even if you are tempted by the increasingly low price.

# ELDER ISSUES

## Opt out of mandatory arbitration in nursing home contracts

Several years ago, *The Wall Street Journal* did a story about nursing homes that harm or kill people through negligence. Surviving family members had no recourse because they signed mandatory arbitration clauses when they were admitting their loved ones that locked them into bogus stacked-deck dispute resolution.

It's getting to the point that nursing homes have no incentive to *not* kill people; there's nothing families can do after the fact. Some nursing homes have even been using multiple holding companies behind the scenes to limit their liability, according to what I've read. There are a lot of things going on in this industry that are unacceptable in a decent society!

Now, *The Wall Street Journal* is not exactly a bleeding-heart liberal-publication—but even they were very angry about mandatory arbitration being written into nursing home contracts.

Before you put a loved one in a nursing home, I want you to carefully vet the admission contract and see if you can opt out of any mandatory arbitration clause. If you can't avoid it, try writing the following next to the clause: "I'm signing this because I was told that I have to." That creates the possibility that you can potentially get out of mandatory arbitration and seek justice in the court system in the event your loved one is harmed or killed while in their care.

Corporations like banks bullying you into mandatory arbitration is bad enough. But it's a whole different story if someone kills your mother.

Interestingly, the demand for beds in nursing homes has been far lower than what demographers anticipated. That's because more families are choosing in-home care options for their elders.

You need to feel confident about who's caring for your senior loved ones.

## Plan for the unexpected with an advance directive

Very few people like to think about the end, but there's an uncontested 100 percent chance that we're all going to die someday. A little preplanning can go a long way in alleviating the burdens both financial and emotional on your loved ones.

Today we're at a point where medical technology can keep people alive even though they are not really functioning. But that may not be the right choice for everyone. For me, I've told my family to pull the plug if I ever enter a vegetative state and have very little chance of coming out. So I've written that down in what's called a "living will" or "advance directive."

A living will is a legal document in which you state your wishes about certain kinds of medical treatments and life-prolonging procedures. The document takes effect if you can't communicate your own health care decisions.

Obtaining the appropriate living will form is easy, and you don't have to pay the $30 or more some lawyers charge. You can obtain your state's form from a local doctor, hospital, or medical clinic. Or you can visit CaringInfo.org (National Hospice and Palliative Care Organization) to download the advance directive free of charge.

This document must be signed by you in the presence of two or more witnesses, but those witnesses cannot be a health care provider or a person who would stand to receive a share of your property in the event of your death.

Once you complete the living will, you can even upload it and have it stored virtually by Google Health, which is another free service. Full details of how to do that are available at CaringInfo.org.

# Homes and Real Estate

W hich way will the housing market go? That's the million-dollar question for so many Americans who are underwater on their mortgages and for the one in three who rents and represents the homeowners of tomorrow.

We've all heard about how real estate prices have crashed. But in every time of hazard, there's also great opportunity to build long-term wealth. You just need the guts to zig when others zag.

In this chapter, I'll show you how you can score a deal on a distressed property, reduce your mortgage interest rate, lower your property taxes, and save money on some of the major purchases for your home, like appliances. I'll also warn you about common pitfalls, including burglar alarm monitoring and home warranties and other things that are way out there, like electronic mortgage fraud.

## BEFORE YOU BUY

### Short sales and deeds in lieu are the new foreclosures

Whether you're a buyer or a seller, a short sale or a deed in lieu of foreclosure may present a way to get out from underneath an upside-down house or get a great deal on distressed real estate.

For a seller, a short sale is one in which you work with a lender to market your home and sell it for less than the mortgage balance. While short sales were once considered more favorable than foreclosures, now both harm your credit to the same degree, lowering your score by roughly 140 to 150 points. As a mark on your credit file, they'll each stay with you for seven years.

For a buyer, a short sale can mean getting a home at a great price if you're willing to play what can be a long waiting game. About two years ago, lenders agreed to guidelines in which they were supposed to acknowledge an offer on a short sale in four days and answer back in forty-five. But that never happened in practice, and typical wait times on an offer are substantially longer.

Joel Larsgaard, at twenty-seven years old the youngest producer on my radio show, recently put bids in on seven short-sale properties, month after month, for the better part of a year. All his offers were turned down. Finally, his eighth attempt worked, and he got his short sale for $89,000 with a fifteen-year loan at 4.375 percent. The property had last sold for $155,000!

It took great sacrifices for Joel to come to the closing table with enough money for a 20 percent down payment. But he did it, and now his monthly mortgage note is $560, not including taxes and insurance. Think about that. Some people have monthly car payments that are higher than his mortgage payment.

One special warning for sellers: Be careful with the paperwork your lender gives you as part of the short-sale agreement. Some lenders are behaving immorally and slipping in legalese that makes their financial loss your legal obligation to pay back. That is not the intent or purpose of a short sale.

In today's market, deeds in lieu offer what I believe is a better alternative to short sales for sellers. With deeds in lieu, the bank agrees to take your home back without foreclosing on it. It also agrees not to seek deficiency, which is loss on the loan that banks are entitled to in most states. As a bonus, deeds in lieu have much less impact on your credit score than does a short sale or a foreclosure.

So at this point I'm recommending that if you absolutely need to get out from under your house, a deed in lieu should be your first choice and a short sale your second.

## Consider distressed real estate

There is just so much opportunity in buying foreclosures, short sales, and other distressed real estate at this point. But a few words of caution are also necessary.

The Internet gives the false impression that you have access to every bit of info and every tool you need to determine real estate value. But as a real estate investor of more than thirty years, I say that you should never buy by remote control. You've got to know the community, the neighborhood, and even the street where you plan to buy. My rule of thumb is to buy 20 percent below fair market value for homes and 30 percent below fair market value for condos.

Distressed real estate in the condo market has a lot of hazards in particular. For example, when you buy a condo, you're buying an obligation and a commitment in a condo association. Do not buy in a building that has been constructed recently. You want to look for established condo buildings that have been there six years or longer. With established buildings, you know that most people are paying their condo fees.

In fact, you should never buy early in any new development. If you do and the builder goes belly-up, you could be living next to scarred earth that's been homogenized for development and looks just awful.

If you're looking for distressed property in the single-family home market, you want several things: an established neighborhood that's ten years or older, a neighborhood where it's mostly owner occupied, not rental, and a house that is structurally sound with cosmetic damage only.

I'm not a fan of buying foreclosures on the courthouse steps because you're competing against too many skilled buyers who do that for a living. HomeSales.gov will allow you to check out foreclosures in your area. Once you find a property you're interested in, you have to work with a real estate agent, broker, or servicing representative to submit an offer.

One final warning about buying foreclosures: Most foreclosures are bought outright with cash. It's very important to protect yourself from the possibility that someone might come along and contest your ownership of a foreclosure. You do this by purchasing owner's title insurance (aka simultaneous title insurance). Don't rely on the title insurance the lender buys; you need your own.

*When the company I worked for shut its doors in 2008, my wife and I were in pretty good shape financially. We had saved up a rainy day fund and held no debt other than our mortgage and one car loan. During the nine-month span that it took me to land another job, I realized my long-held goal to buy and manage some rental property.*

*After taking out a HELOC against our primary home, we bought 3 houses. Each house was an REO foreclosure that had spent a long time on the market. I made fixing these houses my full-time job. I left home each day to fix the houses up (and listened to the Clark Howard Show while working).*

*Being a landlord is not easy, but I am proud of our rental homes. The rental income is slowly helping us replenish our depleted savings and allowing us to pay down the HELOC. Before recently having to evict a tenant, we enjoyed an occupancy rate of 37 out of 38 possible rental months.*

*The best part? The fact that we bought the homes from some of the "giant monster mega-banks" for an average of about 10 cents on the dollar from what they sold for in the peak of the market!*

*Mike M., GA*

## Never buy property without looking at it

Over the years, con artists got notoriously rich by selling people Florida swampland. This rip-off was especially popular in the 1960s and 1970s when future retirees bought property that was basically worthless because it was all wet. It became such a well-known scam that it didn't work anymore—until the mid-2000s when what was old became new again and the con artists came back to prey on another generation.

Sometimes people are all too quick to buy a dream and will suspend disbelief to buy land without seeing it. One of the new equivalents of swampland in Florida has been desert land in Utah. *The New York Times* reported that Box Elder County, Utah, intended to file charges against cons who had sold parcels of land over the phone and Internet to three thousand people in the United States, Europe, and Australia.

The land was supposedly adjacent to a metropolitan city. But when people would go to Utah to see their new homestead, they'd find that no such city even existed. Worse still, the land they'd purchased could not be developed because to do so would violate local and state zoning laws.

This new twist on the old rip-off scheme of land speculation started when cons took advantage of a Utah land rush and bought up property that was parched and desolate. Then they illegally subdivided the land and sold five-acre spreads.

The *New York Times* article was cute in a way. They sent a reporter to find one of these "conveniently located" parcels in Lucin, Utah. The reporter got to the location—some 150 miles away from the nearest big city—and found an area where the only inhabitants were a snake, a beetle, and large ants!

I have two simple rules to follow when buying land. First, never buy property without seeing it. Second, make sure the land has water rights or it's going to be useless to you. This second caveat is especially important if you're buying in one of the mountain states, like Utah.

## Use a home inspector before buying or selling

If you are considering buying a house, I urge you to have your own inspection. First-time homeowners often skip the inspection because they think government workers have somehow inspected the house. Although they have, these kinds of inspections are not enough.

Think about when a hospital, school, or office building is erected. There is a construction manager who makes sure things are being done as they should be. You want someone who does the same thing for you. It's especially important if you're having the house built.

Be sure you don't hire an inspector that your real estate agent recommends. Recent reports show that 70 percent of people do this. Agents suggest only those inspectors who they know will not kill their deal, and that is not in your best interest. You want someone who will kill the deal if the house is not in good shape.

Two sites that offer great referrals are the American Society of Home Inspectors' website at ASHI.com and the National Institute of Building Inspectors at NIBI.com. NIBI requires that its inspectors carry errors and omissions liability insurance, which means they accept responsibility for any oversight.

You also want someone who is certified by the Council of American Building Officials (CABO), which means they are current on all building codes.

Spend some additional money when buying a house and get an inspection. It's worth it. And before you sign a contract with a home builder, make sure you inspect the contract.

Some builders forbid you from hiring an inspector and that wording is included in the contract. So if you see it in there, give that builder the boot.

The same idea applies when you're selling a home. Before you go to market, you should hire an inspector to carefully vet your home. Be sure to fix whatever needs repair, and have the inspector's report and your receipts available for prospective buyers to examine.

As a seller, you have to psychologically try to get inside the head of a buyer. Even though a buyer might consider a used home, they still want it to be as perfect as a doll house. So let's say a corner of your roof needs repair and you don't spend the money to fix it. When their inspector finds it, the buyer is more likely to blow the cost of the potential repair out of proportion and make a lower offer on your house accordingly.

## Determine your best mortgage rate

Figuring out if you have the best possible rate when you go for a mortgage or refinance can be a difficult process. The industry has made it particularly hard to comparison shop in this arena. But TransUnion has a new website called TrueCredit.com that aims to level the playing field with a tool called the "Mortgage Simulator." Visit TrueCredit.com/Mortgage to access this tool directly.

For $10, you can buy a month of service that allows you to get a true indication of the rate you should get on a traditional fifteen- or thirty-year fixed mortgage or refinance. TransUnion takes into account info such as the location of the house, the purchase price, the amount of your down payment, your income, and your credit score.

I have to admit that it's historically been tough to get the best deal. I've had lenders try to cheat me every which way in my real estate dealings. But hopefully this tool can be an equalizer for you.

Two last notes of caution here.

First, you'll probably want to cancel this service in writing after you're done with it or the $10 fee will continue to be automatically deducted from your credit card or checking account each month.

Second, you might see a pitch to pay $14.95 for your credit score and report while at TrueCredit.com. Don't fall for it! Remember that the only site for your free credit report is AnnualCreditReport.com, as I've noted elsewhere in this book.

## Spend only 90 percent of your approval mortagage amount

There's a simple rule of thumb I tell people to follow when shopping for a mortgage: See what you qualify for when it comes to a traditional thirty-year fixed rate loan. Then back off and go house shopping at only 90 percent of that dollar amount. So if you qualify for a $200,000 mortgage, for example, don't look at houses above $180,000.

By doing that, you will help create extra financial breathing room in your life. In the past, people mistakenly thought that stretching to buy a home would create wealth for them.

Historically, however, home values go up only at the rate of inflation plus a little smidge more each year. Yet at the peak of the real estate bubble in 2006, most real estate was overvalued by 50 percent. Something had to give.

In 2011, we're going through what economists call a correction period: Prices went out of sight, they came crashing down, and now recovery will be gradual. We'll eventually get back on track with traditional increases in home values when jobs return and the rate of natural household formation soaks up all the excess housing built by speculators across the nation.

The expense of housing is like a rubber band—stretch it too far and it will break. Stay at 90 percent or lower and your wallet will smile.

## Buy a vacation home during the off-season

When it comes to buying a second home or a vacation home, it's best to know the cycles of the market where you want to buy. There are certain times of year that are better to buy than others—and it's all based on your desired location.

The best times of year are generally the opposite of peak season. For example, try looking between the summer and the fall if you want a vacation home in a mountain state that has winter ski activity. On the other hand, midwinter is the best time to buy in the Great Lakes, the Northeast, or Canada; hardly anyone else will be looking and you might meet up with a desperate seller.

If you'd like to own on a particular lake, ski resort, beach, or mountain, study the rhythms of the local market and know when to strike. Knowing the calendar could save you tens of thousands of dollars. Do not buy during peak season!

Aside from the cyclical nature of hunting for a vacation home, we are right now in the midst of great opportunity because of the housing slump and the Great Recession. When push came to shove and the real estate market fell apart over the last four years, people who owned more than one home tended to hold on to their primary home and let their vacation home go into foreclosure.

I've personally benefited from a bank-owned foreclosure in a mountain community that I bought in early 2008 for 42 percent below the most recent asking price. Some have said that I'm taking advantage of another's misfortune. But I've never understood that point of view; the home was already in foreclosure when I bought it, it's not as if I caused it. I was just there to take advantage of the opportunity.

Only in the last year have people seized the day as I've suggested. I read a recent story in *The Wall Street Journal* about how second-home communities are seeing sales rise by 40 to 50 percent. I guess banks are now seeing reality and selling the foreclosed properties on their books at great prices.

The big overhang of supply in vacation homes is going to whittle down over time, though it's not as if all the opportunity will end tomorrow. I think we will still be in a sweet spot into 2012 to get a great deal on the second home of your dreams.

# ONCE YOU'RE IN THE HOME

### Reduce mortgage interest by switching to a fifteen-year loan

One of the most frequent calls I get on my show is about how and when to refinance your mortgage. There's been great interest in refinancing, as mortgage rates hit historic lows and stayed in very favorable territory during 2009, 2010, and 2011. People used to go by the general rule that if you can shave at least half a point off your current interest rate, it is a good idea to refinance. But that formula has changed slightly over the years.

The easiest way to decide whether to refinance is to measure the cost of refinancing against the potential savings. If you can lower your mortgage rate through a no-cost refinance, that's easy. With no costs to refinance, you'll start saving right away. But the rate you pay will usually be higher than the market average.

If you go the other end of the route and decide to  pay closing costs on your new loan, compare your closing costs to the following: the monthly savings from your new mortgage multiplied by the number of months you expect to stay in the house. If it takes longer than thirty months for your savings to top your closing costs, you might not want to refinance.

One of my favorite kinds of refinancing is going from a thirty-year loan to a fifteen-year loan. If you have twenty-three years left on a thirty-year mortgage and you refinance into a new thirty-year loan, you'll extend the time you're in debt. If you choose a fifteen-year loan instead, you'll cut your interest rate even more and pay off the mortgage sooner. You'll have to pay more per month, though. If you can't afford the payments on a fifteen-year loan, consider a twenty-year loan instead.

Because house prices fell nationwide during the Great Recession, check the value of your house before you refinance. Lenders often will loan no more than 80 percent of what you owe on your mortgage. If an appraisal comes in too low, 80 percent of the appraised value might not be enough to pay off your existing mortgage. Unless you have enough cash available to make up the difference, you might not be able to refinance.

That's why more and more people have started doing cash-in refinances, where they bring their own money to the table at closing. This can be a great way to take advantage of low mortgage interest rates when you might otherwise be locked out because your house won't appraise out.

In fact, with today's very low interest rates, we're in a situation right now where I think you should do a cash-in refinance even if you have to borrow against your 401(k)—gasp!—to pay down that mortgage and get a new, ultra-low interest rate. It's unknown how much longer we have in this window of very low mortgage rates. So if you plan to stay in your house and can scrounge up the money, do it!

*From listening to Clark, I learned that I could refinance my mortgage and possibly get a lower interest rate with a shorter term. I went from 23 years left at 5.5 percent to a 15-year mortgage at 3.875 percent. My house will be paid off just as my oldest child enters his senior year of high school and I'll save tens of thousands of dollars in interest! My payment is slightly higher now, but using some of Clark's other tips I've been able to offset this. For*

*example, by switching my Internet provider I'm saving $10 a month and it's faster than my*
*previous Internet service.*

*Michelle P., OH*

## Avoid accelerated mortgages and set up your own plan

Over the years, I've received a lot of questions about accelerated mortgage offers. People wonder if these offers are a new kind of scam. "Scam" is probably too strong a word, but I do think this is a serious rip-off and I want to show you how to avoid it!

First, let's take a look at the offer. It arrives as a friendly letter inviting you to pay off your mortgage years earlier than you normally would. The deal is that you have to pay your bank or an appointed marketing company $200 to $400 to set you up on a biweekly payment plan. It also stipulates that you'll be billed another couple of bucks each time you make a payment. Or you may be told there are no start-up costs, but every biweekly payment will be assessed a fee.

In essence, this plan will have you paying half your monthly mortgage payment every two weeks. That's equivalent to 26 half-payments in a year. At the end of year, the marketing company or bank makes one additional payment toward your mortgage. So the end result is that you make thirteen months of mortgage payments in a twelve-month period. But because you probably paid an initial fee to set this up, the bank held some of your money all year long and got rich off the interest.

Here's what you should do instead. Keep making monthly mortgage payments and add one-twelfth extra in the additional principal box on your monthly coupon. So if your monthly payment is $1,200, pay $1,300 instead. That way you'll do for free what your bank wants to charge you for and you'll bring your principal down sooner.

## See if you're owed a HUD refund on an FHA mortgage

The collapse of the private mortgage market that accompanied the bank bailouts and the Great Recession put a heavy burden on the government.

According to figures I've seen, the Federal Housing Administration (FHA) accounted for about one in three mortgages written in the United States at the end of last decade. If you've ever had an FHA-backed loan in the past, here's a tip that could potentially be in the "found money" category for you.

Some FHA homeowners are due refunds from mortgage insurance premiums they paid to protect the FHA from the risk of owner default.

In some cases, people who are owed the money will be contacted by third-party companies saying they'll obtain the refund for a cut of it. Don't give your money away—get it for free by visiting the U.S. Department of Housing and Urban Development's website at HUD.gov.

Click on the A–Z Index, go to the R section, and select "Refunds." You can then search by your last name or FHA case number. Call 800-697-6967 if you need additional assistance.

## Appeal your property tax appraisal

A lot of homeowners got a lump of coal from their local government recently. Your home might have gone down in value during the mortgage meltdown and foreclosure crisis of the last few years, but there's little chance your property tax assessment went down with it. You're probably still being billed on old numbers.

The appraisals are out of date and they use faulty data from boom-year sales. The net effect is that your local government is ripping you off. There's simply no other way to say it.

So do you have to just sit there and take it? No way. You can appeal your appraisal. The rules for appeal vary by jurisdiction. In most cases, the appeal process begins informally with your filling out paperwork at the property tax assessor's office. This is your chance to state what you believe the value of your home to be.

But before you set foot in your local tax assessor's office, you'll want to have the "comps" that indicate the prices of recently sold homes in your neighborhood. Search out comps on the Internet or consult a local real estate agent for help pulling these numbers.

Comps should be a real apples-to-apples kind of thing, so if you have a three-bedroom, two-bath home, you'll want the comps for neighborhood properties of the same or similar layout and square footage and property acreage. You'll want to get your hands on two to five recent comps (the more current, the better) to get a true picture of your home's current value.

If you can get comps for foreclosures in your neighborhood, all the better. They're likely to have sold for very little so that's like having extra ammunition in your arsenal. These are the kinds of numbers that will be the smoking gun to help you get a rollback of your outdated assessment.

If the tax assessor ultimately turns up his or her nose at the value you're telling them, you might be able to appeal their decision through a more formal process where you appear before a board of your fellow taxpayers.

Whatever the protocol in your town, there are a few standard pieces of advice I can share. Never gripe about the government at any point during the process. Nobody wants to hear about how you think your hard-earned tax dollars are being poorly spent. Just present the facts about recent sale prices of homes similar to yours.

If you do have to go before a board of your fellow taxpayers, I suggest dressing business casual. The idea is to dress nicely but not too well, and people will respond to your appearance on a subconscious level.

## Monitor your home mortgage for fraud

Is your house in danger of being stolen right out from under your nose? A new kind of mortgage fraud known as "house theft" or "house stealing" involves criminals assuming your identity and then cashing out the value of your home. But there is a way to protect yourself.

A recent report from the FBI finds that there was a 36 percent increase in mortgage frauds of all types toward the end of the last decade. Nearly 64,000 incidents of this crime were reported in 2008, according to *The New York Times*.

The actual method by which crooks commit house theft is downright scary, as a story in *The Modesto Bee* attests.

"Con artists target a property, then assume the identity of the owner by creating fake identification documents. They use real estate forms sold by office supply stores, then forge signatures and file new property deeds with government authorities. That fraud transfers the property's ownership, then the home can be sold or refinanced without the real owner knowing."

So what can you do to protect yourself? A new website called ePropertyWatch.com has a solution. This free service will alert you if there's any change to public documents related to your home. It also offers regular e-mail updates about your home's value, foreclosure activity in your neighborhood, and more. As with most free things on the Web, ePropertyWatch.com is an ad-supported service.

## Thoroughly investigate a reverse mortgage before doing it

If you know a senior who is "house rich, cash poor" or if that describes you, you might want to consider a reverse mortgage. With a reverse mortgage, the bank pays you each month and gets the equity in your home over time.

Reverse mortgages are done by people who own their homes free and clear (or close to it) and need money to live on each month. Traditionally, this means elderly homeowners who aren't getting enough from Social Security to meet their monthly bills.

But there are a few dangers here. First, there's usually no inheritance to leave behind for family members when someone does a reverse mortgage. It all goes to the bank. Second, the fees on reverse mortgages have historically been way too high. While you might pay fees of up to 1.5 percent on a typical refinance, a reverse mortgage in the past could easily come with fees of up to 10 percent.

As awareness grew of those exorbitant fees, seniors effectively went on a buyer's strike and stopped doing reverse mortgages. That's now forced the banks to lower their fees.

Bank of America, Wells Fargo, MetLife Bank, and Financial Freedom have all waived origination fees and other charges on certain reverse mortgages sold as part of the Federal Housing Administration's Home Equity Conversion program, according to *The New York Times*. So if you're a candidate for a reverse mortgage and the fees were prohibitive before, you might consider reshopping one now.

But one last word of warning: Despite the new lower fees, I don't automatically recommend a reverse mortgage for anyone. You've got to do your own research to see if it makes sense for you and your situation. Remember, even though the FHA has reduced the fees, many lenders can and will still charge their own fees—and those can be outrageous. So you have to comparison shop, even under the new FHA program.

Reverse.org is my "go-to" website for reverse mortgage info. It's a free service of the National Center for Home Equity Conversion, an independent nonprofit organization. You should also thoroughly review the lengthy reverse mortgage guide put out by AARP before making any decision.

## Never sign a long-term contract with an alarm monitoring company

The burglar alarm industry is one that has a lot of honest companies, but there are also scam artists out there that you've got to look out for.

Nothing makes you feel more invaded than coming home to a break-in. Burglar alarm salespeople often read local police reports and might show up with an emotional sales pitch seeking to capitalize on your fear and anxiety after break-ins have taken place in your neighborhood.

Of course, it's better to search for an alarm-monitoring company *before* you need it. I recommend visiting user-generated review sites like Yelp.com and Kudzu.com to find a service that is positively reviewed by multiple people. Or you could drive around your neighborhood and look for signs in front yards of no-name alarm companies. Those kinds of companies are often the ones with the great deals. Finally, you can always try a simple Internet search to find a company, entering the name of your town plus a search term like "alarm no contract."

As you can tell, I have a bias against contract alarm companies. So when you find a company you're thinking about going with, the first question you should always ask is whether the company requires a contract. If it does, it's not the company for you; you never want to sign a long-term contract. If you did, you would open yourself to the danger of hidden rollover provisions.

With rollover provisions, you must contact the company in a very specific way (sometimes even on a certain day) to break your contract without being penalized. If you fail to jump through the hoops laid out in the mice-type of your contract, you're automatically renewed for high-rate monthly monitoring for a period of twelve, twenty-four, or thirty-six months.

Your second question should be about their monthly monitoring fees. You want something in the mid-to-high teens—no more than $20 at the most.

Then you have equipment installation costs. You can usually get a preliminary quote over the phone by counting the number of doors and windows you have to protect. Consider adding an internal motion sensor as well. Initial equipment installation costs can be anywhere from $600 to $800 for a typical home. Beware of supposedly "free" equipment because the costs will be built into your monthly monitoring cost.

Finally, make sure your monitoring station is UL approved and also offers integrated smoke and fire detection.

*Clark mentioned in response to a listener some time ago that security monitoring should
not cost more than in the high teens to low twenties per month. ADT had been charging me
over $30 month for this. They just sent me a letter raising my rate from $34 to $37 per
month. I called and told them that I was seeing ads for ADT on TV with monitoring for
"about $1 per day" and that it looked to me like they were taking advantage of customers
like me who have been with them almost 10 years. The rep's immediate response: "I'm
lowering your rate to $24.99 per month." It's not quite as low as I would like, but it is a
LOT better than an increase. Thanks to Clark's benchmark, I'm saving over $120 per year.*

*Alan J., VA*

## Remove jewelry from your home during an open house

An oldie but baddie scam has become active again in the home-selling market. During an
open house, criminals work together, with one distracting your real estate agent while the
other rifles through drawers and cabinets around the house looking for jewelry. The criminals might arrive separately within minutes of each other or they might come as a couple.

*The Washington Post* reported that in one instance at least $43,000 worth of jewelry was
stolen during five open houses in Fairfax County, Virginia.

My rule is to avoid the problem in the first place. When you list your home, be sure you
also rent a safety deposit box off the premises where you can stash away jewelry or other
valuables. Any important financial papers can be stored in a locked cabinet at your home.

Or as one of my listeners suggested, you could also try posting a sign out front that states,
"All valuables have been removed from this property." That should hopefully make any
criminal opportunists think twice before swooping in for what might look like an easy job.

Of course, most people who go to an open house will be honest potential buyers. But you
still have to protect yourself from the small number of people who aren't. Prevention is not
only the best cure here, but the only one.

## Try virtual picketing to resolve issues with a home builder

How should you deal with a builder who doesn't honor the terms of your warranty after you
close on your home? For the past fifteen years, I have been advising people to picket the
builder at their developments. You used to have to call your jurisdiction to find out how to go

about picketing and make sure that you never said slanderous things about the builder's character.

But today instead of physically picketing, people take their ire online. *BusinessWeek* did a report on homeowners who have set up gripe websites. Some builders have fought back by trying to put clauses in their contracts that aim to silence you if you do business with them. That's an infringement of free speech. A builder who is afraid of the truth is not someone you want as a business partner.

I know that building a house is difficult and involves a lot of micro-management with all the day laborers and subcontractors. That why I advise people *not* to close on their home until all the contractual items are complete. If you're getting pressure to close anyway, consider hiring a lawyer to withhold money in escrow to cover any outstanding issues. This practice, known as "retainage," is set at a standard 10 percent in the commercial market.

Once a builder completes your house, you're yesterday's news. The only reason they have to care about you is their reputation. So consider taking your battle online if need be.

# RENTING

### Shop for an apartment sixty days before your lease expires

If you're among the roughly one in three Americans who rents instead of owning a home, there's good news for you in the marketplace. Toward the end of the last decade, the number of apartment vacancies hit a thirty-year high. It will likely be a while before things get back to normal. This creates great opportunity for tenants if they choose to accept the shopping challenge!

Very often, when your lease expires, you might get a renewal bonus like a gift card to entice you to sign on again. But take a cue from *Jerry Maguire* and say, "Show me the money!" You can get real savings by being willing to walk.

I want you to start searching for a new apartment sixty to ninety days before your lease is up, unless you're required to give more notice. Do a thorough search of traditional apartments and also check out condos, which might be newer and might rent for less per square foot than an apartment.

Take the info you've collected and lay it out for your current landlord or property manager. By showing him or her what's available in the marketplace, you have some ammunition to ask for a better deal on rent when it's time to sign another lease.

You might be surprised at the offer your landlord comes back with to keep you. You might get a free month of rent, a waiver of the security deposit, or a kick-out clause in the event that you're laid-off.

But you get that power only if you're willing to walk out of your current situation at renewal time. Landlords have to spend big bucks to find new tenants or to let an apartment sit vacant, so you hold the power.

If you'd rather stay put where you are, you should still search for apartments and then show your current landlord what you've found. It never hurts to ask if he or she will compete against the other cheaper rents out there.

Finally, when you vacate an apartment, be sure to leave it spotless and make any necessary repairs. Hire a cleaner to get it in order if you must. Just be certain to take pictures or video of the condition so the landlord has no reason to withhold your security deposit.

## Bargain in the "shadow market" for vacant condos

The data on rental apartments shows that the number of vacancies is the highest it's been in a generation. You'd have to go back to the mid-1980s to find a similar glut of empty rentals in the marketplace.

This is actually the complete opposite of what economists expected. Technically, the rash of foreclosures that resulted from job loss in the Great Recession should have created more renters. But there were several factors running interference here.

First, a large "shadow market" of condo owners who bought properties as speculators and now can't sell have been forced into becoming involuntary landlords. That creates competition for the traditional apartment complexes.

Second, many people in their twenties are getting out of school and going straight back home to live with their families because of the job crunch, or else they're boomeranging back home after living on their own once they face a job loss.

You'll find the greatest hazard and opportunity alike in renting from the shadow market. Involuntary landlords usually just need the money and don't know or care much about maintaining a property. You might not get a prompt response on maintenance issues. But involuntary landlords are also likely to offer you cheaper rent than a traditional rental complex.

Other dangers of the shadow market include possible risk of landlord foreclosure. In prior times, paying renters could find themselves on the street in as little as five days after their landlord was served with a foreclosure notice. Fortunately, there's a new federal housing law on the books that provides protection for tenants who are current on their rent even when their landlords are facing foreclosure.

The law permits paying tenants to stay for the remainder of the lease, plus an additional ninety days. If you're renting without a lease, you'll get a ninety-day notice of eviction.

The foreclosing bank essentially becomes your landlord and tells you where to mail your check.

## Crooks might pose as landlords to rent foreclosures

Con artists have been taking advantage of the housing meltdown by acting as bogus landlords and renting foreclosures.

Here's how this rip-off typically plays out: Criminals will call a locksmith out to a foreclosed property and say they locked themselves out. Once they get in the house, they'll pay a locksmith for his or her service, and when the locksmith leaves, they'll call another one to come out to rekey the lock.

When the coast is clear, they'll put up a "For Lease" sign or list the property on Craigslist. Unsuspecting tenants go to look at the property and find it's a steal of a deal. And of course the criminal who is masquerading as the landlord is only too happy to take a deposit and hand over the keys.

The unwitting tenants often continue paying rent each month by sending their check to a post office box. Then one day, out of the blue, someone comes around and asks them, "I'm with such-and-such bank and this is a foreclosure. Why are you living here?"

Special thanks to my listener Raymond for letting me know about this scam. Raymond works as a realtor and reports that some crooks are even scraping info from legit multiple listing service (MLS) entries to enhance their Craigslist come-ons.

Here's what Raymond told us about how this scam affected one of his listings: "I looked up the ad [on] Craigslist, and there was my listing complete with the description from my website and several of the pictures I'd taken. [The criminal] was offering this 2,000-square-foot home in a community that has a swimming pool, park, and tennis courts at $750 per month! Such a home would really rent from $1,250 to $1,500 a month."

How can you as a would-be renter protect yourself? Have your potential new landlord show you a copy of the deed on the property. If you feel awkward about asking to see the deed, you can also check with the county assessor's office. They should be able to help you verify that the person presenting himself or herself as the landlord is in fact the true owner on record.

A few more general warnings apply here as well: Don't ever wire money for a deposit. Be suspicious of post office box addresses as a way to send monthly rent; physical street addresses are much safer. And be sure you have a written and executed lease before occupying any property.

Most of the time, landlords will be on the up and up, but you have to protect yourself in the few cases when they're not.

## Shop around for quotes from movers

The Census Bureau found that only 11 percent of Americans moved in 2008 at the peak of the Great Recession. That's down from the typical annual average of 20 percent, according to the *San Francisco Chronicle*.

Why the dearth of people moving? Homeowners simply couldn't afford to take the loss on selling their homes. Plus, there weren't that many jobs available to prompt people to move! The effect is that the moving industry was in a depression and those who did want to move had real pricing power.

The ways you can move have changed. You can hire movers to pack up your possessions and then drive them yourself, you can do it all yourself, or you can load up a portable on-demand storage unit and have a company move it. And as always, you can hire a traditional mover to do everything for you from start to finish.

One thing I tell people is that there's always variable pricing for moving trucks based on the day of the week, the time of the month, and whether you're moving to or from a particular city. It pays to shop around on the Web or to call around for several quotes.

Begin by checking Moving.org, the official site of the American Moving and Storage Association. That's the industry's nonprofit trade association, and they have the ProMover program to help you connect with reputable movers. This new program tries to weed out the rogue operators who might rip you off.

Even when going with a certified ProMover, be sure you get a "binding estimate" in advance specifying the cost of your move. Also, buy replacement value insurance on your possessions separately in case something breaks; the current payout rate was set in the 1930s and never adjusted for inflation. And, finally, videotape your possessions before you start packing so there are no disputes about what you owned if something goes missing.

If you have particularly bulky items to ship—like a boat or heavy machinery—I have another suggestion. Visit UShip.com to let customer-rated movers bid for your moving job.

# ENERGY AND APPLIANCES

### Set up a repair fund in lieu of a home warranty

When you buy a used home, you'll get a lot of pitches about home warranties that are supposed to pay for unexpected repairs. Though I'm not a fan of them, sales of home warranties were significantly strong during the Great Recession as people looked for ways to control costs throughout a time of economic uncertainty.

The California Home Service Contract Association, for example, reported that in one recent year, nearly nine out of every ten housing transactions in the state included a warranty.

Most basic home warranties will cover a home's major operating systems for one year after you purchase the house. That typically means plumbing, electrical and heating systems, hot water heaters, garage door openers, limited pest control, and most built-in appliances.

I know, however, from the calls I get on my show that too many of the outfits pushing home warranties are more interested in selling their policies than in paying for repairs when something breaks. That's why I've long said that the only good time to buy a policy is if you're selling a used home and you want to give a would-be buyer some extra assurance. Think of it as the cost of doing business in a buyer's market.

For most consumers, home warranties have so many limitations and exclusions that they're just not worth the price. In addition to the $300 to $500 for the policy, you must pay more money for each service call. And oftentimes the company claims you are at fault for the damage and won't pay, or else they'll replace failing appliances with substandard equipment after they play the waiting game with you.

You're better off putting $50 each month into a repair fund account and saving for a rainy day on your own.

> *I purchased a home warranty last year thinking that it would make life easier if anything major happened to my appliances, especially the central heat and air. Clark doesn't recommend doing this, but the contract stated it could be canceled anytime. In addition, if you canceled in the first month, you were supposed to be able to get your first payment back.*
>
> *I didn't use the warranty and decided to cancel the contract, but I never could get through on the phone. Their automated system kept me on hold, saying it would be "more than 15 minutes." I stayed on the line. Finally, when a person answered, I told them I wanted to cancel and then was put on hold again with the system saying it would be another 15 minutes of holding! They never came back on the phone.*
>
> *I had to end up canceling by changing my credit card number for fear they would take out the next premium. A few weeks later, I got a letter from an attorney stating that I had a debt for $450, which was the cost of the entire annual contract! I had 30 days to respond or the debt would be enforced. Immediately I responded to the letter, explaining my situation. I sent it back to them certified mail. A few weeks later, I got a return letter stating the charges were dismissed. This saved $450, not to mention my good credit!*
>
> *Shirley S., GA*

## Shop at a local scratch-and-dent store for appliance deals

I recently had to shop for a new washer/dryer combo when mine croaked after years of loyal service. So where did I go to shop? A "scratch-and-dent" appliance store, of course.

Scratch-and-dent stores offer new appliances that have been sufficiently scuffed up during shipping to the point where they can't be sold in a traditional appliance store.

In my case, I had been pricing the same model I wanted at Costco and ultimately paid *half the price* at the scratch-and-dent—after checking reliability stats in *Consumer Reports*, of course. If you can beat Costco by that much, you know you have a real deal!

Think about it: Who cares if an appliance has a dent? Especially if you're going to put it up against a wall and never see it!

How can you find a scratch-and-dent store near you? Try calling local appliance stores and asking if they have a nearby outlet store or warehouse. Sears operates some of the best scratch-and-dent outlets across the country. There's also a regional chain called Appliance Smart that has locations in Georgia, Minnesota, Ohio, and Texas.

Just be aware that delivery often isn't included in the price, so you'll need to arrange for that on your own or through the scratch-and-dent's own delivery agent at an additional cost.

## Buy gently used or new appliances on Craigslist

Gently used or new appliances can be a real deal on Craigslist, as my executive radio producer, Christa DiBiase, has found. Unfortunately, Christa had to replace all the major appliances in her home after floods swept through the Southeast in September 2009.

By diligently searching online every day, she was able to find brand-new stainless-steel double convection ovens that were never installed or used in a home. She bought them from a man who planned to use them in one of his high-end rental properties in metro Atlanta. But he couldn't install them because the tenants wanted a different finish! So what retails for $2,850 cost Christa a mere $600.

In addition, she picked up a fancy six-burner gas range from an architect who bought it for a client who again opted for a different finish. It was never used and came in its box with warranty. Retail price: $3,200. Christa's price: around $600! She also snatched up a $3,150 Thermador hood for just $500!

The only hazard here is that people selling appliances on Craigslist could be doing so out of their foreclosed homes. Or worse yet, they might be selling stolen goods. Meet with the sellers and use your own judgment. If you think they're offering stolen appliances, don't do business with them.

## Buy appliances without relying on Energy Star labeling

For years, I've encouraged people to buy Energy Star appliances because of their reputation for energy efficiency. But the blue Energy Star label has apparently been cheapened.

Earlier this decade, *The Washington Post* found that far too many appliances bore the Energy Star label. Initially the program was designed to recognize only the top 25 percent of products in any given category. How is it then that 84 percent of LCD displays bore the logo, along with 79 percent of all television sets, according to the newspaper?

No word yet if this is a result of outright dishonesty or just bureaucratic bungling. But it's as if manufacturers are on the honor system when it comes to labeling their appliances.

So how should you be making the best choice when you buy an appliance?

Start by looking for reliability stats by manufacturer in *Consumer Reports* or elsewhere, and then shop at a scratch-and-dent store. (See "Shop at a Local Scratch-and-Dent Store for Appliance Deals" on page 143.) When you're at the store, look at the actual cost of energy consumption, which is usually indicated on a yellow-and-white tag either on the front of or inside the appliance. It's not just the purchase price that matters but the cost of energy or other resources such as water that the appliance will consume over time.

I recently had to buy a new washer. So I wound up willingly paying $180 more for a unit than I would have if I had purchased a similar model that drank tons more water. But I know I'll be making that $180 up (and more) over the lifetime of the washer.

So beware of paying more for an item that has the Energy Star logo versus another smart buy that might not. However, in some cases, there are federal and state rebates for Energy Star products. Then it might make sense to buy one. Visit EnergySavers.gov/Financial to find appliance rebates in your state.

## Use CFLs or LEDs to save on your electric bill

For several years, I've been explaining how my beloved compact fluorescent light (CFL) bulbs are really just a transitional technology until we get to light-emitting diodes (LED) for home use.

With CFLs, you get a product that can save you about $30 over the life of the bulb versus a traditional incandescent bulb. A lot of people have poked fun at me for my enthusiasm about CFLs. I think that's partly because CFLs are more expensive to buy than traditional bulbs. But remember, the cost of a bulb means nothing; it's all about the cost of electricity to run the bulb.

Another hang-up about CFLs has been the mercury content. Now that Home Depot has begun a nationwide recycling program at all of its stores, I can feel better about recommending CFLs. You don't even have to buy the bulb at a Home Depot for them to recycle it at the end of its life! Visit HomeDepot.com for more details. A number of smaller retailers have also stepped up with their own CFL recycling programs now too.

But the real savings action is going to come from LEDs. Being the pioneer that I am, I've already been toying with LEDs around the house. In fact, one of the first things I did was install an LED by my elliptical machine. Turns out the light is so poor, I can't even read a newspaper while I work out!

Obviously, LEDs are not ready for prime time—yet. But they promise to deliver great light down the road at a cost to operate that's even cheaper than CFLs. And they won't have any of the mercury disposal issues.

Lighting accounts for 20 to 25 percent of the average electric bill, but that will drop like a rock in the future. The most efficient LEDs use only 5 percent of the electricity of a regular bulb and they throw off much less heat.

Bridgelux is one company that makes a $20 LED bulb, which could potentially last an entire lifetime. Of course, the company isn't counting on many residential buyers at that price. They figure the market will be commercial users and retailers who have massive electric bills. In warmer climates, such users would also be able to reduce their air-conditioning bill because of the decreased heat generated by the bulb.

### Get a free online quote for residential solar power

The first time I saw solar energy at work was when I was traveling in the Middle East during the late 1970s. Back then I thought, "What are all those funny-looking things on the buildings?"

While much of the world has embraced alternative forms of energy, we're still playing catch-up in America. The problem for homeowners has been figuring out how to implement technologies like solar, wind, and geothermal. You can't exactly just call around for quotes.

That's where the power of the Internet comes in.

Sungevity.com allows you to enter your street address and get a guaranteed quote on the installation of a home solar energy system. The assessment is done by satellite mapping, so no visit to your home is required. As I write this, the service is available only in certain areas of the country.

A team of contractors recently finished installing solar panels at my home. We plan to use solar energy to heat our water, which will allow us to cut our natural gas marketer loose.

The cost of installing solar in homes has dropped dramatically thanks to Chinese over-production of panels. And right now, the government is your partner when it comes to installing solar at home. The feds will eat 30 percent of the cost and many states have their own subsidies as well.

I've crunched the numbers for my house and determined I won't get payback on my solar installation for nine years. Normally, that's not a good return on an investment. But today, with investments earning so little, a nine-year payback is actually decent. After nine years, it's just pure profit going back into my pocket.

So does solar make sense for your life? Well, it's not for the financially faint of heart. I've had to lay out thousands of bucks up front to do this. It's often a smarter move for businesses than for residential customers. If you're doing it for a residential home, it has to be from the heart and not from the head.

## Prefab construction is more cost-effective than stick-built

Modular homes may be the wave of the future if Warren Buffett has his way. Our nation's top-dog investor is pouring his money into the i-house, an ultra-affordable, ultra-energy-efficient home that's built in pieces in a factory and later assembled onsite.

Tradition holds that most homes in America are stick-built at the worksite rather than being prefabricated. But the current housing crisis means upsetting that tradition.

Modular factory-built homes can be far more interesting architecturally because they're built with computer-aided design. We're not talking about single-wide or double-wide mobile homes here; modular homes are championed by high-end architectural publications like *Dwell*.

And talk about the savings on your monthly energy bill! You can heat and cool the i-house for around $30 each month! Visit ClaytoniHouse.com for more details and a virtual tour. Base pricing for the i-house starts at $74,900 before setup costs and installation fees.

There have been so many attempts to do factory-built modular housing in the past. The now defunct Cardinal Industries tried to do a lot of prefab manufacturing in the eastern United States. However, their look was too "cookie cutter" and the company never took off.

In addition, most people have never gotten away from fears about local zoning. But I'm hoping Buffett's support might help create a new day in cheap, green housing.

Zeta Communities is one start-up in San Francisco that's now building zero-energy townhomes. These townhomes use solar energy, among other types of green energy, and also create power that can be sold down the grid. The cost is $250,000, which is actually cheap in the Bay area. Visit ZetaCommunities.com for more info.

I believe zero-energy prefabricated homes are very much a part of our future. It used to be that no one cared about the costs of running a home—they just cared about what the home cost. But that was then and this is now.

# Insurance

Insurance is one of life's obligations. None of us wants insurance, but we buy it because it's necessary. And because of our reluctance to deal with insurance, we tend to buy it hurriedly, purchasing too little of some kinds and too much of others.

In this chapter, I'll tell you the right kinds of insurance you need, how much of it to buy, what to do if your insurer goes bust (as many did during the economic meltdown), and how to identify financially strong insurers that will be around for the long haul. Plus, I'll name a couple of my favorite companies for all your insurance needs.

## AUTO INSURANCE

### Go with a top-tier insurer like USAA or Amica Mutual

Cutesy TV ads do not a good insurer make. We buy insurance because if something goes wrong, we expect the insurer will be there to make it right—be it to repair our home or to fix our car or replace it if it gets stolen.

I particularly love insurance companies that put the focus on the customer, such as USAA and Amica Mutual. Both Amica and USAA are often rated as having just about the best customer service of any company in America by J. D. Power and Associates, *Consumer Reports*, and other sources. It's as if these elite companies get up every morning and think, "How can we please our customers?"

However, USAA and Amica don't earn trust with low premiums; they do it by really help-ing customers when they have claims.

USAA limits its insurance offerings to active military and all honorably discharged members regardless of when they served. I've been a member for more than thirty years now. During that time, my family had three claims (none of them major) and each time the service has been phenomenal. Visit USAA.com for more information.

If you're not military, Amica is often acknowledged in the insurance industry as an equal to USAA. Amica is a mutual, which means you as a shareholder are an owner and Amica is run as a co-op. If it pays out less in claims than it takes in during a given year, it sends a refund check to customers. Visit Amica.com for more information.

Will you pay more with Amica or USAA? Sometimes yes, sometimes no. But you'll be with a company that will stand by you when the chips are down.

If these two insurers don't appeal to you, the key is to get several other quotes before making a decision. Sites like Insure.com, InsWeb.com, and NetQuote.com will give you quotes from multiple auto insurers. If you prefer the human touch, you can find an indepen-dent insurance agent in your area to do the same thing for you. In addition, Costco Whole-sale members can buy group auto coverage at a very good rate, and it's underwritten by Ameriprise Financial, Inc.

## Auto insurance ads are not all they seem to be

GEICO, Progressive, and Allstate are just a few of the auto insurers with ads on TV promising they can save you hundreds over the competition. But how can they all be the cheapest?

There are actually huge differences among insurers based on an individual driver's cir-cumstances. Each insurer uses its own criteria to assess your level of risk and prices your policy accordingly. That's how each insurer can claim to be the cheapest in its ads; they're all assessing different motorists and presenting the results as typical.

*Consumer Reports* put Progressive's claims to be the cheapest to the test. Flo the Progres-sive Girl's "name your price" promise is really more of a "name your coverage" come-on. And it's not necessarily the cheapest; in fact, *Consumer Reports* found Progressive could be twice as expensive for certain motorists. In one hypothetical situation the magazine detailed, Progressive wanted to charge $94 each month on a 2006 Toyota Camry that would have cost $49 for the same coverage with another major insurer.

I'm not saying this to bash Progressive. I'm just saying it to show that you've got to be diligent shopping over the phone and on the Web to find the best deals. Get out your current coverage statement and compare it apples to apples with other insurers' offerings. I recommend shopping for insurance every three years or after an accident or a ticket.

The only time I would *not* recommend jumping ship for a lower premium is if you're with either Amica Mutual or USAA. See my explanation above.

## Develop an independent value for your vehicle

Any call that I take from a listener following an auto accident is what we refer to behind the scenes on the show as an "onion call."

There are so many layers to these questions and they can go in any direction. Chief among them are concerns about whether the car should be totaled, how much you should be compensated for a totaled car, and whether or not the vehicle should be repaired.

Edmunds.com recently ran an article titled "Confessions of an Auto Claims Adjuster" that goes a long way in addressing one common complaint I hear from people after an accident: "I can't get the adjuster to call me back!"

I have long said that adjusters purposely don't call back because they're trying to wear you down. But Edmunds says that's not the case—rather, it's all about adjusters being overworked. Adjusters are racing the clock and the phone every day. The caseloads are heavy and the rate of burnout is high in this industry.

Having said that, I still believe insurance adjusters will lowball you and hope you just take their offer. It's up to you to independently verify that the money they're offering for your car is a fair amount.

The database the industry uses has historically paid about 70 cents on the dollar. But you can visit Edmunds.com, KBB.com, and NADA.com to build an independent value for your vehicle.

Never be rude when you're speaking to the adjuster and explaining your method of calculation. Some adjusters have a real attitude, but for the most part they're just overwhelmed. Just clearly state why you claim your car is worth more than what the adjuster is saying.

Finally, Edmunds disagrees with my long-standing advice that it's acceptable to go to a shop preferred by your insurer for repair so long as the repair is guaranteed for the life of the vehicle. Edmunds instead insists that you pick the repair shop, preferably one that specializes in your brand.

### Skip the rental insurance when renting a car

Car rentals are the one segment of travel that went up in price during the recession, unlike hotels and airfares. When the car rental companies sensed the softening economy at the end of the last decade and the beginning of this one, they simply refused to buy new fleet cars. That drove down supply and drove up price, in addition to leaving customers stuck with older, run-down vehicles.

I recommend booking a rental at the time that you book your air travel. Then one week before your trip, check the rates again and see if you can grab a better deal at a lower price. Car rental fees are completely refundable, so you won't lose anything if you cancel the original booking.

When you get to the rental counter, you'll be hit with a sales pitch for insurance such as a collision damage waiver (CDW), also known by the codes LDW or PDW, and excess liability coverage.

There are two "Clark Smart" ways to get around signing up for this rip-off fee, which can cost you up to $20 a day.

First, your auto insurer might have a clause in your policy that covers you for temporary use of a rental car. It's worth calling them before you take a trip to find out.

Second, certain VISA and American Express cards and MasterCards will provide secondary coverage when you rent a car. If you're a frequent car renter, you might want to pay the $95 annual fee for a Diners Club card because they offer full primary coverage.

So I say waive the additional coverage the car rental company is trying to sell. The only exception to this rule would be when you rent a truck to move because neither your credit card nor your insurer is likely to cover that.


# HEALTH AND RELATED INSURANCES


### Drastically low premiums might indicate a bogus insurance pitch

There are a lot of pseudo—health insurance companies out there selling fake plans to employers and individuals. *The Wall Street Journal* reports that some 200,000 businesses have been taken in by these kinds of rip-offs.

Small businesses crushed by high premiums are very susceptible to the lure of cheaper health care. But when somebody gets sick, the insurance card comes back as a fake and all the bills go unpaid. This has been happening in state after state.

Insurance is regulated by the states, not the federal government, so the rip-off artists can just bounce around from state to state pulling their scams. What do you need to know to stay safe? First off, be wary if you get a pitch for a great deal with premiums that are drastically lower than what others in the marketplace are offering you.

But don't let your skepticism stop there. Contact your state insurance department and ask if a prospective company is licensed to do business in your state. Make sure the name matches exactly because sometimes the rip-off artists will use a name that's very similar to that of a legitimate business.

Seniors also have to be especially careful of fake prescription plans. Once again, call your state insurance department to verify if a health insurance salesperson represents a legitimately licensed company. Preventative steps are the best medicine for your wallet.

If you're starting from scratch in shopping for health insurance, I recommend comparison shopping online for affordable coverage at a site like eHealthInsurance.com. In addition, you might want to check out Kaiser Permanente, one of the nation's largest health maintenance organizations. Kaiser is available if you live in California, Colorado, Georgia, Hawaii, Maryland, Ohio, Oregon, Virginia, Washington D.C., or Washington State. Visit KaiserPermanente.org for more details. Finally, Costco Wholesale offers an affordable health insurance plan administered by Aetna for customers in Georgia, Illinois, Pennsylvania, and Texas.

## Take advantage of PCIP

Having a preexisting condition used to make you a pariah to insurers. But as part of the health care reform law that President Obama supports, those with preexisting conditions would no longer be ignored.

In actuality, there are two programs at work here: States that chose to administer a risk pool themselves and states that opted out and asked the federal government to step in. The majority of the latter states are located throughout the Southeast and the mountain states.

Visit HealthCare.gov to see if the federal pool exists in your state. In order to qualify to buy coverage, you must have been uninsured for at least six months. Premiums will depend on your age and your state of residence. The minimum monthly premium will be $140, while the maximum premium caps out at $900. With the risk pool, you have a cap on what treatments will cost you. That will be roughly around $6,000 annually.

The Pre-Existing Condition Insurance Plan (PCIP) is really just a bridge program through 2014 until the new federal rules kick in and ban insurers from redlining based on preexisting conditions. It's being funded with $5 billion. Now that may sound like a lot of money, but it's supposed to last through 2014, and that's very unlikely to happen.

## Bump up your FSA during open enrollment

Each November, many employees choose their benefits during open enrollment at their workplace. Don't forget about those flexible spending accounts (FSAs)! This is a way to take tax money back from Uncle Sam. It's like getting an automatic raise.

Here's how it works: You elect to have your employer automatically deduct money out of your gross pay. That money is essentially put into a savings account funded with pretax dollars. Then over the course of the following year, you can take those pretax dollars and use them for qualified medical expenses.

One caveat: You've got to use it or lose it. If there's unused FSA money left over at the end of the year, *you won't get it back*.

There are two major types of FSAs. The health care FSA can be used to take care of unreimbursed medical bills like deductibles, copays, medications, eyeglasses, dental care, etc. While there's no government-imposed limit on how much you can contribute, most employers will limit your annual contributions to $5,000. However, beginning in 2013, the FSA cap will drop from $5,000 to $2,500, with annual inflation increases.

The second type of FSA is for dependent care. For example, you can use the money in this FSA to pay for day care or a legal nanny. The same $5,000 limit ($2,500 beginning in 2013 and going forward, with annual inflation increases) and forfeiture rules apply. Other qualifying uses of this money include paying for an elderly relative or other adult who needs special care.

In addition, new rules governing the amount of pretax money you can put into FSAs—not to mention health savings accounts or health reimbursement accounts—went into effect in 2011.

You'll no longer be allowed to buy over-the-counter medications with your tax-free money. In addition, the use of your pretax money will be tightened steadily for unreimbursed purchases of prescription meds, with the only exceptions being medical equipment and supplies. That includes "over-the-counter medical supplies such as crutches, medical-testing kits and joint supports, and standard medicine cabinet stock, such as Band-Aids, contact lens solution and hearing-aid batteries," according to financial writer Greg Karp.

My advice with FSAs is to choose wisely how much you put in; you don't want to overestimate and wind up losing your money.

## Buy disability insurance at 60 percent of current pay

Your odds of being disabled are far greater than your odds of dying during your working years. That makes disability insurance more important than life insurance.

I know that a lot of people find the idea of disability insurance to be distasteful, because no one likes to consider that they might become disabled. But this could happen to you, and you need to be prepared if it does. In fact, you can visit WhatsMyPDQ.org to assess your "personal disability quotient" (PDQ). This is a free service of the Council of Disability Awareness. Your PDQ will predict the likelihood of your needing to use disability insurance during your working lifetime.

When purchasing disability insurance, it's best to get a disability policy that begins making payments three or six months after you are disabled and continues until age sixty-five. Buy coverage that's equal to 60 percent of your current pay before taxes, because that will approximate what you're taking home after taxes.

Be sure you get a policy that uses a more liberal definition of disability than the one used by the Social Security Administration. Social Security pays only about one-third of the claims it receives.

Finally, don't make the mistake of buying disability insurance (or life insurance) through your employer. It might be more costly and it won't follow you if you change jobs. Worse still, if you develop a health condition that makes you ineligible to buy disability and life insurance, you'll have lost your chance to buy them when you were healthy.

## Buy long-term care insurance in your late fifties and early sixties

I have long encouraged people in their late fifties and early sixties to consider buying long-term care (LTC) insurance, which pays for care in a nursing home, assisted living facility, or your own home. LTC policies are not for everyone. It depends on your age, health status, overall retirement objectives, income, and wealth.

There's a misconception that Medicare will pay for this kind of care, but it won't. Medicaid, meanwhile, requires you to impoverish yourself before the government will pick up the tab for a nursing home. But what happens when you get better and you suddenly find you're broke? LTC insurance takes the worry out of the equation.

However, the industry has been littered with fly-by-night operations and other unstable players. One textbook example of the latter came in late 2008 amid the insurance industry meltdown. An insurer called Conseco worked out a deal with Pennsylvania to dump its LTC obligations and essentially turn people over as wards of the state. It was a troubling situation that scared a lot of people.

The solution is to buy LTC insurance only from a solid company, preferably one that has an A.M. Best rating of A++ or A+. A.M. Best is one of the most respected rating agencies for the world of insurance. Visit AMBest.com and sign up for free to view their ratings.

While it might cost you more now, decades down the road you'll have a greater likelihood that A++ and A+ companies will be around to provide the benefits you paid for.

One final note: LTC insurance isn't necessary if you're so wealthy that money is no object to getting the best care, or if you're so poor that being a ward of the state makes sense. That still leaves between 65 and 80 percent of Americans in the middle who could benefit from it.

## Avoid single-issue insurance policies

Single-issue insurance policies are considered a rip-off by some consumer advocates. I also agree that you should avoid them. Examples of single-issue policies include mortgage life insurance, cancer insurance, and accident insurance.

In the case of cancer insurance, insurers use the power of the C-word to sell the policy. Years ago, people wouldn't even utter the word "cancer." They would just say that you had a malignant tumor, because a diagnosis was often considered fatal. But today, many people survive cancer. Insurers, however, have learned that they can still capitalize on people's fear of the disease.

Accident policies are also a tremendous rip-off. The reality is that general insurance—of the life, disability, and/or health variety—represents a better choice.

Mortgage life insurance (aka "croak and choke" insurance), meanwhile, is garbage too. The premiums are about ten times what life insurance should cost. The worst part of it is that you're insuring the mortgage company, not yourself; mortgage life insurance pays off the lender in the event of your death! But your survivors likely will have more pressing financial needs at that time. That's why plain-vanilla term life insurance would be a much better choice than expensive mortgage life that doesn't provide any benefit to your survivors.

# HOME INSURANCE

## Update your amount of homeowners coverage every few years

If you've been in a house for five years or longer, chances are you might be grossly under-insured for homeowners coverage. Discovering that fact *after* a catastrophic loss is not the answer.

I want you to read the coverage limits when your policy comes up for renewal every year. Let your insurer know if there is no way you could rebuild your house for the specified amount. Write down the name of the representative you speak to and the date/time of the call. That way if your insurer refuses to raise your limits and a catastrophic loss happens, you've already begun building a case against them.

My insurer would not raise my limits on my primary residence, so I triggered a clause in my contract and got a third-party appraiser to look at my home. The appraiser said my home had appreciated in value beyond my coverage. Only then did the insurer accept the appraisal and comply by raising my coverage—and even though the extra coverage raised my premiums, I was happy to pay.

The scary reality is that insurance companies are not required to rebuild your home in the event of catastrophic damage if you're grossly underinsured. Say you purchased your home ten years ago for $100,000. Now your home might be worth $200,000. But your insurance has probably not kept pace. So you'll be destroyed financially if you have a catastrophic loss.

It gets even worse if you have a mortgage on your property. You can lose your home in a disaster through foreclosure and be sued by the lender for losses on the loan. Am I scaring you yet? That's my intention.

A couple of years ago I bought a foreclosure in a mountain community. In that case, the insurer sent an appraiser out and told me I needed more insurance because of the expense of rebuilding on a mountain. Again, I was happy to comply.

The possibilities of a catastrophic loss are minimal, but why take the chance of having your wallet disrupted just as terribly as your life in the case of the unthinkable?

## Document your belongings with a video camera or online

Every year on her birthday, my wife grabs a video camera and does a "walk and talk" around our home to document all of our belongings. No, my wife isn't showing off. She just knows that if you have legitimate losses from a house fire or other catastrophes, the insurance adjuster might assume you're trying to put something over on him—even if you're not. Videotaping your belongings helps you prove what you say you've lost.

When Lane is done, she then stores the tape at her parents' home. After all, that tape won't do you any good if it melts in your home or apartment during a fire! A fireproof safe is another great place to store the tape.

Now, obviously, her choice of day is entirely arbitrary; you can do this any day of the year. It's just important to remember to get it done once a year so you can account for new possessions.

Video cameras can be had for $100 or less these days, but they can save you thousands of dollars if your house was to ever catch fire. That videotape becomes an insurance policy for your insurance policy.

KnowYourStuff.org is a free website that lets you document all your belongings online and store the info on a secure server. It is a free service of the Insurance Information Institute.

## Consider flood insurance if you live near a flood zone

Every year seems to bring a rash of flooding in our country. In 2009, it was in the Southeast. The year before that, it was in the Midwest. And who can forget the hurricane season of 2005 with Katrina, Rita, and Wilma?

On my show team, we experienced the devastation of the flooding in 2009. The entire ground floor of my executive producer's Atlanta home was flooded while she and her husband were enjoying their tenth anniversary in Cancún.

Our associate producer Joel Larsgaard, a slew of Christa's neighbors, and I helped move furniture and other belongings to higher ground at her home while she was stuck in Mexico. Joel had a vested interest in what happened at the house because Christa was allowing him to store some of his belongings in her garage while he was house hunting.

Here's an important lesson for you: There's no excuse for *not* buying flood insurance through the National Flood Insurance Program if you are adjacent to a floodplain. Simply visit FEMA.gov and look for "flood insurance" in their quick-links section.

Flood insurance is subsidized at extra-cheap rates by your fellow taxpayers and covers damage for up to $250,000. Renters can buy a special version of flood insurance that's also subsidized.

Insurers will *not* offer you additional coverage unless you first have this separate coverage from the feds. Typically, there's a thirty-day waiting period from the time you purchase a flood policy before it becomes effective.

## Buy renters insurance if you rent

More than one in three of us now rent a home. That makes renters insurance a necessity that you need to know about.

In general, landlords are *not* responsible for your belongings. The sole exception is in the case of "negligence" on the part of the landlord, which is very hard to prove in a court of law. So you're on the hook if your belongings are stolen, damaged, or destroyed in a fire. That's where renters insurance comes in.

You'll typically pay around $15 per month, or $150–$250 annually, for renters insurance. One of my TV producers recently sold her house and moved into an apartment where she was actually *required* by the landlord to have renters insurance.

Be certain that your policy includes relocation assistance and replacement value coverage. The latter will help avoid protracted battles over the price of depreciating assets like old electronics. You'll just get one lump-sum payout to replace your items rather than having to haggle over the depreciated value of a three-year-old TV.

## A free C.L.U.E. report shows what insurers know about you

Knowledge is power, as the old saying goes, and the more access you have to what insurers know about you, the better off you are. Some insurance companies, when you call up and ask questions, will log it on your Comprehensive Loss Underwriting Exchange (C.L.U.E.) report. This is a tactic that makes other insurance companies not want to insure you.

But you can order your free C.L.U.E. report once a year just like you can order your credit report, and if something turns up false, challenge it. A giant research firm called LexisNexis recently took over operations for ChoiceTrust, which is a group I used to talk about that gives you free access to your C.L.U.E. reports once a year.

C.L.U.E reports come in two flavors. There's one for personal property loss pertaining to your house and one for auto loss. You must be the owner of the home or vehicle you're requesting a report on; you can't do it speculatively for a car or property you're thinking about buying.

Here's how a C.L.U.E. report can benefit you: Sellers need every advantage they can get in today's tight real estate market. I think a C.L.U.E. report can be one piece of the puzzle. If you're trying to sell your home, why not request the personal property report on your residence and make it available for prospective buyers to see?

Sure, the buyers will get the property inspected as a condition of purchase, but having the C.L.U.E. report handy is just another way to assure them they're not buying a property loaded with hidden problems that got passed on to the insurer.

Visit PersonalReports.LexisNexis.com to request your C.L.U.E. reports. You will have to give your Social Security number and you will be charged if you need a homeowners report on more than one address. While you're there, you can also request an employment history report and resident history report on yourself for nada.


# LIFE INSURANCE


## Buy level-term life insurance

Simple is better when it comes to buying life insurance, and level-term insurance is just about as simple as you can get. "Level term" means you buy insurance for a set number of years depending on your age and your family, and the premium remains the same for that number of years. The only purpose of life insurance is to replace your income (or your spouse's) for your family if you die.

For example, if you have young kids and you want to provide financial security for them until they are adults, you would want a twenty-year term policy. If you're thirty-five and it's just you and your spouse, you might want to provide for the remainder of your spouse's life in the event of your death. So you'd probably want a thirty-year term policy. Or not. It's really a personal family choice.

If you have no dependents at all, you don't need to buy any life insurance. And don't buy insurance on children. A three-year-old doesn't earn a salary, so there's no need to replace his or her income.

Life insurance has gotten much cheaper over the years, in part because people are living longer. Add into the mix the Internet, which has made it ultra-easy to compare prices when shopping for life insurance. The result is that term life insurance costs have dropped by two-thirds in the last fifteen years. That's a great deal!

So if you bought a policy when you were thirty and now you're forty-five, you can get a new life insurance policy at a much lower rate than fifteen years ago. As long as your health hasn't declined, you'll still be able to get great deals. Visit AccuQuote.com, Insure.com, or QuickQuote.com to comparison shop for term coverage.

## Buy ten times your annual income with term life

As I said in the tip above, life insurance is meant to replace your income. My rule of thumb is to buy an amount equal to six to ten times your annual salary, before taxes.

So if you make $40,000 a year, get $400,000 of life insurance to replace your income. If that's too rich for your blood, make sure you buy at least six times your salary. In this example, that would be $240,000.

If you decide to get term life insurance, the best way to buy is by checking for a financially strong company that offers low premiums. AMBest.com is a good site for research purposes. Free registration is required to use this site.

If you are in a whole life policy (sometimes referred to as "permanent insurance") with a substandard company, you can borrow the cash value and use those proceeds to buy a term policy from a strong company. Don't cancel a whole life policy. Once you've purchased it, it's best to keep it. If you're changing insurers, do not cancel your existing policy until you pass the medical underwriting for the new policy.

## Look for a financially solid insurer

During the financial meltdown of 2008, a lot of people fell into a life insurance purgatory when several big insurers went bust. This is a very difficult and precarious position to be in as a policyholder.

The insurance industry has long been regulated by the states. But it became clear that state guaranty funds would not be adequate to handle the insolvency of large providers. So the federal government had to cough up additional taxpayer money as a backstop.

Who would have ever thought you'd need insurance for your insurance?! See my next entry for more details on what happens when a life insurer fails.

The best way to avoid this problem is to do all you can to never face it in the first place. That means you need to make smart choices when you're buying insurance. I recommend buying only from companies that are rated A++ or A+ by A.M. Best—one of the top companies when it comes to making pronouncements about different insurers' relative financial strength.

Be sure you have the company's *exact* name when you're checking out its rating. For example, a search for "Prudential" on A.M. Best's website turns up more than fifty results that detail all of the company's holdings and its sub-companies. You need to know that you're really looking for "Prudential Insurance Co. of America," which, incidentally, is rated A+ as I write this.

Remember, anything less than an A+—even an A—is unacceptable. Don't be tempted by low premiums when you're shopping around. Stick with insurers of top strength, even if you have to pay more for it.

## If you're a veteran, get USAA

The brave men and women in our all-volunteer military have long had access to USAA, a one-branch bank in Texas that provides top-tier banking and insurance services to military customers all over the world.

At one time, you had to apply for membership in USAA within 180 days after an honorable separation from the military. Now, however, that requirement has changed and all honorably discharged members of the military (and their families) can join regardless of how long ago they served.

This highly respected company—which offers banking, auto insurance, homeowners insurance, and life insurance—is often rated as having just about the best customer service of any company in America by J. D. Power and Associates, *Consumer Reports*, and other sources.

USAA's new expanded membership policy opens the doors for so many more people. But what can you do if you've never served in the military and still want a great company? I recommend checking out Amica Mutual. Amica is often acknowledged in the industry as an equal to USAA.

With both Amica and USAA, it's *not* about getting the lowest premiums on insurance. But both offer service that is great when the chips are down and you need an insurer to stand by you.

## Know your level of state guaranty coverage if your insurer fails

What happens when a life insurer fails? Unlike banks, insurance companies are regulated at the state level, not the federal level. So there's no FDIC as there is for banks that can step in with money if an insurer goes insolvent. A state guaranty association is the last line of defense in the event of a failure.

Most states have coverage levels of $100,000 to $300,000 for individual policyholders. The National Organization of Life and Health Insurance Guaranty Associations (NOLHGA) can help determine the level of protection your state provides. Visit NOLHGA.com and click on the "Policyholder Info" tab to see a drop-down menu with links to each state's guaranty fund.

However, there is one caution about state guaranty associations. In the very unlikely event your insurer fails, the associations usually won't have enough money on hand to make everyone whole right away. So there might be an indeterminate waiting period until you get your money. Contrast that with the FDIC approach: If a bank goes bust today, you get your insured money tomorrow.

If you're going to buy substantial insurance, then be sure to have it split up among different insurers to be proactive about protecting yourself. Never exceed your state's guaranty fund coverage level in any one policy.

Again, though, the best advice I can give is to avoid the threat of having to wait for your money if an insurer goes bust. And do that in the first place by sticking with companies that are rated A++ or A+ by A.M. Best.

## Don't buy insurance from commissioned salespeople

The insurance industry is one in which bad apples exist right alongside good apples. Ultimately, however, this is an industry that would not exist if not for a real need. For some families, a life insurance policy can mean the difference between poverty and financial survival when a primary provider dies. Still, I want to alert you to some dangers.

Insurance salespeople are exempt from what's called "fiduciary responsibility," much like full-commission stockbrokers. Fiduciary responsibility simply means your interests must be put first in all business dealings . . . and sadly, insurance salespeople are *not* required to do that.

Let me go off on a tangent for a moment to really drive home a point about what this means. Let's say you go to a full-commission stock brokerage. Under what used to be called the "Merrill Lynch rule" in the industry, investment firms are allowed to do what helps them first as long as the investment they put you in is "generally suitable" for your situation. So if, for example, it would be great for you to own a stock fund, the full-commission brokerage can pick the most expensive, lowest-performing stock fund for you that earns the firm a big commission. They might be more motivated to do that than to guide you to a high-performing fund that keeps its expenses low.

The same thing is true when you talk to an insurance salesperson. When it comes to life insurance, 98 percent of us would be well served with a plain, simple level-term insurance policy. But in huge numbers, we're pushed to buy whole life. Why? Because it has huge commissions, not like the tiny commissions on level-term insurance.

I'm not saying that there aren't a lot of fine, decent people selling insurance. There are. And honest commissioned salespeople will rise above their personal interests and sell what's right for you. But you've got to at least be aware that insurance salespeople are not held to fiduciary standards, no matter how nice and charming they might seem.

## Don't sell your life insurance policy for quick cash

More and more people who are elderly or ill are selling their life insurance policies to score some quick cash. Yet the world of death futures contracts, or life settlements as they're also known, is fraught with dangers.

Let's say you have a $100,000 policy. Your insurer might quote the cash value of your policy at only $5,000 if you were to turn it in. But someone in the free market might offer you $15,000 or $20,000 for your policy if you sign over the rights to them.

The company or person you sell to then pays your premiums and hopes you die in a hurry! Unfortunately, when you do, your heirs won't get any payment. It all goes to the new policyholder.

For investors, death futures are pitched as a way to earn a great return on your money. Beware that there are untold numbers of scams in this field, and there's no way to be certain you're dealing with legit players.

If you have a policy and insist on selling it, start by finding out the cash value from your insurance company. If you want to sell it in the free market, be sure to get quotes from multiple companies who buy life insurance policies. The quotes will likely be all over the board, and there might be tax consequences in taking a payout.

Finally, beware the example of Larry King. The media personality sold his policies and is now worried he'll be knocked off for the proceeds. Don't sell a policy if you're subject to paranoia.

## Know the "true" investment return on your life insurance policy

If you have an old life insurance policy that you've been paying the premiums on for years, it can be difficult to know whether it's beneficial to keep paying for it or to dump the thing.

That's where a service from the Consumer Federation of America (CFA) can come in handy. For $80, there's a man named James Hunt who will run an analysis to determine the true investment returns on any cash-value life insurance policy—be it whole life, universal life, or variable life.

Hunt will compare the cash-value policy with the alternative of buying lower-premium term insurance and investing the premium savings in a bank account or a mutual fund. You get a computer printout comparing average annual rates of return over five-, ten-, fifteen-, and twenty-year periods with detailed explanations.

At just $80, it's got to be a money loser for the CFA. But it could represent thousands of dollars in savings to you over time. Simply visit EvaluateLifeInsurance.org or call 603-224-2805 to get started.

## Get a quote for an immediate annuity

If you've listened to my radio show anytime during the past twenty years, you know that an annuity is a four-letter word in my mind. Most annuities have massive commissions and massive expenses. That's why they're pushed by commissioned salespeople, especially those in banks who target customers complaining about puny interest rates on CDs.

But there's one annuity that might be a great deal for a lot of people. It's called an "immediate payout annuity" (aka life annuity).

When you retire, you might not have enough money to provide for your monthly needs from savings. So there are companies that turn a supply of money into a lifetime stream of income. Immediate payout annuities are entirely legitimate, but they have so little in the way of commissions that they're never pushed by salespeople.

As with anything else, there are good providers and bad providers of life annuities out there. *SmartMoney* magazine recently ranked the top immediate annuity providers, based on who gives the highest monthly income and who is the financially strongest insurer. Their top four included USAA, State Farm, New York Life, and Penn Mutual Life.

If you'd like to check out some quotes on your own, try visiting ImmediateAnnuities.com for their instant annuity quote calculator.

One knock against life annuities that I often hear is, "What if I pour all my money into an immediate payout annuity and then I die next week?" It's true that all the money will be gone and there will be none for your heirs.

That's why you can opt for a special provision called "period certain," which means that there will be a guaranteed payout to heirs (typically for twenty years) even in the event of your death. The monthly benefit will drop by about 10 percent if you take the period certain option, but at least it guarantees to provide something for your survivors.

> *My banker was very persuasive in trying to sell me a $300,000 variable annuity with a*
> *death benefit wrapper as well as a $200,000 life insurance policy on my 79-year-old*
> *mother. I am the co-trustee of a large estate and my mom is the trustee. She depends on me*

*to make the right decisions. I have heard Clark talk about red flags where variable annuities are concerned. I talked this over with my banker and he told me that different investments work for different situations and there is no such thing as a bad investment . . . RED FLAG. He showed me how the annuity would make tons of money in 7 years and the $300,000 would never go down and would always go up. This stuff was very complicated. We talked for 1 hour one day and 1 1/2 hours the next on this dry subject. What did I do? Played it safe and put all the money in a one-year CD and told the banker that I wasn't comfortable with annuities and life insurance policies and I didn't understand them well enough to invest. End of story. Thanks, Clark!*

*Debbie W., CA*

# Personal Finance

Since the Wall Street meltdown and the Great Recession, Americans have been trying hard to watch their dollars. We've been trying to pay down debt, save more, and live more frugally. Many of us have realized that the free-spending ways of the past don't work in the new decade.

In this chapter, I'll show you how to track your spending, saving, and debt online with free tools; how to handle your investments yourself; and how to boost your credit score, including why you should use your "back of the wallet" credit cards at least twice a year.

## BANKS AND BUDGETING

### Triage your finances

When you get into financial trouble, who do you pay first? Human nature dictates that people will pay the person who screams the loudest. That often means we pay our credit cards and skip the mortgage payment. Bad move.

Credit card debt is unsecured, meaning there's not much a lender can do to you if you don't pay—other than ruin your credit. Debtor's prison is very rare in the United States.

That's why the banks that control the majority of credit cards in the United States use bully psychology to force you into paying up. Mortgage lenders, on the other hand, can take your house away from you if you don't pay up. So they're typically very nonconfrontational when you don't pay because they're the ones who can actually hold your feet to the fire by doing something tangible.

I want you to start thinking about your finances like you would a triage room at a hospital. In the emergency room, the staff determines who has a life-threatening situation like a bullet wound, who has a fractured bone, and who is just there for a headache. Obviously, the wound victim will be seen immediately while the guy with the headache is likely to be all but ignored until after everybody else is seen. That's how I want you to prioritize your monthly bills.

Basic grocery expenses should always come first. You've got to eat, right? That should be followed by your transportation bill or car loan so you can get to work and keep earning. I used to tell people that paying your mortgage or rent was the highest priority. But nowadays paying your car note might actually be a higher priority than your housing debt. After all, most Americans need a car to get to job interviews. And if your situation is really desperate, you might need to live with friends or relatives until you can get back on your feet—in which case you'll have few or no housing expenses.

After you take care of those basics each month, I want you to drop your credit card debt a few notches down the totem pole and ignore the lenders if you don't have enough money to go around. People immediately say, "Well, I'll ruin my credit if I do that." But if you don't have enough money to pay your mortgage or car loan, chances are your credit is already being messed up.

If your wallet is still ailing after triaging your finances, you might need to seek free or low-cost debt counseling. Read the tip "Get Free Credit Counseling" (see page 185) for details on that.

## A CLARK FAVORITE
### *Track your finances online with free budgeting tools*

One of the most frequent complaints I hear from people is that they have no idea where their money goes each pay period. There's such a sense of powerlessness in that statement. I have several free tools to share with you that will help you gain control of your wallet again.

In another age, I recommended the old-fashioned envelope method or the notebook method of keeping track of your expenses. But it's much harder now to keep track of balances with the ATM, checks, auto-drafts, debit card transactions, and more all clearing at different times.

Banking has gone from being linear to something that moves in so many different directions that it's easy to lose control. Because almost everything we do today is online, it's only natural that the Internet offers a way to help you gain control over your spending.

One of the best free online budgeting tools I've found is Mint.com. You register all your financial accounts with them anonymously, without using your name or other personally identifiable info. It's a "read-only" service, as their website explains, and no money transfers are allowed via Mint—either in or out.

Once you've signed up, Mint uses artificial intelligence software to analyze where your money goes on a daily basis. In addition to tracking your spending, the service will also send you simple reminders when your bills are due. One of my credit card bills got lost in the mail, but Mint reminded me it was due, so I didn't have to pay a late fee.

My executive radio producer, Christa DiBiase, likes the automated reminder from Mint that tells her if she's approaching the limits of her monthly budget for groceries or entertainment. Mint allows Christa to then review her monthly spending and see exactly where her money has disappeared.

There are other Mint competitors that I've been playing around with, ClearCheckBook.com and Yodlee.com. JustThrive.com is another site that seems to target the twentysomething crowd and should appeal to people who like social networking.

People always ask me about safety concerns with these online budgeting tools that require access to your accounts. All these sites say they're safe for you to use. But are they really? Well, I'm willing to take the chance because I believe the greater risk here is the one posed by uncontrolled spending.

*I use a trick that I believe that I adapted from Clark, but I've been a listener for so long that it's possible that I just created it based on Clark's "budgeting brain" leaking into mine.*

*Trick: I don't use a debit card, but use a point-earning credit card, almost exclusively. I then record it in my electronic check register with a code of CCHOLD and deduct it as IF I wrote a check. Then, when the credit card bill arrives, I simply add back in the held balance and I have all the money I need to pay the credit card bill. I haven't paid interest in a decade using this approach and I have a clear idea of how much available cash I have without letting credit card purchases get in the way of my budget.*

*Plus, I get the points, which I'm saving for an anniversary trip to Ireland! My family is never surprised when I bark, "Clark Says . . ."!*

*Beverlee A., FL*

## Find the best CD rates online

Throughout the beginning of this decade, CD rates were looking anemic across the nation. At one point, the national average was just a little north of a measly 1 percent! But there are a number of smaller banks, credit unions, and some wholly unusual sources that offer rates above the norm.

How do you find these deals? Many of the best ones are at community banks and credit unions in your hometown. Look on billboards or signs when you're driving around. So long as the bank is FDIC insured (or NCUA insured for credit unions), your money is protected up to $250,000.

If you want to cast the net a little wider, Bankrate.com is one of the best national clearinghouses I know for rates. Once you establish what Bankrate.com says is the best national average, I'd like you to go one better (hopefully) and put your business into an online auction marketplace where small banks will compete for it. That service is available for free at MoneyAisle.com.

At MoneyAisle.com, you simply pop in your deposit amount, pick a CD duration, and enter your state and zip code. Then banks and credit unions start bidding for your business online and in real time. The bidding process takes about sixty seconds or less, and you can watch the competitors driving up your interest rate right before your eyes!

CD rates are sure to go up from here, but no one knows exactly when. It could be in the very near future or it could be further down the road. That's why I recommend laddering your CDs. The easiest way to do that is to split your money into three piles—a money-market or savings account, a one-year CD, and a five-year CD.

A more sophisticated laddering approach would involve a six-tier setup. Splitting your money into six even piles, you'd have the following setup: a money-market or savings account, then a one-year CD, two-year CD, three-year CD, four-year CD, and five-year CD.

Taking the latter example, when your one-year CD comes due, you have that money available to take advantage of a better rate—if there is one. Ditto for your two-year CD when it comes due, your three-year CD, and so on. This way you don't lock all your money into a lengthy CD if rates go up in the near future, and you'll still be earning the rates you lock in today in the very unlikely event that they go slightly lower down the road.

## Lend or borrow money without banks through P2P online lending

What do you do if you need money but want to avoid borrowing from the banks? In the past, I've always recommended credit unions. But now there are even more options available thanks to what's called peer-to-peer (P2P) lending.

In P2P lending, individuals willing to take the risk will lend their money to others online—once a potential borrower's credit standing is carefully vetted. The best P2P websites incorporate elements of social networking (users create their own pages detailing why they need the money and upload photos of themselves) and elements of an online auction (borrowers advertise how much interest they're willing to pay).

A single borrower will typically get little slices and dices of cash from multiple lenders online. That helps lower an individual lender's risk in the case of default. The P2P sites make their money by charging a loan origination fee and taking a small cut for loan administration, which includes pursuing collections if need be.

Before I go any further, I want to underscore the possible risk here for lenders. Some of these sites have high failure rates and might be gone by the time you read this. But others will surely take their place; this idea isn't going to go away!

Prosper.com was one of the earliest P2P lenders to gain traction in the marketplace. After some early trouble, Prosper now claims nearly one million members and nearly $200 million in loan funding at the time of this writing. *Barron's* reports the site has a 5 percent default rate among borrowers.

LendingClub.com has a 3 percent default rate, meanwhile, but turns down 90 percent of potential borrowers in an effort to cull the herd and find the most creditworthy.

This all begs the question: Why would anyone go the P2P route if they're creditworthy? Generally, you can get a better deal with a P2P lender versus a bank. Yet it's roughly equivalent to the kind of deal you'd get at a credit union.

The returns you might get as a lender can be enticing. Prosper.com says their average lender earns 7 percent on his money, net after expenses and charge-offs. But those who are really into this virtual underwriting boast that they can make a 12 percent return.

My advice? Be skeptical and do your research if you want to get involved. There are already blogs and message boards dedicated to P2P lending. Study them and be sure to know your risk. There will always be people trying to clean up a mess in their life with somebody else's money.

## Don't exceed FDIC limits on your bank deposits

During 2009 and 2010, nearly three hundred banks failed and were taken over by the Federal Deposit Insurance Corporation (FDIC). That hurt a lot of people who had money on deposit in excess of current FDIC protections.

The FDIC guarantees that any money on deposit in an FDIC-insured account will be repaid even if the bank fails, as long as the amount doesn't exceed $250,000. Back in 2008, before the big wave of bank failures, the FDIC limit was $100,000.

One of the earliest bank failures of the Great Recession was IndyMac, which had $541 million in uninsured deposits at the time of failure. That's $541 million that went up in smoke and there's been no way for ruined customers to get it back.

During our last rash of bank collapses in the 1980s, approximately 8 to 12 percent of the money was uninsured. Today that figure has ballooned to nearly 40 percent—especially among organizations, nonprofits, and small businesses.

The reality is that a large number of banks will continue to go insolvent during the next couple of years. Many will be invisibly absorbed or merged into larger banks. Customers will be fine as long as they don't exceed the FDIC limit.

Though FDIC insurance is available on deposits up to $250,000, I advise people to put no more than $225,000 in a single account. That way you don't forfeit a penny of interest in the event of a bank failure.

If you have multiple accounts at one institution that are all titled differently for ownership, don't just assume each one is protected. You can find out for certain at FDIC.gov by using the Electronic Deposit Insurance Estimator (EDIE) at FDIC.gov/EDIE.

Meanwhile, in the world of credit unions, the National Credit Union Administration has an insurance fund that protects deposits at the same limits as the FDIC. But be aware that in some instances, certain credit unions might be covered only by a state guaranty pool. Check with NCUA.gov to determine coverage.

If you do have a lot of money to keep on deposit—and I mean *a lot*—I suggest using the Certificate of Deposit Account Registry Service (CDARS). With CDARS, you can put in up to $50 million and it will be spread around to multiple financial institutions in FDIC-protected CDs so that no one account exceeds the traditional $250,000 protection limit. Obviously this is a very good problem to have! Visit CDARS.com for more info on the program.

## Never give out your checking account info

Toward the end of the last decade, the Federal Trade Commission announced the largest ever bust of telemarketers as part of its "Operation Tele-PHONEY."

Here's the scoop: Scammers were trying to sell people all kinds of things over the phone, from advance-fee loans to big savings on prescriptions, from magazine subscriptions to household products for seniors. Though there were many independent telemarketers, the common thread here was that they all sought to get your checking account information. Once they had it, they would bill you and try to empty out your account.

The banking industry continues to have zero security in place for drafts on your account. A legitimate person trying to cash a hard-copy check will be put through the ringer at a bank if they're a noncustomer—including being asked to provide a fingerprint in addition to two proofs of identification.

But if you just have an account number and make an electronic draft, they'll pay it with no questions asked. This is a true Achilles' heel that can easily be exploited by criminals.

The takeaway here is simple: Never give out your check routing number over the phone or on the Web. If you're dealing with a collection agency, consider paying by money order rather than by check. You might pay a nominal fee to do so, but this is the only truly safe way to settle your debt.

## Suspend automatic drafts from your account

Too often, I talk to people who have allowed a company to automatically deduct money from their checking or savings account each month. It could be a utility company, a health club, a mortgage lender, a cable provider, a cell provider, or any other business.

That business might continue to make monthly Automated Clearing House (ACH) debits from your account once your contract with them ends. Giving authorization to regularly draft an account is an open-ended arrangement, regardless of your contract. And getting that money back can be a grueling process. The problem with ACH payments is that there are no consumer protection statutes governing what happens if you're cheated on purpose or in error.

*The New York Times* reported the story of one consumer who had a real nightmare with a car loan. The note was paid in full, yet the loan servicer continued to take monthly payments! The customer's own bank was no help and it was a fight every month to get the money back.

Another recent report I saw in the *Chicago Tribune* detailed how a health club franchise that had fallen on hard times was tapping into the accounts of former members in order to keep its doors open. One woman reported her checking account was raided on three occasions for a total of $117—this despite the fact that she hadn't been a member in more than five years!

The gym's parent organization said they wouldn't take responsibility for the actions of a franchise. In fact, I've heard more complaints about the health club industry than any other when it comes to these wrongful automatic drafts.

So what's the solution? I have two for you actually. First, use electronic bill pay that you set up so you can shut it down anytime you want. That's the distinction between e-bill pay and traditional ACH payments. The former you control, the latter is out of your control.

Second, if you're already finding your account being dinged every month without your permission, you can write your bank and tell it to stop unauthorized drafts. (You'll want to be sure you've already canceled the account in writing with the offending business, of course.) The Federal Reserve has special rules governing preauthorized transfers.

If you need to write your bank about this, I suggest you send the following simple three-paragraph letter by certified mail, return receipt requested:

"I am writing to request that you stop [insert company's name] from making future automatic withdrawals from my checking account. These charges are unauthorized. I canceled my contract in writing with [insert company's name] on [list the date of cancellation].

"The Federal Reserve's rules governing preauthorized transfers (part of Regulation E) state the following: 'Once a financial institution has been notified that the customer's authorization is no longer valid, it must block all future payments for the particular debit trans-mitted by the designated payee-originator.'

"I would appreciate your immediate compliance with this federal law. Please contact me if you have any further questions."

Upon receipt of this letter, the bank has ten business days to give you back the money that was wrongfully taken from your account, give you a provisional credit, or deny your request (I don't see why they would). So the bank effectively becomes liable for refunding your money. It may not want to, but now you have the form letter to hold the bank's feet to the fire!

There's a larger problem here, of course: The rules on drafting accounts are set up for the benefit of businesses with zero consumer protections.

So if you sign up with a new company, be sure to give only your credit card number. That way you can dispute any bogus zombie transactions it might try to pull. Look through your bank statements and discontinue any automatic drafts that come out of your savings or checking accounts.

## File a complaint against your bank

When monster mega-banks misbehave, the average person will just sit there and take it. That's not the right response! You should really fire your bank if it can't resolve an outstand-ing problem, and take your business to a credit union or small community bank.

Many big banks seem to pride themselves on customer no-service. Well, after you've given them a chance to do what's right and they still haven't done it, you have one final recourse: You can file a complaint with the Office of the Comptroller of the Currency, which charters and disciplines all of the nation's banks. Visit OCC.gov and click on "Consumer Complaints" to get started. It's a six-page form and the OCC makes it very user friendly.

I've found that once you register your complaint at OCC.gov, it's helpful to go back to the bank and explain what you've done. The banks will usually start falling all over themselves to help you at this point instead of trying to ignore you. That's the power of complaining to the right entity!

When the new Consumer Financial Protection Bureau created by President Obama's financial overhaul law gets up and running, it will likely be the one to handle complaints against banks. But keep using OCC.gov until further notice.

*I thank you for directing me to the Office of the Comptroller of the Currency in the U.S. Treasury Department. I had them contact my bank after I tried for 24 months to correct an error they made in not crediting a $30 payment to my account.*

*This escalated to $270 in late fees that I refused to pay and, after a dozen letters and faxes, they sold the account to a collection agency. They reported to the credit rating agencies that I was delinquent.*

*The OCC got the matter cleared up in 14 days! The bank sent me a letter confirming that the $30 was never properly credited to my account, but they did not apologize for trying to ruin my credit or making a mistake.*

*I have canceled the card and will never use anything connected with the bank or recommend them to anyone.*

*I wrote the collection agency and sent them a copy of the letter and told them never to contact me again regarding this matter or I would report them to Washington!*

*Mace F., CA*

# CREDIT CARDS AND CREDIT USE

## A CLARK FAVORITE
### *Get a free approximation of your credit score*

So often when I'm talking to someone, they'll tell me what their credit score is. Immediately, I come back with something that makes them get that glazed look in their eyes: "Which credit score are you talking about?" No one knows there are about a gazillion different credit scores out there. But there's only a single "real" one that's used by most lenders.

Your true credit score is a number between 350 and 850 that evaluates your risk as a borrower. The FICO people (formerly known as Fair Isaac Corporation) are the one and only source for your true credit score—known simply as your FICO score.

A score of above 700 on the FICO scale is like getting a B+ in school. Anyone with a FICO score of 760–850 is an A student, or what's called "golden" in the industry, which means you're a very safe credit risk for a lender.

To complicate things, you have a FICO score with Equifax, a separate one with Experian, and another one with TransUnion! Each bureau's score will vary slightly because of differences in the way they compile information on you. However, they'll all be similar in range.

The credit score most used by lenders is the Equifax FICO score. You can purchase your Equifax FICO score for $7.95 by calling 1-877-SCORE-11. I recommend doing this if you're about to apply for a serious loan like a mortgage or a car note.

But if you're the kind of person who just wants to keep a general tab on your credit, I recommend getting a free non-FICO score that's available instantly online. I know of three main outlets for this: Credit.com, CreditKarma.com, and Quizzle.com.

Credit.com gives you a "report card" based on your TransUnion score once a month. It includes a letter grade and a number that roughly equates to your true FICO score. CreditKarma.com will give a score based on your TransUnion report once daily. And Quizzle.com will give you a score based on your Experian report twice a year. Again, these are all approximations of your true FICO, not the real deal.

Each of these free services will try to up-sell you on a variety of additional services. That's how they make their money and can offer their services for free. Be sure to read the terms of use closely on each site if you have privacy concerns. By using these services, you're allowing them to contact you—even if you're on the federal government's "do not call" list. But there's no obligation to buy anything ever to get your free non-FICO score.

## Get free credit reports at the one legitimate site

When is the last time you checked your credit report? Some people never do. And as it usually turns out, those are the ones who could become susceptible to deceptive loan tactics.

For example, let's say you're at a car dealership. When it comes time to talk financing, the salesman might put on a big show during which he or she says how difficult it was to get you financing, but that they finally found a lender who will write your loan at 14 percent. But all along you had great credit and could have found yourself a loan elsewhere at 4 percent—if you'd only checked your credit!

Each of the three main credit bureaus—Equifax, Experian, and TransUnion—maintains a credit file on you. You have a right under federal law to see each of your three credit files once a year for free. The federally sanctioned site for this is AnnualCreditReport.com. It is the only truly free website to check your credit report. The same service is also available over the phone for free by calling 877-322-8228.

Longtime listeners of my show might think this news is old hat, but I still get tons of calls from those who were taken in by the other (not so) "free" credit report sites. You know the ones I'm talking about—with the catchy jingle and the promise of a free credit report. The catch is that you enroll in a subscription service to have your credit monitored at a price of up to $200 annually. The public has been so deceived by these ads, particularly those put out by FreeCreditReport.com.

I want you to check your report periodically through AnnualCreditReport.com. I suggest you make a note on your calendar to check one of the three credit files every four months, like clockwork. If that's not realistic, at least make sure to pull all three at once, once a year. You might find it very illuminating: You'll learn how often you make late payments, which issues are aging off (most credit issues stay on your report for a maximum of seven years), and more. All of this will help you get your finances in better order and possibly eliminate credit problems down the road!

## Pay your bills on time to boost your credit score

To get your credit healthy again, you've got to actively manage and manipulate your credit. Yes, that's right, I said "manipulate." This is the kind of instance where manipulation does *not* have a negative connotation!

Everybody wants to have a good credit score. Fortunately, the keys to making the grade are relatively simple. When you consider that credit scores remain central to getting good rates on insurance, on a mortgage, and on future credit and could even cause you to be turned down for a job offer, well, I think it's one of the simplest and most effective things you can tweak in your life.

One big thing you can do to improve your credit score is to pay your bills on time. Even if you have some late pays on your report, just focus on paying your current bills on time. Making timely payments accounts for about 35 percent of your overall score, and the most recent bills count more. If you remember anything from reading this book, remember this one! This is the single most important rule for having a good credit score.

*I started listening to Coach Clark about four years ago. (I call him Coach because he IS my financial coach.) In general, I had no interest in finances or credit before I started listening. In fact, I didn't even know what a credit score was. I guess I had always assumed banks and other lenders had access to information but they kept all of that under wraps.*

*On Clark's advice, I decided to check my FICO score and see where I stood. To my dismay, my credit score was 386! So I developed a plan using Clark's advice.*

*Clark always said that your payment history was one of the biggest factors in your credit score, so I began by simply paying my bills on time.*

*With the few collection accounts I had, I again took Clark's advice and contacted the creditor and got all of those taken care of. I just took my time.*

*Clark always said that the late pays on a credit report hurt less and less as time goes by, so I just waited. I continued to pay all of my bills on time, got a secured credit card (again at Clark's suggestion), didn't use the card except two times a year, and waited.*

*After about 18 months or so, I noticed a dramatic increase to about 570. I continued to wait it out and after about 30 months applied for a mortgage. My credit score was 656 at that time, which was still good enough to qualify back then. Now, just four years later, I can look at my credit score and proudly say that I stand at 736 and rising!*

*Joe R., NC*

## Don't use too much of your credit

In addition to paying your bills on time, you should aim to use less of your available credit.

If you have a credit card with a $10,000 limit and you have a balance of around $3,000, you're using 30 percent of your available credit. You want to stay at or below that level.

Your credit utilization rate accounts for about 30 percent of your overall score. So if you pay your bills on time and don't use too much of your available credit, you're good to go, because those two factors account for 65 percent of your credit score.

Unfortunately, during the Great Recession many people found their credit limits inexplicably lowered at what seemed like the whim of the banks. So if your credit limit gets cut to $3,000 and you have a $3,000 outstanding balance, then suddenly you're using 100 percent of your available credit. Lenders do not like maxed-out borrowers, so a change like this can be disastrous to your credit score.

This is yet another reason to pay down credit card debt as quickly as possible. Under the new credit card rules that went into effect in 2010, if you have multiple interest rates on a credit card (balance transfers, cash advances, etc.), anything you pay over the minimum balance will be applied to the highest rate first. But beware, if you pay only the minimum, the banks are still allowed to apply the money to the lowest rate first. I want you paying more than minimums each month!

*At a time in my life when I was barely making $27,000 a year, I managed to accumulate $25,000 in credit card debt. The fear and shame and helplessness I felt kept me up at night. Were it not for Clark and his advice, I don't know what I would have done.*

*Per Clark's suggestion, I first tackled the credit card with the highest interest rate, even though it wasn't the card with the highest balance.*

*Taking care of the former gave me a psychological boost more than anything. Because I had deprived a bank the ability to charge me more money in interest, I now felt confident taking on the other banks.*

*Best of all, once I got used to paying off my debt regularly (twice a month, not once— another of Clark's suggestions), I found I could pay even more without breaking a sweat. By the end of two years, I was so used to frugality, I was actually paying off most of my last months in debt.*

*I want to thank Clark for throwing me a lifeline. And I'm happy to report I have not been in debt since.*

*Kevin C., TX*

## Keep credit card accounts open if there's no annual fee

When people dig themselves out of credit card debt, one of the first things they want to do is cut up all their cards and close out the accounts. I understand the sentiment, but don't do it!

Closing existing accounts only reduces your available credit and drives your score down. Keeping the credit line open helps your credit score. Open lines of credit account for about 15 percent of your overall credit score.

You want to have four to six lines of credit in today's economic climate. And as I note later in this chapter, you've got to do more than just have them hanging around; you've got to actively use them. Be sure to use all your cards twice a year—even if it's just for a dollar store purchase or to grab some food on the go—and then pay them off right away online or when the bill comes in the mail. That will keep those cards active in your credit mix.

A lot of people have asked me what to do when facing a huge new annual fee on a card that has a zero balance. I suggest "leapfrogging." That's my term for using the forty-five-day window you have before any new terms of service go into effect to shop around for a better deal. So once you get a notice about a new annual fee, start looking around for other no-fee credit cards. Submit your applications, and once you get your new no-fee card, then go ahead and shut down the original one that wanted to spring a huge new fee on you.

By doing this, you're replacing like with like and substituting new open lines of credit to keep your credit score healthy.

> *I always thought that closing credit card accounts was the best way to increase your FICO score. Boy, was I wrong!! I closed some of my accounts, thinking, "Wow, this will really help my credit rating." I listen to Clark Howard every day and watch him on HLN on the weekend. When he advised to leave the credit card account open, I almost fell off of my seat!! I had it all backwards. Now I keep my account open, use it twice a year, and pay off the balance as soon as possible (another awesome tip from Clark).*
>
> *In these days of tight credit, and credit card companies getting tough on their faithful customers, Clark not only saved me from a plummeting credit score, but also put me in a much better position. I am getting ready to send my daughter off to college this fall. Thanks to Clark's wonderful advice, my credit rating was saved! Now I can focus on saving for my daughter's education, not my credit score.*
>
> *Frances B., FL*

## Find the best reward card for you

People with good credit get a lot of pitches for reward cards—those credit cards that promise cash back or gift points for every dollar you charge. But reward cards typically have higher interest rates and benefit only those who pay the bill in full each month.

If you carry a balance, however, having a reward card is like trying to collect fool's gold. You'll pay more in interest charges than you get back in benefits. Try instead to get a nonreward card with the lowest interest rate possible. Look at small community banks and credit unions for the best offers in this regard.

There's also the question of airline mileage cards. My advice is to avoid these kinds of cards because it's difficult to redeem miles and the airlines keep raising the number of miles you need to get a seat. The only exception to this might be a business owner or executive who has a high charge volume and travels often.

Right now, high-net-worth people with good credit scores (740–850 on the FICO scale) are receiving solicitations for cards with high annual fees and a lot of rewards. The fees might be anywhere from $200 to $500. Some offers from American Express have annual fees of $1,500. A card had better offer you *amazing* rewards to make that fee worthwhile!

CreditCardTuneUp.com can help you determine the best reward card for you. When you're at the site, you can enter the amount you charge each month by category—restaurants, grocery stores, gas stations, airfare, hotels, vehicle rental, and more—and their system will crunch the numbers to see what the thirty most popular reward cards will give you during your first year of use. The site even converts rewards like points or mileage into a cash-back equivalent so you can do a straight apples-to-apples comparison across a variety of card offerings.

There's a new competitor, NerdWallet.com, that I read about on *The New York Times*' Bucks blog. NerdWallet.com uses a slightly different routine from CreditCardTuneUp to find the best card for you. I particularly like that if you know your credit score, you can enter it on NerdWallet.com and that will change your list of potential best cards.

I recommending using both CreditCardTuneUp and NerdWallet and comparing the results. If both sites find the same card(s) as the first, second, or third choice for you, that would be great independent validation. At any rate, it sure beats picking a card based on the fancy envelope that comes in the mail, as many people do. CreditCardTuneUp and NerdWallet give you a way to methodically and scientifically select the right credit card for you.

## Use your "back of the wallet" cards twice a year

Many of us have what are called in the lingo of the credit card industry "back of the wallet" cards. Those are the cards you hardly ever use that might be buried somewhere in your wallet or in a drawer at home.

The typical American has about a dozen cards but uses only two of them frequently. The rest are ignored until they go dormant. In fact, you might not even activate a new card when you get it in the mail.

Banks used to just let a dormant account sit and hope you'd someday use the card again—but that was not how it played out during the recession. If an account went stale, the bank just closed that account. Unfortunately, that meant a double whammy for you; it hurt your credit score and it limited your access to funds.

To avoid having a dormant account closed, use your "back of the wallet" cards twice a year about six months apart. Charge a nominal amount and then pay it off. Mark it on a calendar if you have to in order to remember.

This is not just a silly assignment. You'll be helping your credit score, which is very important in getting lower interest rates and future lines of credit and securing job offers.

## Get free credit counseling

If you watch bad late-night TV, you've probably seen those ads being run by the debt-settlement outfits. Their promises scream out in the night about reducing your outstanding debt to just pennies on the dollar without making you file for bankruptcy—no matter how much outstanding debt you have.

That promise, however, is just an illusion. The debt-settlement firms' typical modus operandi goes like this: You pay an up-front fee to them, plus a monthly retainer. They then tell you to stop paying on your bills, stash the money you would have used to pay bills into a bank account, and just sit on it. The idea is to make the credit card companies so desperate that they'll cry uncle and want to settle with you at a reduced rate. The reality, however, is that too often you wind up just damaging your credit.

In the worst-case scenario, the more unsavory players in the debt-settlement business will take your up-front fee and first month's retainer and then ignore you when you try to initiate further contact with them. Beware!

It's so easy to want to believe that somebody has a magic bullet to solve all your problems. But that's simply not the case.

So what do you do? Get in touch with the National Foundation for Credit Counseling (NFCC) at NFCC.org or call 1-800-388-2227 to find a local affiliate office near you. NFCC affiliates offer free or low-cost debt counseling. About one in three clients just needs some budgeting help to get their lives back on track. Beyond simple budgeting, the NFCC can also get you set up on a hardship debt-management plan (DMP) if you qualify.

In the case of a hardship DMP, lenders agree to modify the terms and conditions of their repayment policies. That means they might waive late and over-the-limit fees, in addition to reducing interest rates. They will not, however, agree to a reduction of your outstanding balance. But it could be worth a look if you meet the eligibility requirements. Get in touch with a local affiliate of the NFCC today to find out.

> *I was solicited by a credit consolidation company. It sounded like just what we needed to get our monthly bills down just a bit. I talked to him, gave him all my info and he told me how he could help. I called my wife very excited after I arranged a call back with the representative.*
>
> *However, my wife, who watched Clark's show, was suspicious and she had questions. The representative I spoke with wanted us to ignore creditors while our "deal" was being settled. My wife called several times with questions and kept saying, "Clark Howard says this isn't a good idea, I know—I watched a show on it!" So she looked up your site, called the hot line and confirmed she was right. We told the man what we did when he called back and, boy, he turned nasty quick—he actually said we were going to hell.*
>
> *Well, we won't be going to hell for scamming anybody! And thanks to Clark we still have a credit score in the 780s. Our bills are still a little bit high, but our credit is safe!*
>
> *Nathan & Misty L., MO*

## Send bill collectors a "drop dead letter"

While I acknowledge there are some decent, honest, hardworking bill collectors operating in the collections industry, I routinely trash their counterparts who break the law when trying to collect outstanding debts.

Before I go any further, let me say that I actually paid my way through grad school working as a bill collector. I did commercial collections for IBM and really enjoyed my work. I got to use my own style of getting to know the people at the organizations that owed my employer money. Basically, I used my naturally friendly personality to get debtors to pay up.

Later when I owned my own chain of travel agencies, I would dedicate Thursday mornings to showing up in person at the doors of people who owed me money. I was always respectful, and you know what? It worked. But many others in the collections business are not as respectful.

Too often, collectors play dirty pool—threatening jail or even telling children that their parents are going to the slammer because they can't honor their debts. Both are practices that disgust me to no end. To say that to a child is just sadistic, and the reality is that the likelihood of going to debtor's prison is rare in the United States . Be sure to record any abusive messages from collectors. If you think they've violated the law, contact your state attorney general's office by visiting NAAG.org and the Federal Trade Commission at FTC.gov.

It's usually the third-party companies who buy outstanding debts for pennies on the dollar that use these threatening tactics even though they're illegal. But sometimes, even the banks can legitimately behave like creeps.

The banking industry's powerful lobby won an exemption under the rules of the Fair Debt Collection Practices Act (FDCPA) that actually allows their in-house collectors to do *anything* to collect on a debt—short of harming you physically or threatening to do so. Fortunately, that's the only exemption in the entire collections industry.

Everybody else is governed under the normal provisions of the FDCPA. So once you tell non–bank employee collectors to stop harassing you about an unpaid debt, they are required to do so. Now, they may not heed the law as it's written; some collectors care about the law while others do not. But I say it's worth a try to get them off your back.

You can do that by sending them a "drop dead letter" by certified mail, return receipt requested, that states the following: "I have been contacted by your company about a debt you allege I owe. I am instructing you not to contact me further in connection with this debt. Under the Fair Debt Collection Practices Act, a federal law, you may not contact me further once I have notified you not to do so."

They can still sue you or ruin your credit even if you've restricted contact. And you still owe the money, of course. But a drop dead letter can be a way to get them to stop bugging you until you can get some funds together to honor your debt.

# IDENTITY THEFT

## Freeze your credit to protect against identity theft

People often ask me if they should sign up for LifeLock or a similar service in order to avoid identity theft. If you've ever seen or heard a LifeLock ad, you know that CEO Todd Davis proudly announces his Social Security number—essentially challenging thieves to steal his identity. It's brilliant marketing that's won his company a lot of customers.

While Lifelock is completely legitimate and in no way a scam, I think you're paying for false security. I have a better way to get the job done and it's very low cost or might even be free for you.

First, though, a little background: LifeLock's business model is based on offering a glorified monitoring service and putting fraud alerts on your credit files. These alerts are meant to raise a flag to potential creditors so they carefully verify an applicant's identity before granting credit. Too often, however, the alerts are ignored and credit is granted anyway to thieves using your name.

So what's my solution? It's called a credit freeze and it's one of the most effective tools against financial identity theft available to consumers today.

As you probably know, each of the three main credit bureaus maintains an active dossier on you that contains info about your payment history, lines of credit, and more. A credit freeze allows you to seal your credit reports with each bureau. It does not affect your current use of credit in any way.

When you do a freeze, you get a personal identification number (PIN) that only you know. That added layer of security means that crooks can't establish new lines of credit in your name even if they are able to take over other elements of your identity—because they don't have your secret PIN.

Then when you actually want to apply for a new line of credit, you simply use your PIN to temporarily "thaw" your files. That makes them accessible to the creditor who's considering you as a customer.

The cost to freeze your credit ranges from free to $10 per bureau, depending on your state. When you multiply that by three credit bureaus, you could pay anywhere from nothing to $30 for a freeze. Victims of identity theft can get any fees waived, and seniors are often exempt from the fees in most states.

If you visit ClarkHoward.com and search the keyword "credit freeze," you can link to a guide I've prepared that will give you the cost in your state. My guide also offers full details on how to get in touch with each of the bureaus to request your credit freeze.

## Beware of the worst corporations for identity theft

Several years ago, the Berkeley Center for Law and Technology analyzed corporate America to see which companies have the highest incidence of identity theft. The top company? Bank of America.

Bank of America is the nation's largest bank. By comparison, Citibank—another of the nation's largest banks—had about one-third fewer incidences of identity theft than BOA, and it came in sixth, according to the Berkeley study!

AT&T occupies the second slot following BOA. After that, Sprint, JPMorgan Chase, and Capital One round out the top five. (You can view the complete list online at eScholarship .org by searching the keywords "Measuring Identity Theft at Top Banks.")

So three of the top five are banks, which is understandable. But why are two phone companies way up there? It's because they do a credit check when you apply for phone service. That opens you up as a potential target after they get hold of your info.

Now the inevitable question: Why do these institutions have high rates of identity theft? I believe it has to do with the way they handle your information internally.

Quite interestingly, the Berkeley study revealed that the bank with the lowest incidence of identity theft was ING DIRECT. You would think they'd be up at the top of the list since they're an Internet-only institution with no branches in the United States. But being a newer entry to our banking market, ING DIRECT has been dealing with outsmarting identity thieves since it launched. It's much tougher for a legacy financial institution to retroactively patch good protection into banking systems that were built decades ago before the computer age.

I'm not raising this info to make you overly fearful about the companies you do business with, nor do I want you to feel that your "safe" options are limited in the marketplace. In reality, identity theft has not grown significantly since it emerged. It continues to hold steady at about 10 million people a year, which is about 3 percent of the population of the United States. But it's still a major issue, nonetheless.

As I explained earlier, a credit freeze is the best tool that's available today to curtail your chances of economic identity theft.

## Beware of bogus mobile apps for online banking

Online banking is shifting from computers to smartphones such as the iPhone and all the Android phones. Along with that transition comes the threat of bogus mobile applications and downloads that aren't from legitimate sources.

As a member of USAA, I first heard about this threat from that esteemed institution. Apparently there was a phony USAA app floating around that mimicked the true app from USAA. Criminals have discovered this can be a lucrative way to get rich in a hurry by stealing other people's money.

Meanwhile, Dow Jones has reported that there are dozens of phony sites offering apps for the Google phones, which run on the Android platform. Android is an open platform, meaning that people can post whatever apps they wish. Only after someone gets taken and files a formal complaint will the bad apps be removed.

Interestingly, the iPhone is on a closed system, but that hasn't made it any safer when it comes to the threat of bogus mobile banking apps.

So is mobile banking on your smartphone a smart idea? The techie answer is yes, but be sure to download apps only directly from your bank, brokerage house, or mutual fund company's website. Don't trust Apple's App Store or the Google Apps website.

## Automatically send sensitive financial info to survivors

What happens to your accounts, usernames, and passwords when you die? An article I saw in *Time* magazine titled "How to Manage Your Online Life When You're Dead" addresses this thoroughly modern dilemma.

A variety of new online services have popped up with solutions. Deathswitch.com is a service that repeatedly prompts you for your password to make sure you're still living. You choose the frequency of the prompts, and it can be anywhere from a daily message to a once-a-year checkup. If you fail to reply to multiple prompts sent by DeathSwitch's servers, their system will then e-blast out a message you've precomposed (containing usernames, passwords, special messages to loved ones, sensitive financial info, etc.) to let those you wish know of your demise! You're in complete control of the digital "beneficiaries" who will get your message, and your communication can include videos, pictures, and documents, in addition to a simple e-mail message.

The service is free if you have only one message you need sent to one person upon your death. A premium subscription that allows up to thirty messages (and ten recipients per message) is $20 annually. Similar services (all with different price points) are available from AssetLock.net, LegacyLocker.com, MyWebWill.com, and WeRemember.org.

But what if you sign up with one of these services and it goes bust? What becomes of your sensitive info? There is no clear law in the United States to govern this at the time of this writing. Hopefully some protections will be put into place in the future. I should warn you that in similar instances, user info has sometimes been sold to make creditors whole!

Obviously, there's no perfect solution yet. If you're a brainiac, there's a great business opportunity here helping people preplan how to handle their digital lives after they're gone, I promise you.

I handle the whole dilemma in a very analog way. I've given one of my lifelong friends an envelope that has all my usernames and accounts in the event of my death. He'll then see to it that the info is shared with the right parties. Luckily, I really trust my friend, because if he's not trustworthy, I could be broke in a minute considering all the info he has on me!

# INVESTING AND RETIREMENT

## Pick up matching 401(k) contributions from your employer

We as a country can't continue to pay for the Social Security, Medicare, and Medicaid obligations that we've promised our citizens. The math simply *isn't* going to work, especially as we enjoy longer life spans.

When you get right down to it, you are the only person who can provide for your retirement—particularly if you're under forty. So you can either start saving money now, or face the fact that you might not get to retire. Not retiring is *not* the worst thing in the world; after all, retirement itself is a relatively new concept in human history.

But if you can save as little as a dime on every dollar you make, you'll put yourself in good stead for retirement. Do you have an employer match through your 401(k)? Make sure you're putting in at least enough to pick up the match. If you're not, you're leaving money on the table that could be yours.

What if your employer doesn't offer any retirement plan at all? That's the predicament nearly 80 million people face, according to a study from the Employee Benefit Research Institute.

For those people, I have two suggestions. The first is to open up a simplified employee pension (SEP). The paperwork to set up a SEP is simple, and you can typically open it wherever you want—at a low-cost investment house, for example—at no cost. SEPs work like a traditional IRA, with a current year tax deduction, but withdrawals are taxed at retirement. They also offer flexibility, in that investors can put in nothing in a year or as much as $49,000.

The other option I like when you don't have access to a retirement plan through work is to open a Roth IRA. See my No. 6 tip, "Help Me Now, Clark," for more on that option.

## A CLARK FAVORITE
### *Increase your savings rate gradually*

A recent report from CNNMoney.com showed that more than one in four American workers have zero savings. Now, this could be a personal choice, or maybe it's because of a series of circumstances like health woes or divorce. But getting financial breathing room in your life is absolutely essential. Otherwise, you're one whisker away from financial disaster in the event of a job loss.

I often talk about setting up automatic withdrawals from your check each pay period to a 401(k) or a Roth IRA. Somewhere around half of us work for employers that offer a 401(k) plan. Employers that do so often mandate their employees contribute to it. In addition, the employer might even periodically bump up the level of your contributions. I'm in favor of this heavy-handed approach because it forces at least half of us to save for retirement.

Bumping up your savings rate—whether you do it or your employer does it for you—doesn't have to be a painful thing. Most people find it pretty comfortable to increase their savings rate by one percentage point every six months. So if you save nothing currently, start by saving 1 percent of your pay, then increase to 2 percent in six months. With automatic withdrawals the money is gone before you ever see it. You probably won't miss it!

It used to be an article of faith that as Americans made more money, we saved more money. But our culture has become one of immediate gratification for everything from houses to cars. Now as our income rises, many of us just spend and borrow more.

So how about you—are you in this category? Are you going for the instant store line of credit every time it's offered? If so, I want you to take a new approach. Think about saving money before making a purchase instead of borrowing and then having another monthly obligation to meet. Greater long-term satisfaction comes from buying only what you can afford, when you have the dough, than from buying something on credit that you can't afford, for which you get merely a momentary adrenaline rush.

## Start a Roth with $100 or less

When I talk with someone who is trying to save for the future, I notice their eyes start to glaze over as I answer their questions. I can even tell when this is happening as I talk to someone on the radio!

Investing can seem so complicated that you might shut down and do nothing when you hit that wall—or feel you need to hire someone to guide you.

However, it doesn't need to be complicated, nor does it have to be prohibitively expensive, either. Many investment houses charge up to $3,000 to open an account. But you don't need big bucks to get started.

The Vanguard Star Fund, one of my favorite picks as a custodial account for a child, can be opened with as little as $1,000. Still too rich for your blood? Schwab is now requiring *just $100* to open an account. And T. Rowe Price has no minimum requirement at all if you commit to regular contributions of $50 every pay period.

You can find out more about the Vanguard Star Fund at Vanguard.com or call 877-662-7447. Visit "Chuck" at Schwab.com or call 866-232-9890 for info on their plans. The T. Rowe Price option is called the Automatic Asset Builder plan. Visit TRowePrice.com and search that keyword or call 800-638-5660 to get signed up.

If you don't have that employer forcing you into a 401(k), you might never do it. I want you to do what it takes to be the master of your own destiny.

### CLARK'S GREATEST HITS

*Dollar cost average and diversify in your investment choices*

Once you start saving for retirement with a Roth IRA or a 401(k), my goal for you is to automatically put in a set amount of money each month to build the habit and reduce the risk of investing.

By making regular contributions monthly in equal amounts, you are doing what's called "dollar cost averaging." That's just a fancy way of saying you're not trying to time the market. In months that the stock market is diving, your money buys more shares. In months that the market is climbing, your money buys a smaller number of shares, but the shares you already own are worth more.

Dollar cost averaging is a way to pace your investing so that you're buying shares when prices are low, high, or in between.

Over time, putting money in this way reduces the possibility that you will panic and either sell or stop investing; it keeps you steady as you go. And staying in the game makes you more money over the long haul.

When the Dow Jones Industrial Average dropped to 6,547 on March 9, 2009, a lot of investors had their willpower tested. But people who didn't sell out and kept putting in their $50 or $100 saw big gains on their shares when the Dow surged back. No one knows what the markets will do, but putting in cash every month really cuts your risk.

## Don't tap into your retirement account when you're unemployed

With the hard economic times, many people have taken to raiding their retirement savings without fully understanding the repercussions. If you do choose to cash out your 401(k), know that you'll typically get hit with taxes and penalties that can eat up some 40 percent of your money.

For example, if you take a 401(k) with $10,000 in it and cash it out, you get a tax bill for 20 percent up front. Then when you file your tax return the following year, you get hit with another 20 percent in taxes and penalties.

That means your $10,000 becomes more like $6,000 and you have zero saved for retirement. Very bad math, right?

So you can see my bias against cashing out your retirement account when the going gets tough. In fact, it should be done only if you've absolutely exhausted every other resource and can't put a roof over your head or food on your family's table.

There are some circumstances where you can withdraw retirement money and pay only tax and no penalty.

For IRA holders, these circumstances include buying a home (as a first-time home buyer); paying educational expenses for immediate family; and some select instances involving unreimbursed medical expenses and health insurance.

When it comes to your 401(k), you can make a penalty-free early withdrawal in only two circumstances: if you turn fifty-five or older the same year that you leave your employer and for some unreimbursed medical expenses.

The problem is that I find the circumstances are little understood by the average person and all too often disregarded. You should consult with a tax professional before making any decisions.

## Never take a 401(k) check yourself

The average worker no longer spends a lifetime with a single employer. That raises a dilemma when you do leave a job: What to do with your 401(k)?

The best strategies are to leave it with the old employer's plan or to roll it over to your new employer's plan.

Recent estimates from Hewitt Associates, a human resources consulting firm, suggest that 46 percent of people spend their 401(k) when they move on from an employer.

If you do need to get at that money—which obviously flies in the face of my advice in the previous tip—there are two smart ways to do it.

First, you can have your 401(k) rolled over to an IRA and draw only what you need to live on. By doing this, you reduce the tax and penalties you'll face. Be sure you're doing what's called a "trustee to trustee transfer" when you move the money. That means the money goes from your current plan administrator to your new plan administrator and never enters your hands. You never want to receive a check yourself—even if you go ahead and deposit it in a new retirement account—unless you want to be eaten alive on taxes and penalties.

If you haven't lost your job and need cash, you could try borrowing from your 401(k). Now, a lot of people have argued that this is a wonderful option because it's like you're paying yourself back as you pay back the loan. However, I don't think it's as great as it seems. You're paying yourself back with after-tax dollars that will be taxed again during retirement. So you're effectively being taxed twice instead of only once when the money is spent during retirement. And if you should leave your employer before you've paid back the loan, the balance becomes immediately due in full with tax.

## Avoid "can't lose" investments

The name Bernie Madoff has become instantly recognizable even to those people who don't know anything about investing. That's because Madoff operated an infamous $50 billion Ponzi scheme (the largest ever in history), promising his victims the "Madoff 10"—completely safe returns of 10 percent annually regardless of market conditions.

Madoff wouldn't divulge the proprietary investing techniques behind "the Madoff 10" during the decades that he was in operation. Why? Because there weren't any techniques! In classic Ponzi style, early investors were simply paid with money from those who later got on the gravy train.

You'd think after all the Madoff publicity, investors would be wary of Ponzi schemes. But *The Orlando Sentinel* reports there's been a 175 percent increase in the number of investment-fraud complaints in the last few years, citing numbers from Florida's attorney general. The FBI concurs with that assessment of the spike in Ponzi scheme activity.

Here's what you need to know: You should be suspicious anytime you're told about a method of investing that's completely "safe" and promises returns that are higher than what the marketplace offers. Usually with a Ponzi, the floor is 10 percent a month. Maybe that's why Madoff was able to fly under the radar for so long; he was promising only 10 percent annually.

Consider this: If the average savings account is paying about 1 percent annually as I write this, some "opportunity" promising well above that could easily be a fraud.

No one can promise you returns without risk. Beware of the "can't lose" promises—no matter how small or great they are.

And don't buy complicated investments that you don't understand. If you follow this simple rule, you'll avoid most of the scams out there. If you can't explain the investment to a fifth grader, don't buy it!

## Limit your investments in gold or precious metals

I've gotten so many calls since the recession began from people asking about investing in gold or other precious metals. But buying gold because you saw a cheesy ad on late-night TV is not really an investment; it's more of a speculative venture.

I recommend putting no more than 5 or 10 percent of your portfolio into gold or other precious metals. Anything above that is too risky. As I write this, gold has been trading at amazing prices—over $1,486 an ounce! That's a huge sum. You might read this and think, "I've got to get a piece of the action." But even if the price keeps going up from here, you've got to realize that the good news about gold is already baked in the cake. For those who already own gold, they're showing good profits, on paper at least.

If you buy now, however, there's a chance that values could start to decline. Prices could go higher still, of course, but that would likely be contingent on unfavorable world conditions such as a brutal world war. Gold trades on fear and bad fundamentals in the marketplace. We've already seen the bad fundamentals during the economic meltdown. That's why I have to reiterate that this is *not* a great time to hop in—despite those amazing numbers.

If you still want to buy gold, do not buy the actual bars. Storage can be cumbersome, and there's a huge spread on the buy and the sell. You typically have to buy at 5 percent above the market price and sell at 5 to 6 percent less than current value.

My preferred way to own gold is through a gold exchange-traded fund (ETF). ETFs are the fastest-growing area of investing, and I think of them as mutual funds for the next generation. Just as mutual funds have exploded in popularity over the last thirty years, so too will ETFs as we move into the future.

You buy ETFs exactly as you would a stock, preferably through a zero-commission broker, and you can sell them at any time. The fund stores the physical bars of gold at minimal cost to you. And then you can buy and sell at will, without worrying about getting clobbered on the spread.

If you want to get in the gold game, I like Fidelity's PowerShares DB Precious Metals Fund, iShares COMEX Gold Trust, Central Fund of Canada, and SPDR Gold Shares because they all hold actual physical bars of gold in their reserves. Just pop any of those names into your favorite search engine and you'll be able to link to their webpages.

## Currency trading is just another get-rich-quick scheme

If you're afraid of the stock market and tired of puny returns on CDs, you might be tempted to get into currency trading. Bad idea. For example, let's say you bought Iraqi dinar during the Persian Gulf War years ago with the hopes that you'd become a millionaire when the country's economy turned around. Today that currency is essentially worthless.

Currency trading is one of the latest Dare to Be Rich schemes making the rounds in a down economy, much as buying and flipping houses was all the rage before the real estate bubble burst.

First, it's important to understand that there is a legitimate business here. The main purpose of currency trading is to allow businesses that operate in multiple countries to lower the risk of exchange movement and its effect on their profits.

But the only people making money on currency trading are the ones who push a variety of "how to" info tapes and seminars. They want you to believe that you, as an individual in your spare time, can take their course, watch their tape, or complete their webinar to learn this tricky business.

The reality is that currency trading is extremely high-risk territory. It's not the "insta-business" it seems.

The *New York Post* recently did a story about the currency trading frenzy. According to the article, one trading desk did nearly $7 trillion in trades for clients in 2008. Another company claimed one top employee earned monthly returns of 1,951 percent on his money.

Those kinds of numbers really get your attention and make you think you can make big money. But don't believe the hype. At their worst, currency trading operations can very easily be fronts for Ponzi scheme operators. Even in the best-case scenario, you as an individual trader are up against large institutions that have a lot of resources at their fingertips. That makes it very easy to lose money.

As one securities industry attorney told the *New York Post*, "[Individuals] could be trading against professional traders with a lot of research, charts and sophisticated computer programs—and these pros could fleece them. I am now hearing cases of folks like these small investors losing $5,000, $15,000, $20,000, $25,000."

I want you to stay safe and preserve your capital! The best way to get ahead is with sound principles like spending less than you make and saving for retirement little by little each pay period. There's no fix-all solution that's going to make you rich overnight.

# TAXES

## Prepare and e-file your income taxes online for free

Almost all Americans are eligible for free e-filing of their federal income tax. Generally, the IRS allows up to 90 percent of people to participate; it's only the top 10 percent of income earners who are forbidden. Yet America currently has one of the lowest rates of e-filing among developed countries. I actually prefer that you e-file because errors are less likely thanks to software improvements.

Everyone knows our tax code is incredibly complex. My tax return is typically around 170 pages in length! If your return is simpler, you might also have an opportunity to have your federal tax return done for free by a professional service.

The IRS website offers a list of about twenty companies that will prepare and e-file your taxes for free if you earn an adjusted gross income of a little less than $60,000. It's part of the IRS's annual Free File initiative. Visit IRS.gov and do a keyword search for "Free File" to see the list. You can even try your return with more than one company to see who does the best job for you—just be sure you don't file more than once!

Finally, if you're not Internet-savvy, free income tax prep is also offered offline by AARP and the IRS. The latter's Volunteer Income Tax Assistance (VITA) program caters to those with low income, the elderly, the disabled, and limited English speakers. VITA can be reached at 800-906-9887.

## Pay dimes on the dollar on back taxes

If you owe back taxes, you've probably seen ads from companies promising to help you pay just pennies on the dollar and settle your debt with the IRS.

While that offer is doubtful at best, there is a way for you to pay dimes on the dollar in back taxes with an officially sanctioned IRS program called Offer in Compromise (OIC).

The OIC program—designed to allow delinquent taxpayers to negotiate a lump-sum settlement—was something of a joke in the past. Most offers in compromise were flat-out denied because the IRS assumed people were lying. In many cases, taxpayers who were sitting in homes that had appreciated in value were told they should take out a second mortgage to pay their tax bill. Well, we all know how that scenario played out after the real estate bubble burst and the recession hit.

Now the IRS is beginning to consider all reasonable OICs as a result of the dismal economic climate. The IRS knows that home values have plummeted and is now reviewing each OIC on its individual merits—not redlining it because officials are looking at an outdated valuation of your house.

There is a $150 application fee when you want to do an OIC. But you can wind up saving thousands in the process based on your individual circumstances and back taxes. Visit IRS .gov and search keyword "Offer in Compromise" for more information.

## Beware of the bogus IRS e-mail scam

Have you gotten an e-mail that appears to be from the IRS and says you're owed a small refund?

Crooks faithfully come out of the woodwork the first few months of each year pretending they're the IRS and need to track you down with money that's supposedly yours. I've heard several figures over the years for the dollar amount they promise, such as $63.80 and $139.50. But it can be any dollar amount that's relatively small, say below $200 or $300.

These bogus e-mails are typically branded with the IRS logo and look very legit. They sometimes originate from an address that ends in ".us," which most people think is a sign of authenticity. A ".us" domain name, however, is the same as a ".com"—it could be set up by anybody. Some of these e-mails might even come from an address that ends in ".gov," falsely (in this case) signifying a government organization.

But know this: The IRS does not send e-mails to taxpayers or request detailed personal info through e-mail.

The fake e-mails explain that the money you're supposedly owed will be deposited into your account—provided that you send your account number and secret access code. Do not respond, click on any links, or open any attachments. If you comply, your account will be cleaned out by cyber-criminals.

# Telephones and Television

Technology has created a world where mobile phones are getting cheaper and more sophisticated all the time, allowing social networking and text messaging on the go to become the preferred way of communicating. It's also ushered in a new era of the television age, where price points are constantly dropping on flat screens that offer jaw-dropping high-definition possibilities.

In this chapter, I'll show you how to get into a cheap unlimited phone plan with no contract, use your computer to make calls for extra cheap, and even make and receive international calls while traveling for next to nothing. Plus, I'll show you how you can fire your cable or satellite provider and start enjoying a flood of cheaper programming that's available over the Internet.

## PHONES AND MOBILE DEVICES

### Don't sign a twenty-four-month cell phone contract

New cellular industry data from FierceWireless.com shows that two out of every three customers who signed up for service toward the end of the last decade did so with a noncontract carrier.

The Big Four carriers—AT&T, Sprint, T-Mobile, and Verizon—had a long love affair with twenty-four-month contracts or "service agreements," as they were euphemistically called.

For the longest time, the Big Four argued that contracts were necessary because they helped subsidize the cost of cell phones. But this explanation turned out to be bogus; early iPhone customers had to pay full market price for their phones, and they were still forced into a contract!

Let's face it, in capitalism, contracts are for cowards. Carriers *had* to default to them because of the industry's spotty record of customer service. It was their way of preventing you from fleeing. But Americans have grown tired of contracts.

Interestingly, T-Mobile (the smallest of the Big Four) has been experimenting with a European-style plan called Even More Plus. This plans allows you to bring your own phone to their network; there's no contract; and you typically pay $10 less than someone who's in a contract. No word yet on how successful this market initiative will be.

Remember, there are also a whole host of no-contract providers out there, such as MetroPCS, Cricket Communications, Straight Talk, Boost Mobile, and Virgin Mobile. See the "Switch to a Cheap No-Contract Cell Phone Provider" entry in the "Help Me Now, Clark" chapter at the beginning of this book (see page 9).

Contracts will eventually go the way of the dodo bird. But don't wait for that to happen down the road. If you're out of a contract, why not go noncontract instead of re-upping with a service agreement that just handcuffs you for another twenty-four months?

## Don't buy cell phone insurance

With how expensive some iPhones and Android phones can be, a lot of consumers are tempted to buy cell phone insurance. They end up paying about $5 or $7 per month for the insurance, plus a deductible of up to $100 or more if the phone gets damaged or lost.

Insurance should just be for catastrophic kinds of things that you could never afford to replace. Let's face it, if your smartphone goes kaput, you could always get a cheaper phone or activate an old one you might have sitting in a drawer somewhere.

Most phones come with a one-year manufacturer's warranty anyway. As I told you in "Help Me Now, Clarke," you can extend a manufacturer's original warranty for free. You do this by using a credit card to double it up to one additional year at the time of purchase. That's two years of the equivalent of insurance for free.

Several years ago, there was a lawsuit alleging that cell phone insurance is fraud. The suit states that you're paying for insurance *on a used phone*. That's right—when you turn in your damaged phone and get another one, it's usually "refurbished" anyway. *Consumer Reports* weighed in on this topic, saying that people should get cell phone insurance only if they own a very expensive phone. Insurance rates are the same for a $500 phone and a $50 phone. So it definitely makes no sense if you're at the lower end of the scale. And they found that only one in five people actually used the insurance.

## Consider a prepaid cell phone plan for light-volume calling

If you need a cell phone for only occasional use, there's almost no reason to be with one of the Big Four cell providers, who generally give you a block of minutes and eat you alive if you go over those minutes.

For light cell phone users, there are so many options in the market. One of the old stand-bys has been Net10.com. No roaming charges, no long distance charges, no monthly fees, and a flat 10 cents per minute for calls.

Net10 plans start at $15 per month for 150 minutes. Their phones start at around $20 and are available online and at Walmart stores. If you want one with a keyboard for texting, you'll pay $79 and up.

The Common Cents phones start at around $19 and are available online and at Walmart stores. If you want a phone that has a keyboard for texting, those start at $69.

These are all no-contract plans and no-contract is the wave of the future in the industry. Find out when your contract ends and reshop the market!

*Thanks to Clark's recommendation, I ditched a contract phone plan and went to a prepaid plan from T-Mobile. I found that was the only way to take control of my outrageously expensive cell phone bill. Now, not only do I decide how much I pay, I decide when I want to buy more minutes. To make it ever sweeter, Clark told me about CallingMart.com. I use it to buy my minutes without paying sales tax, and it often has promotions where I get 10 percent off. I buy 1,000 minutes at a time (they're good for a year) and they usually cost me only 9 cents a minute. Since switching over a year ago, I've cut my monthly cell phone cost from $58 to about $15. I tell everyone I know about this and many have made the switch too. Thanks, Clark!! You rock!!!*

*Nathan D., UT*

## Try Google Voice

One of Google's latest free services, Google Voice, is the search engine giant's attempt to get into the phone business. This free service offers users a single number for their cell, home phone, office phone, and any other phones to ring on. There are no monthly fees, no minimums, and no sign-up fees. As always, going forward, this service is likely to be monetized with ads.

Other Google Voice features include free voice mail, free call forwarding, and free conference calling. With the voice mail feature, you're able to listen in as voice mails are being left for you and pick up in the middle of the call—just like you would with an answering machine. You can also have voice mails automatically converted into text messages.

Google Voice is likely to get the wireless carriers twisted into pretzels. FierceWireless.com reports that the service might allow you to stop paying big bucks for unlimited calling to a select group of "favorite" numbers. You'll be able to route your calls through Google Voice for nada, thereby freeing you up to cut your plan down to the lowest level for unlimited calling. I'm figuring that will be about $29 per month on most plans. But wait, there's more! You can also do international calling using Google Voice at a tiny fraction of the cost of what it is with your wireless provider.

This is a lot of functionality wrapped up into one package. So how do you get it? Go to Google.com/voice (the lowercase "v" in "voice" is case sensitive) to watch an introductory video and sign up.

## Vet your cell phone bill for the cram

There could be a scam lurking in your cell phone bill that's ugly yet quite preventable; it's called the "cram." Cramming is the practice by which crooks set up third-party marketing groups to post bogus charges to your monthly bill. Once limited to the monopoly landline industry, the cram is now popping up on cell phone bills, according to the Federal Trade Commission. With more and more Americans disconnecting their landlines, criminals have unfortunately migrated to where there is opportunity.

One Florida man who was running a cram operation from his jail cell (!) managed to steal $35 million by posting charges on the last pages of cell phone bills that consumers didn't even notice. That's probably because the hieroglyphics of your bill are almost unintelligible. Cram charges on a cellular statement may be masked with an innocuous term like "Internet advertising," "service fee," "calling plan," "premium content," "direct bill charge," or "minimum monthly usage fee."

The FTC also busted another cram scheme that netted $19 million over a five-year period, with fake charges that ranged from $12.95 to $39.95 per month. An operation called Inc21 outsourced its cram business to foreign telemarketers who called people to offer "free" trials for website hosting, directory listings, search engine advertising, and Internet-based faxing. The telemarketers offered no disclosure that unsuspecting customers would have to take steps to avoid charges.

No one should be calling you on your cell phone offering supposedly "free" services. Be especially careful of fill-out sweepstakes entry forms or toll-free services like a date line or a psychic line. Buried in the mice-type of your terms of services could be a clause that says you give permission to have your account dinged each month for a certain number of dollars.

So what's the alternative to getting ripped off? Either be sure to go through your bill every month page by page to vet out any cram charges or, better yet, call your wireless carrier and tell them to block access for third-party charges. This block is usually free.

> *After hearing Clark's comment on cramming, I decided to check my Verizon [Wireless] bill.*
> *Under "Usage Charges, Data" I found a $9.99 charge from a ringtone company called*
> *Flycell. So I called Verizon to ask about the reason for the charge. They said that it had*
> *been going on for over a year and it is something that I authorized. I said, "Heck no," and*
> *the operator replied, "I can give you a $50 refund, but I can't go over that without*
> *supervisor approval." But they won't grant approval because I am supposed to check my*
> *bill. I can't get all the horses that have been stolen, but I stopped more from being stolen!*
> *Harvey C., WA*

## Avoid "off deck" charges on your kids' cell phones

Half of all children age twelve and up now have a cell phone, according to the global connectivity research outfit Yankee Group. That means parents have to be especially wary of what are being termed "off deck" deals, where the cell phone provider partners with marketers who offer supposedly free ringtones, jokes of the day, and other services.

A recent article in *The New York Times* reported on a consumer whose child responded for a "free" joke of the day that cost $20!

The business model here is that the cell providers split the money in half with the marketers. Cell providers particularly love those cheap add-a-phone offers for kids that tend to price out around $10 each month because the parent must also accept responsibility for any charges that are incurred.

So it's incumbent on you to teach your kids that they are not to respond to any "free" offers that are being pitched on their cell phone.

If you get hit with off deck charges, call your cell phone company and tell them to remove the charge. Try explaining that you know they're in cahoots with the marketer. Even my executive radio producer, Christa DiBiase, got taken in by one of these rip-offs. But I get the monthly bill for her cell phone as a business expense! It took me three months of calls (and three months of charges) before I finally got the cell phone company to behave.

This is why it's so important to read through your cell bill page by page, as I've mentioned elsewhere in this book. Don't get taken advantage of because of how confusing the bills can be.

*The New York Times* also reported that some cell providers offer a $60 per year service in which they agree *not* to rip you off with all these off deck charges.

In just one example, AT&T's Smart Limits option lets you control the dollar amount of downloads purchased and put constraints on the number of text and instant messages and more for a monthly fee of $5. But why should you have to pay a fee to prevent a company from ripping you off as a customer? That's outrageous!

## Use free directory assistance

Do you remember when it was free to call directory assistance? Some free services are making a comeback thanks to new ad-based business models.

Several years ago, my eldest daughter called old-fashioned directory assistance and was charged $1.80! That was until I told her about a variety of free alternatives.

For the longest time, one of my favorites was 800-FREE-411 (800-373-3411) because you only had to listen to an advertisement to get the number you wanted. Another free option I'm aware of is the ad-supported 800-YELLOWPAGES (800-935-5697).

People sometimes gripe that the numbers they get from these free services aren't always correct. But several years ago I saw a study that found that the numbers you get from paid services are just as likely to be wrong. So why pay extra for the chance of a wrong number?

I often turn to the Internet when I'm looking for a number. I practically never look in a phone book anymore. In the 1979 move *The Jerk*, starring Steve Martin, there is a scene where the new phone book arrives and Martin goes running for it, looks up his name, and shouts, "I am somebody! I'm in the phone book!" Pretty soon people won't know what the whole phone book phenomenon was about. In the future there might not be any phone books, because the costs to print and distribute them are so high compared with the costs of looking up phone numbers on the Internet.

## Jailbreak your iPhone

Adding unauthorized apps to an iPhone has been deemed a legal activity by the Library of Congress during a recent routine review of copyright rules.

The process of adding non-Apple-approved apps to the iPhone or other Apple devices is known as "jailbreaking." The term also denotes unlocking a locked device so it can be used on another network, such as taking your iPhone and making it work on T-Mobile.

Doing so had been considered illegal under an existing interpretation of the rules. But that didn't stop iPhone owners from doing it! More than 4 million iPhones and iPod Touch devices were jailbroken by the end of the last decade, according to the *Los Angeles Times*.

One word of caution: Jailbreaking your iPhone will void your warranty. So if the iPhone is damaged in the process, Apple is not required to provide technical support to help you resolve any issues.

But in general, I love that jailbreaking has gotten the thumbs-up on legal grounds. If you want to jailbreak a phone, one listener to my radio show recently suggested searching for tutorial videos on YouTube that will have step-by-step instructions. I would add that you should read the user comments below any video you're considering following to make sure others who have tried the advice give it a thumbs-up.

## Get better home cell reception with a femtocell

Cell phones are great, but they can be a real pain if you get a lousy signal at home. That's where a "femtocell" can come in handy. Femtocells are like tiny cell towers you can put in your home to improve cellular reception. They should *not* be confused with those "fembots" with the exploding heads from the *Austin Powers* movies!

Most cell phone companies now offer this product, but you have to ask for it. Depending on your company, they will either give you the device for free with no monthly fee, charge you for it up front with no monthly fee, or charge you both for the device and a monthly fee.

A femtocell will use your broadband connection to deliver a reliable, crystal-clear connection. I've used Sprint's femtocell at home and my wife and I are now getting nine bars on our cells! The ads show five bars—who knew you could have nine?

An alternative is third-party antenna boosters that can blast a signal through your house or office for no monthly fee. Fair warning, though, these third-party signal boosters are very expensive, usually $200 to $400.

A website called Wi-Ex.com offers a femtocell called the zBoost for $169 that works with most popular phones. But you must have an existing signal outside your home for a femtocell to amplify; if you don't have a signal, it won't be of any help.

A femtocell might be able to give you enough signal on your cell that you'll want to disconnect your landline and drop your monopoly local phone company. Femtocells are the next step in the evolution of the cell phone's destroying the need for an antiquated home landline. There's almost *no* reason left to have a home phone from a local company in today's world.


## Moisture strips in cell phones can be inaccurate

There are moisture strips inside cell phones that show whether your phone has gotten wet or been submerged. Cell phone companies use these like law to void your warranty and deny you repair service.

The cell companies claim the moisture strips are foolproof, but in fact, according to the *New York Post*, they are faulty. It's been proven that just by putting a damp cloth next to the phone, you can change the color of the strip!

So if you have a problem with your cell phone, and you are told your warranty is void because you got it wet (when you know you really didn't), here's what I recommend. Find an old cell phone you're not using anymore, take it back to the store, put a damp cloth near the strip on the battery, and prove to them right there that the strip is not accurate!

# LANDLINE AND VoIP

## Get cheap VoIP calling for $20 per year

Being a cheap guy, I'm often willing to take a chance on the next great thrifty thing—including dubious tech services that soon fail and go into Clark's Graveyard! (See page 241 for the complete body count!)

One of the things I've tried in recent years is magicJack.com, a Voice over Internet Protocol (VoIP) service. VoIPs are a lot less complicated than their name suggests. These kinds of plans work just like traditional calls. The only difference is that you're using your high-speed Internet as your connection to make and receive the calls.

With magicJack, a scant $40 buys you one year of unlimited local/long distance phone service through your computer. You simply plug a landline phone into the magicJack USB device and then plug it into your computer's USB port to start making calls. A subsequent year of service costs about $20.

I've used magicJack on four continents with the free Internet connection in my hotel rooms. It's allowed me to call back to the United States for nada. Boy, have I loved the money that it's saved me!

The ultimate test is when I'm overseas and call my college-age daughter on magicJack. She'll start telling me a story about what happened in class that day, like I'm in the room with her! These ultra-inexpensive phone services eliminate the long-distance charges. Likewise, when my wife and I were in Italy, we had magicJack hooked up in Sorrento and the phone would ring and it would be one of the kids or my wife's parents calling to say hello!

The magicJack business model is a complete mystery to me, and I long ago expected it to be in the Graveyard. But I sure hope it stays around.

One caveat to share with you: Along with ZenniOptical.com, magicJack is one of the most polarizing things I talk about on my show. A lot of people love that magicJack allows them to make unlimited long distance calls over the Internet for about $3 and change per month. Others have griped endlessly about the call quality and lack of customer service.

So let the buyer beware on this one. As for me, I'm perfectly willing to accept lower quality for a lower price!

---

## A CLARK FAVORITE
### *Drop your landline*

If you're looking for an easy way to reduce your monthly budget, consider dropping your landline and going cell phone only. About one in five Americans have disconnected their home phone, while an additional 13 percent say they have a home phone that they *never* use. That's about one-third of all Americans who have gone cell phone only or are very close to it.

What about you? Can you go cell phone only—with a VoIP service like Skype, magicJack, or Ooma as a backup—and get rid of your home phone?

Whenever I discuss this issue, I hear from those who say, "Well, what do I do after a natural disaster when my cell phone doesn't work?" I did medical evacuations in New Orleans after Hurricane Katrina. There were no working cell phones. However, the cable operator was still working. Vonage saved the day for many people who would have been otherwise cut off. Today many emergency personnel have satellite phones in the event of an emergency.

Another common objection to dropping the landline comes from people who say they need it for their burglar alarm system. But professional burglars will simply cut the phone line before going in. That's why security consultants routinely recommend wireless monitoring instead.

Other people tell me they need a landline for Internet access and for pay satellite TV. But you can get naked DSL for the Internet (see page 50) and then watch free TV and movies over the Internet (see page 2). There's always a way to get around having a landline at home!

The typical local phone bill is $30 to $50 each month. That could be $360 or $600 back in your pocket annually if you make the jump.

---

## Vet your landline bill for the cram

For those of you who still have a landline, you've got to be extra careful about that oldie but baddie scam involving false charges being posted to your bill I mentioned earlier—the practice that's known as cramming.

Businesses with landlines face typical cram charges, perhaps for a bogus 800 or 900 number, of $10 or $15. For a consumer with a home phone, it's more like $5 to $10. But here's the dirty secret: The monopoly phone company that does the "courtesy" third-party billing for these crooks takes a cut of the proceeds. It's to their benefit to cram these charges on your bill! Worse yet, if you call their bluff, they'll give you back only a month or two of the money you've lost—no matter how long you've been getting ripped off.

Verizon and AT&T are the two big monopoly local phone companies across much of the nation. Fortunately, Verizon does offer a free Bill Block service where they effectively prevent themselves from putting third-party charges on your bill. If you're a Verizon customer, simply get in touch with them and request this free service. Special thanks to Mitch Lipka of *The Boston Globe* for reporting this tidbit.

AT&T, however, refuses to follow Verizon with the bill blocking. When my show staff questioned them on this, their statement read in part, "Currently we do not have the ability to automatically block third-party charges."

The ability or the desire? AT&T needs to wake up and realize it's not a good idea for a corporate citizen to be in business with criminals. How much could they possibly make from cram charges, and is it worth the price of their reputation? AT&T went on to explain in a page of corporate doublespeak that you can work with customer service to have the cram charges removed from your bill. But I say, just do the right thing in the first place, AT&T. It's your job to go through your phone bill line by line each month and make sure you're not on the hook for cram charges, especially if you're a business customer.

# TELEVISION

## Know your flat-screen TVs before buying

Several years ago, I made a statement on my radio show to the effect that most women would rather buy and receive jewelry than electronics. Boy, did I get an earful from that! A poll on ClarkHoward.com about who was purchasing flat-screen televisions proved that my statement was a chauvinistic one.

Now when I'm in stores, more women than men ask me for advice on buying high-definition TVs. Both sexes have their heads spinning like Linda Blair in *The Exorcist* with all the choices out there. With that in mind, I want to offer you a primer on the three types of HDTVs that dominate the market: LCDs (liquid crystal display), DLPs (digital light processing), and plasma TVs.

Get an LCD if you're looking to reduce energy consumption and want something with a small cabinet. LCDs are also good if there's a lot of natural sunlight available.

DLPs are great if you have space for foot-long cabinets and huge screens. They might look huge, but they are actually very light. One drawback with DLPs is that you have to look straight at your TV to see the image. They're not good if your room has lots of side-viewing angles. In that instance, you probably want a plasma because the picture is rich and true from any angle. But plasmas are bad in rooms with natural sunlight, which washes out the picture.

For my money, I prefer plasmas over LCDs for picture quality. But keep in mind that plasmas use more energy than LCDs.

A lot of shoppers also get confused by the 1080p versus 720p resolution issue. The manufacturing industry is moving toward 1080p, but all the programming is in 720p. My advice is to buy a cheaper 720p set for now. By the time all the programming switches over, 1080p sets will be more affordable than they are now. Don't overbuy at today's prices for something that will steadily be cheaper tomorrow.

Finally, here are some target price points to keep in mind. For 32-inch LCDs, look for deals in the $400s. Don't pay more than $600. The 42-inch plasmas should go for around $700, while 50-inch ones will go up to $900. If you're going to spend around $900 for a DLP, make sure you get a 60-inch set. DLPs tend to have more repair issues than the other two, but they're all basically reliable. Do not under any circumstances buy an extended warranty! (See my tip "Avoid extended warranties" on page 8.)

---

### CLARK'S GREATEST HITS

## *Go back to rabbit ears and fire your pay TV provider*

With all the talk of where TV is going in the future, it's easy to forget that it's also extra cheap where it's been in the past. Don't overlook the original option: using an old-fashioned pair of rabbit-ear antennas to pick up local channels over the air for free!

---

> The process is actually really simple. Go to AntennaWeb.org, click the "Choose an antenna" button, and enter your street address. They'll tell you what channels will be available to you and what kind of antenna would be best for you.
>
> Then you simply need to buy the antenna and a converter box to get the digital signal. Both are routinely available at any major electronics store. Just follow AntennaWeb's recommendations about the best equipment for your home.

*My family was fed up with paying so much for a television service when, in reality, we only ended up watching our local channels. Out of curiosity, I changed my newer televisions' input over to digital antenna mode and was stunned by what I saw! I had a couple of stunning HD channels without even having an antenna hooked up! I was sold.*

*I went to AntennaWeb.org and found out what kind of antenna I would need. I hooked it up and now I have lots of quality channels. Most channels were HD. I did some research and discovered that TIVO will work with over-the-air service.*

*The only snag I ran into was my homeowners association not allowing me to put an antenna on my house. I did some more research and discovered that they were in the wrong and breaking the law by saying I could not have a reasonable-sized antenna on my house (do a search for "FCC OTARD" and you'll see what I mean). So I am saving lots of money and with the DVR, I am enjoying my television service more than I ever have.*

*Jeffrey E., WA*

## Dump your cable or satellite provider for cheaper high-tech options

I love Netflix.com and its on-demand video service. But there's another option called Vudu .com that has a slightly different business model.

With Netflix on demand, you sit down with a remote, select the movie you want to see, and then it streams to your computer or TV over the Internet via your Wii console. Wait times for a movie are generally less than one minute, and most subscription plans start at $8 per month. They also have a limited plan at $4.99 that offers one DVD a month and two hours of on-demand content.

Vudu, however, doesn't lock you into any monthly contract. You pay for what you choose to watch. That means you can pay $1 for an older movie or up to about $8 for a hot title in full 1080p HD format, all streamed over the Internet through your HDTV or Blu-ray player.

Vudu became a real threat to Walmart, the nation's largest seller of DVDs. That prompted the retail giant to buy out Vudu, with plans to keep the service fully operational and extra cheap!

Another way to beat hefty bills for pay TV is to watch at least some of your TV online for free. In the next few years it will get easier and easier to get programming from the Internet to your TV without being a techno-geek. For now, we have an interim technology called TVersity.com that lets you stream Internet video and more to your TV, Xbox, Wii, or PlayStation console.

The next wave of innovation will likely come from Google—who else? Sony has teamed up with Google to work on a new open-source method for getting Internet programming on your TV in a seamless, easy fashion.

By Christmas of 2011, it will be so easy to get Internet shows on your TV—regardless of your technical know-how—that it will be common and mainstream. Now this doesn't mean that all Internet programming will be free. Hulu.com, for example, has begun charging for content. But at least these new solutions will render the middleman—the cable and satellite companies—unnecessary.

## Watch Internet programming on your TV if you're not tech-savvy

So much of where TV is headed involves getting content over the Internet. That's great, but what if the only thing you know about computers is how to turn them on? Several years ago, I talked about a service called Sezmi.com on my radio show. Sezmi uses the Internet to provide some cable channels and all local broadcast stations right on your big screen with a fancy DVR. (Though there's no ESPN, sports fans!) No technical know-how is required.

This service is now testing in select markets for $19.99 per month. It's a good option for those who aren't that tech-savvy but still want to watch some Web-based programming. High-speed Internet access is required. The DVR does have a cost of about $149 or more up front, but after that investment you pay only the monthly fee.

The real savings are for those who want limited Internet programming, because Sezmi also has a $4.99 per month option. With the cheaper plan, you get all your local channels (no cable), YouTube, video podcasts, and on-demand movies and TV shows from all the major

Hollywood studios on your TV—all without any technical know-how on your part. (Most on-demand TV shows are free. The movies rent from less than a buck for older titles to up to $5 for new releases.)

Sezmi is available in thirty-six metro areas as I write this. Visit the website to see if it's available in your town. This could be a great excuse to fire your cable or satellite provider and stop paying those hefty bills.

# Travel

Before launching my radio and TV career, I founded a successful chain of travel agencies in the early 1980s. I still travel nearly every week of my life for personal pleasure or professional obligations. So over the years I've picked up a thing or two about saving money on travel.

In this chapter, I'll show you how to avoid those hefty baggage fees most airlines love to charge, how to find the cheapest rates on four- and five-star hotel accommodations, how to get access to your money while overseas without paying an arm and a leg, and how to unload an unwanted timeshare.

## ACCOMMODATIONS

### Check message boards before you bid on Priceline or Hotwire

I have obsessive-compulsive disorder when it comes to saving on hotels. When I travel for work, I book 95 percent of the hotels I stay in through Priceline.com or Hotwire.com. Priceline and Hotwire might not be for everyone; there's something of a guess factor involved when using either one because you're bidding on hotel rooms but don't find out which brand you're getting until after you pay nonrefundable money. The only information you see is a hotel's ranking based on a five-star system.

Before I get ready to do any online bidding, I first check out a couple of related message boards. For Priceline, my first stop is BiddingForTravel.com to get a feel for what other people are bidding. BiddingForTravel.com is a forum where travelers help one another and share knowledge, including tips on how to bid multiple times a day. There's a similar forum for Hotwire called BetterBidding.com. It also offers a Priceline forum, but it's far from the authority on Priceline that BiddingForTravel can be.

Once I've done research on BiddingForTravel, I go to Hotwire and see what's available. While BiddingForTravel gives me a general range of price, Hotwire lets me know what it's making available for that same night. Then for the equivalent level of hotel, I bid 30 percent less on Priceline. It's the usual math formula that I apply.

Let's say I'm looking at a city, and Hotwire has a four-star hotel at $100 per night; I've seen what people are doing on BiddingForTravel, so I will bid $70 as my first bid on Priceline.

With Priceline, there will be multiple hotel zones in most cities. A major metropolitan area might have eight different zones in the central part of the city, and I look at which ones I'm willing to stay in. I also look for other zones that don't have four-star hotels.

So I'm able to do first all the zones I want to stay in and then all the zones I don't want to stay in that don't have four-star hotels, because I know that even if I add a zone I don't want as an additional free rebid, I won't get that zone.

Let's say my initial Priceline bid of $70 gets turned down; if there are six zones in the metro area and I know that BiddingForTravel says the most anybody has been paying for a four-star hotel is $90, I'll add another neighborhood and go up a few dollars each bid. Eventually, barring a sellout in that town, I'll get my room. And if I don't, I already knew that the worst I'd do is $100 on Hotwire.

Make no doubt about it, this is work and it takes time to do it. But the savings are so great.

Besides, this the closest I get to the thrill people have in a casino! The cool thing is it never costs me any money, it only saves me money. If my bid is turned down, I didn't lose any money, I just lost that round of bidding. You have to have the patience of knowing you can always come back and fight another day.

Here are examples of some of the latest deals I've landed using this strategy:

- a three-star hotel in Albuquerque, New Mexico, for $42
- a three-star hotel in Memphis for $42

- a three-and-a-half-star hotel in Westchester County, New York, for $80
- a three-and-a-half-star hotel in Connecticut for $69
- a four-star hotel in Rome for $85 (roughly 58 euros at the time)
- a four-star hotel in San Francisco for $99
- a five-star hotel in London for $95

My experience is that most people prefer the certainty of Hotwire over the bidding process on Priceline. And if you do, it's much less hassle on Hotwire, though their rating system of stars tends to be more inflated than Priceline. When you go below three-star hotels or below, the accommodations can be a little dicey. I've found that the sweet spot is three and a half stars.

When it comes to Hotwire, I have a little tip to help you figure out what hotel you *might* get: Select the dates you want to go; click on the "build a package" option for a rental car (even if you don't plan on renting one); and then it'll show you what hotels would come with the car rental. This trick will work about 75 percent of the time. Just remember it is nonrefundable once you buy.

The savings you get in exchange for booking "blind" on Priceline or Hotwire can be up to 35 to 60 percent off the usual price. However, many people don't like the whole idea of the blind bidding sites.

A lot of entrepreneurs travel for business, and there's a particular site that I really like called QuikBook.com. With this discount hotel reservation site, you get access to the equivalent of corporate-negotiated hotel rates at a lower price than you would normally have available to you as someone with a very small company. I've used QuikBook for both business and leisure travel and it's saved me a decent amount of money.

## Find cheap vacation rentals by owners

The soft real estate market means that rentals in prime vacation spots like the mountains and the beach come at a deep discount these days. But even when the economy firms up again, there's a way to get a deal on a great vacation spot.

As longtime listeners to my show are aware, it's now become commonplace when you're looking for a deal to rent a condo or a home directly from the homeowner rather than renting a traditional hotel room. I love VRBO.com (aka Vacation Rentals by Owner) for this purpose. As the name suggests, this website helps you rent straight from the owner—whether you're talking about a home, condo, cabin, villa, or apartment!

I always look for places that were built in the last five years (or renovated in the last four) and that have a lot of pictures posted online. Both factors help ensure that the rental will be in tip-top shape. But at the same time, you want to be somewhat wary of the pictures of the accommodations supplied by the owner; photography can cover up a lot of sins. Don't be shy about asking for more pictures beyond just what's posted online. What you get initially might be misleading, so watch out!

This is another case where you want to cull the collective wisdom of the public to find a real winner. Make sure any rental you consider is accompanied by a lot of positive reviews from satisfied customers. And book only if you plan to pay by credit card, so you have the right to do a charge back with the card issuer if the accommodations turn out to not be what was promised.

> *My mom is an avid Clark listener and is the one who turned me on to the show about a year ago. But because of my job I am unable to listen every day. When she found out that I was shopping around for a weekend vacation spot, she told me about VRBO.com. I checked it out and found a beachfront condo in Carolina Beach, North Carolina, for a Friday and Saturday night. Price paid: $200. And that's not all; the owner also had a bottle of wine for me on the coffee table. Thank you, Clark . . . and Mom.*
>
> *Matt P., NC*

## Stay with newfound friends for free

I'm not thrifty, I'm downright cheap. But there are some lines even I won't cross. For example, I won't bunk with a stranger. However, it is my duty in my line of work to bring you ideas that could save you money.

CouchSurfing.com is a site that allows people to meet others around the world and stay at their homes for free. It's like crashing at a friend's pad, but you don't know the friend. This site—with its MySpace-like interface that lets community wisdom vet out any potential unsafe travelers or hosts—is free to use. Talk about doing a good job of making hostels seem expensive!

To tell you the truth, though, I wouldn't have done this even in my young, mostly broke days. But that's just me. A couple of producers on my show, Joel Larsgaard and Kimberly Drobes, had some animated discussions about the possible dangers of CouchSurfing.com when I mentioned it in a staff meeting.

Joel says he has stayed with people he didn't know before, but he didn't meet them through CouchSurfing.com. He does, however, tentatively have plans to try out this site and see how the experience goes.

Kim, meanwhile, found an article on the ABC News site that reports CouchSurfing.com has been around since 2004 and had only one minor theft incident in all that time. The website uses a system of reference, vouching, and verification to ensure the safety of all its members. While it is not a dating site, CouchSurfing.com has resulted in at least one known baby that's come about as a result of a host/traveler connection.

Fortunately, CouchSurfing.com doesn't have an exclusive corner on the sleeping-in-strangers-homes thing. HospitalityClub.org is another site that's free to use, while Evergreen Club.com is a pay portal geared toward more mature travelers looking for a home in which to crash.

## A CLARK FAVORITE
### Use social media to resolve hotel issues

Travelers are using technology to get new leverage when they're faced with an unsatisfactory hotel stay, according to *The Wall Street Journal*. We all know that Facebook and Twitter give people the opportunity to post gripes (or praise) about anything online in real time. And I've already discussed the impact of the United Breaks Guitars viral campaign earlier in this book (see "Take Your Gripes Online with the Power of the Internet" on page 73). But now some hotel chains are monitoring social networking sites for instances of their name and responding to customer grievances, according to the newspaper.

Say you get to your hotel and you need some extra towels, just as an example. If you call down to the front desk, you might be ignored if it's during a high-occupancy time and there are no hands on deck to help you. But if you make a comment about the lack of towels on the hotel's official Twitter or Facebook page, hotel management might ring your room and offer, "We're sorry you were unhappy with the lack of clean towels today. Can we come by now and drop some off for you?" This works particularly well if you as a blogger, Tweeter, or

Facebooker have a large following of "friends" who could potentially be swayed by your posts.

Social media policies vary widely by chain and even within chains. *The Wall Street Journal* noted that customers got particularly good responses to gripes by Tweeting when they stayed at the Marriott Orlando World Center Resort in Florida and the Atlantis, Paradise Island in the Bahamas. Social media is only poised to grow, so making a post on Twitter or Facebook is worth a try.

And you shouldn't wait until you have a problem to post; writing something online saying you're greatly anticipating your stay before you get to your hotel is a good way to put yourself on their radar and possibly get some upgrades.

## Try a home exchange arrangement when traveling

If you're a little wary of staying with people you don't know, perhaps you'd consider staying in their homes by yourself. There are a variety of exchange services that pair families in different countries who want to swap homes for a week or so each year.

HomeExchange.com is the graybeard in the business. If you've ever seen the romantic comedy *The Holiday* with Cameron Diaz and Kate Winslet, this is the service they were using to swap homes in Los Angeles and London.

Homes in the United States are often much nicer and more spacious than accommodations in European countries, so be realistic in your expectations. You can also use the service for domestic swaps.

There's a fee of $9.95 per month with a one-year contract that gives you the opportunity to make unlimited exchanges for a year. If you don't find a home exchange partner during the year, your second year is free. If that's still too rich for your blood, there's also a three-month membership option priced at $15.95 per month.

Other sites that offer similar services include Airbnb.com, HomeLink.org, Exchange-Homes.com, JewettStreet.com, and SabbaticalHomes.com; the latter is geared toward the ivory tower crowd.

# AIR TRAVEL

## Be flexible to find the best deals

If you want to save the most money on travel, you might have to do something many people either can't or won't do—not pick a specific travel destination or date. The more flexibility you have about *when* and *where* you want to travel, the more likely you will find a great deal.

The key is to buy the deal and then figure out why you want to go there. That's been my travel philosophy since the airlines deregulated in 1978. Let the deal drive the trip instead of picking one place and time and trying to find an airfare deal to get there.

This is also the philosophy I use when I book an annual staff trip for the employees who make me look good every day. Our team simply waits for a deal to pop up and then we buy it. By doing this, we've gone on trips, at bargain rates, to Japan, Hawaii, the Caribbean, Spain, China, Budapest, Italy, Switzerland, England, France, Holland, and Argentina.

Where should you look for a deal? Travelzoo.com, AirGorilla.com, Momondo.com and Kayak.com are all good options. Mobissimo.com is a good option if you're looking for an international destination.

Great travel deals often pop up and then disappear quickly. When you see one, pounce on it.

*We took an all-inclusive (air, meals and 4-star lodging) to Cancún in March for only $650/person for 7 days. Normally it goes for over $2,000 a person. First, we checked out the best days to fly by using Travelocity flexible dates option. Then, on Orbitz we searched for vacation packages during the cheapest flight dates. Then, on RetailMeNot.com we found a coupon for Orbitz good for $100 off per person. The place was wonderful and the cheap price made it more memorable.*

*Chuck M., OH*

## Fly the discount airlines—not the full-fare fleets

You get what you pay for, right? That's a perception that many people have about the airline industry, where you have the expensive full-fare airlines on the one hand and the much cheaper discount airlines on the other. But *USA Today* has done an exhaustive analysis of government and consumer survey data for the industry going back to 2004 and found that, as a general rule, the cheaper the airline, the better the service.

The newspaper has come up with a new tally of the airlines, ranked on quality and service. Here's the breakdown from best to worst: JetBlue, Hawaiian, Southwest, Frontier, Alaska, Continental, Northwest (before the Delta merger), American, Delta, United, and US Airways.

The data was overwhelming that you get a *much* better experience on the discounters than the full-fare airlines, regardless of price. As *USA Today* put it, "Despite lower fares, passengers consistently rank discount airlines higher in quality and service than better-known traditional carriers." JetBlue, Southwest (which has since absorbed AirTran), and Frontier are all discounters, while the remaining ones on the list are full-fare airlines.

How is it that the discounters can offer their superior services so much more cheaply? Typically, they run a much simpler business. The full-fares fly up to eight or ten types of airplanes in their fleets. Discounters, however, will fly only one or two types of jets. That move alone can save big bucks in terms of maintenance and upkeep of the aircraft. In addition, the discounters put the focus on customers by offering deals instead of trying to come up with new ways to fee you to death like the full-fares do.

When a discounter goes into a market, airfares start dropping like flies. When they're absent, boy, can it hurt your wallet. Recently, I had to take an hour-long flight to a market that was served only by full-fare airlines. I paid $1,350 round-trip! If I'd had access to a discounter, I would have paid at most a few hundred dollars for the same trip.

Little wonder then that discounters were the only ones making money during the Great Recession as people dialed back on discretionary travel. The full-fares, meanwhile, were reporting quarterly losses of up to $250 million each at the peak of the recession.

Longtime listeners to my show know that I love Southwest. In addition to no baggage fees, Southwest does not charge customers to change nonrefundable tickets. It also has a simplified boarding process that makes it an oasis of calm at the gate. So I think you can expect to see Southwest back up at the top of the list soon!

## Use hard discounter airlines to travel around Europe

Visiting Europe is one of my favorite things to do. I simply love places like western Ireland, Lucerne, Switzerland, and all of Italy, to name a few spots. The key to cheap travel to and around Europe is to fly into Ireland, Britain, or Germany during the off-peak season when fares are low and then use hard discounter airlines like Ryanair and easyJet to fly around the continent for unbelievably low rates. (Ireland is the real key here, because sometimes the taxes on a ticket into Britain can really take the price up into the stratosphere.)

Ryanair is widely acknowledged as the world's cheapest airline. I've flown them extensively around Europe, but they're something of an acquired taste. They've stripped every frill out of their planes to deliver the lowest fares. For example, the seats don't recline, there are no seat-back pockets, and you won't find any window shades. They even cram 199 seats onto a 737 that usually holds only 150 people. You can expect to be uncomfortable if you weigh more than one hundred pounds or are taller than four feet, eight inches. I'm kidding of course, but you get the idea. And don't even mention the boarding process; it's as frenzied as a rugby scrum. But, oh, what savings: I took a flight from England to Ireland for the equivalent of $1.75!

The company's chief executive is a wild man with a foul mouth named Michael O'Leary. He hires flight attendants from formerly communist Eastern European countries and pays them on commissions from the in-flight sales of goods. So you have these stewardesses running around the plane in five-inch heels trying to sell cigarettes, lottery tickets, trinkets, and more during the entire flight.

A word about airfares to Europe in general. When we went to the Open Skies policy, part of the deal was that all international airlines could enter into co-ops or alliances. Today there are three main ones—Oneworld, SkyTeam, and Star Alliance—that actually work to the detriment of the flying public.

Airlines within these co-ops coordinate schedules, routes, and fares, which has greatly reduced competition when you want to fly between the United States and especially Europe. This makes it more important than ever to fly wherever in Europe you find a deal, if you don't mind the inconvenience, and then take Ryanair or easyJet.

The truth is that these three co-op cartels have raised the fares so much to Europe that there's a giant opportunity for one of the European hard discounters to start service to the United States and blow them out of the water. Ryanair has made noise about flying to the U.S. with eye-popping fares as low as $15. So far it's just talk, but at some point it will happen.

## Track fares online and get a refund if the price drops

Have you heard of airfare envy? That's when you buy a ticket and find the same itinerary for less money afterward. The good news is that there are a handful of airlines that will give you a voucher for the difference if you ask. These include Alaska Air, JetBlue, Southwest, United, and US Airways.

Each airline picks a price point at which they'll dole out. For Alaska and JetBlue, you'll get a refund for any price drop whatsoever. For US Airways, however, the price drop has to be $150 or more before they'll shell out.

But unless you religiously follow airfares after you've made your purchase, you might not even know that you've overpaid. That's where Yapta.com comes in handy. After completing the free registration, Yapta will e-mail you when your flight goes down in price and help you get a refund for the difference.

One caveat here. Some airlines will charge big fees if you want to process a refund. United and US Air both charge a whopping $150. So make sure it's worth your while before you get involved.

## Ditch the frequent-flyer miles credit card

I have a long-standing beef with my nephew David, who is addicted to frequent-flyer mileage programs and jumps through all kinds of hoops to accumulate miles. Here's what David doesn't understand: There's an industry-wide trend of airlines to devalue frequent-flyer miles by making the miles tougher to redeem and earn.

Having a stockpile of miles is like having a reverse savings account—the value leaches out of it every day. If you use a credit card that earns frequent-flyer miles, I would prefer that you ditch it and get a card that pays you cash instead. With cash, there are no restrictions on when you can use it.

My senior producer Kimberly Drobes is also one of those people conned by the mileage programs. She once redeemed miles and had to fly to the wrong city, while changing planes two times to get there and two more times to get home. That's a lot of work to take a "free" trip.

So what should you do with your mileage balances? The full-fare airlines are adding international routes all the time, so look for new service announcements on their websites and jump when you get the opportunity. Then jump at a credit card that pays cash dividends, not miles.

## Know when to buy trip insurance

The 2010 volcanic eruption in Iceland that left millions of travelers stranded on both sides of the Atlantic presented one compelling argument for buying trip insurance.

Policies are designed to protect consumers by giving them refunds in the event of illness of the traveler or immediate family member, or to provide a refund in the case of company, tour operator, or airline default.

These policies should always be purchased when you are taking a cruise, a tour, or traveling on a trip that requires prepayment of thousands of dollars. Just be sure you purchase a policy independent of the cruise, tour, or vacation planner. Never purchase the trip protection plan from the trip organizer. Those types of policies are designed to protect the company, not the consumer!

You can expect a policy to cost around 6 percent of the total cost of the trip. Of course, it's possible to run that number way up. Visit InsureMyTrip.com to comparison shop for policies.

Flight delays are sometimes an unavoidable fact of life when you're traveling. Yet often, they're more of an annoyance or a nuisance, not a disaster. My advice is to try to keep your perspective. Let little hassles roll off your back if you can. If you miss a connection or are delayed with a flight cancellation, do not stand in line at the airport. People will queue up for a tenth of a mile to talk to customer no-service and it does no good. Get on the phone or online and see what you can accomplish instead.

> *Recently, I traveled from Alabama to California. The week before I had heard Clark talking about what to do if your flight was cancelled—not to stand in lines, but call reservations. Well, my flight going into Dallas from Huntsville was rerouted to Oklahoma (due to storms). While on the long wait on the runway at Oklahoma, my connecting flight to*

*Orange County's John Wayne Airport was cancelled. I called reservations and they got me*
*on a later flight to LAX. When we finally got to Dallas, I was able to get on the plane to LAX*
*and there was a mad scramble and a long line because so many were messed up because of*
*the weather. Thank you so much for the advice! I had to be there for surgery on a close*
*family member so it was very important for me to get there.*

*Betty J., AL*

## Save on airport parking

Parking at the airport can be a real headache—driving up and down mile-long lines of already parked vehicles in the economy section. Using off-site parking and taking advantage of free shuttles to the terminal can be a much better idea. But with so many off-site parking lots competing for your business, how do you know which one offers the best deal? Sites like BestParking.com and LongTermParking.com have a solution.

BestParking.com is a free parking search engine that steers drivers toward the cheapest and most convenient parking facilities in sixteen cities and sixty-six airports. Addresses, phone numbers, photos, rates, and other attributes are provided for all facilities, and some of the nation's largest parking operators also offer exclusive discounts and reservations through the service.

Using BestParking is a cinch. Simply select your desired airport and your arrival and departure dates/times. BestParking will crunch the numbers and pop up the dollar amounts of all available parking vendors on a Google map. Saving money can be that simple! And save you can, especially when you consider that in midtown Manhattan, motorists can spend anywhere between $12 and $87 for a full day of parking, or that a week's stay at Los Angeles International Airport can range from $53 to $210.

Like everything else these days, BestParking also offers a free app for iPhone, Android, and select BlackBerry users.

Of course, the default option is to do a simple Web search for "airport parking coupons + [the name of the airport or city]" or something similar. For example, I had to leave a car in Jacksonville, Florida, for three weeks and couldn't find any parking that was less than $4.99 each day. When I did a Bing search for "Jacksonsville airport parking discount," I found a deal for $2.75 each day! It's like a treasure hunt just looking around for things.

Only two discount airlines—JetBlue and Southwest—allow you to check a bag without paying a fee. Your first bag is free on JetBlue, while a second bag will cost you $30. Southwest, meanwhile, allows up to two checked bags absolutely free. Nobody knows if Southwest will continue with their liberal "no baggage fees" policy. But it certainly has made for some strong imaging for them. You can see their "no baggage fees" commercials in constant rotation during heavily watched sports events like the NFL play-offs.

Not everyone lives in a market served by JetBlue or Southwest. So there's still one other way to avoid baggage fees no matter which carrier you're flying: Don't check a bag! I travel only with what an airline permits free as a single carry-on—usually a 22 x 14 x 8-inch piece of luggage. Another plus is I never worry about the airline losing my baggage.

Sometimes getting everything you need into a carry-on can be an extreme test. When you fly Ryanair, the European discounter, your suitcase must be less than twenty-two pounds—or you'll pay a nearly $50 fee to check it in at the airport ($20 online). So my favorite Ryanair story involves the time I had to wear multiple layers of clothing in Dublin to make sure I avoided that hefty $50 fee! That meant three pairs of pants, two shirts, and a sweatshirt on top of that while flying. My wife even has the pictures to prove it!

# CAR RENTALS AND OTHER TRANSPORTATION

### Ride the bus around the country for $1!

There is a real market demand for cheap, reliable, and safe city-to-city bus transportation. The push for cheap fares among big cities really started with bus lines running in the Washington D.C./New York/Boston corridor that were geared toward ethnic Chinese customers. But if "bus service" makes you think of a Greyhound terminal in a seedy part of town, boy, have things changed!

Greyhound has launched a new line called BoltBus.com with eight daily trips between Washington, D.C., and New York, plus other Northeast Corridor routes. Online fares start at

$1, and onboard amenities include free Wi-Fi and extra legroom because they've removed some seats.

There's also a European player in the game called Megabus.com that serves a large swath of the country from New Hampshire to North Carolina and all the way out to the midwestern states of Missouri, Minnesota, Iowa, and Missouri (inclusive of everything in between, from the East Coast to the Midwest).

A select number of seats on every bus sells for about $1, with the deals typically going to passengers who book six or more days in advance. A *Washington Post* reporter went from Washington, D.C., to midtown Manhattan for $1.50! Of course, there are only a limited number of seats at those kinds of prices. Other seats can run up to the $20 range. Still, any of these options offer great alternatives to flight delays and high gas prices the next time you have to move around.

These new breeds of bus lines are trying to attract customers out of their cars by avoiding traditional crime-ridden bus terminals. They instead pick up in high-income commercial districts and drop passengers off at other high-income areas at the end of the line.

With BoltBus.com, the irony is that it's owned by the same parent company that owns Greyhound. They were obviously smart enough to ditch the Greyhound reputation and go with new branding and a new fleet of buses!

*My wife and I decided to go to Boston and see a nephew of ours who was coming from out of the country for a medical convention. We were going to use our car, taking turns driving on what would be a four-hour road trip for us. That was the plan until we heard Clark talk about Megabus. After a quick visit to the website, we made reservations from New York to Boston that weekend.*

*On the day of our travel, we took the ferry from Fort Lee to Manhattan and at the corner of 9th Avenue and 31st Street we got on the bus with our 2 suitcases. In four hours we were at Boston's South Station (Gate 11)! The bus was indeed "mega" (2 decks) and clean, the seats were comfortable and the view from the second deck kept me awake the whole trip. There was a toilet, electric outlets, television and free Wi-Fi. Total cost for the both of us? $52 round trip!*

*We were so pleased with the experience that when we wanted to go to Philadelphia about a month later, we looked at each other and said, "Megabus!" Previously, we used to* *drive there. The trip was two hours (same as with the car) and the final cost for the both of us? $26.50 round trip!! Who can beat that?*

*Paul K., NJ*

## Find a $10 to $20 car rental before peak travel times at select locations

There are still some ways to beat the high cost of rental cars, despite the fact that they represent the one segment of the travel business that has gone up in price during the Great Recession.

Ahead of peak travel seasons in November-December and late April, there's often a mad rush to get cars from across the nation to hot vacation destinations like Florida. You might find companies like Dollar Rent A Car and Thrifty Car Rental offering rentals for as little as $10 or $20 per day if you can move their vehicles from the Northeast and Midwest to the Sunshine State.

There might also be similar deals to reposition cars from the West to vacation destinations like Arizona and Southern California. It's certainly to the benefit of the rental companies to offer these deals. Otherwise they'd have to fly paid employees out to do the same work or load cars on trucks to move them around.

With these kinds of deals, you want to be ahead of the curve. So call around to a few agencies that are located at airports several weeks before a peak travel time and ask if they're participating and where they need their cars moved.

Now, because of the cheap price, there will be a lot of restrictions on these deals, plus additional taxes and fees. But if you can make it work, this is a real steal.

Here's another way you can save money on car rentals: Pay a cab to take you off an airport property and get into the town. For example, my family and I booked a Colorado ski trip right before Christmas last year. Cars at Denver Airport were as much as a few hundred dollars a day. So I checked and found we could rent a car in the town of Denver for $24 a day.

Both Enterprise and Hertz have a huge network of in-town rental locations that are geared to locals with completely different pricing than what's available at airports.

In another example, my brother once couldn't find a decent car rental in Dallas because there was some convention going on. All the rentals were more than $100 a day. So I told him to take an airport shuttle from Dallas/Fort Worth Airport to downtown Dallas and he got a car for $22 a day. Giving up convenience in exchange for saving money must run in the family!

*I recently visited the San Francisco area and needed to rent a car for a week. I got quotes from several agencies BUT what I did was compare their prices for picking up the car at different local airports. One particular agency's prices—FOR THE SAME CAR—were: SFO $525, SJO (San Jose Airport) $600, and OAK (Oakland) $200! I took the Bay Area Rapid Transit (BART) system over to Oakland and picked up the rental car there. After my trip was done, I returned the car to Oakland and the agency gave me a free ride to the BART station and I hopped the train back to SFO. Taking BART (round-trip to both airports) cost me $16 and I saved over $300!*

*Dayle V., FL*

## A CLARK FAVORITE
### *Use a Diners Club card if you frequently rent cars*

Certain VISA and American Express cards and MasterCards will provide secondary coverage when you rent a car. But if you're a frequent car renter, you might want to pay the huge annual fee of $95 for a Diners Club card because they offer full primary coverage.

Diners Club makes it easy. You simply decline the collision damage waiver (CDW) at the desk when you're renting and charge the rental to your Diners Club card. In the event of an accident, they'll step in with full primary coverage on cars valued up to $50,000 for a basic cardholder account.

That can be a savings of up to $20 per day; if you rent often enough, I think this is a no-brainer. Best of all, because Diners Club is primary, any accident that occurs won't be reported to your insurance company. So you save again by avoiding a premium hike.

There are now a small number of individual issuers of Visas and MasterCards that are doing primary coverage. My experience is that when they do, they trumpet it. So if you get a solicitation for a card and you're looking at their car rental coverage, it will say "primary" in big, bold type. If it's not primary, they aren't going to mention it.

# TIMESHARES

## Timeshare solicitations are now posing as fake birthday postcards

David Lazarus of the *Los Angeles Times* has uncovered a new wrinkle in the mail pitches being sent out for timeshares. Have you received a postcard around your birthday with an offer of two round-trip airfares to any U.S. location, plus a car rental? Don't dial that number in an attempt to redeem it! It's very likely a timeshare solicitation disguised as a free trip.

If you take the bait, you'll need to sit through a ninety-minute strong-arm pitch. And those free tickets aren't really free. You can go only where they say and when. Why the smoke and mirrors? "If we said 'timeshare,' our response rate would probably go down," one marketer told Lazarus. "That's why we say, 'Call for details.'"

You never want to buy a timeshare new from the original developer. The only way to buy a timeshare is used from an existing owner. Visit the Timeshare Users Group at TUG2.net and check out their Timeshare Marketplace forum for a listing of timeshares being sold at a discount. Just beware that if the operator of the timeshare is insolvent, you'll likely have problems with maintenance of amenities like pools or tennis courts. This is very dicey territory. You have been warned!

## Beware of promises to help you resell your timeshare

Buying a timeshare is a bad enough rip-off. But imagine getting ripped off twice or three times by crooks promising to help you resell your timeshare!

Florida is the epicenter of the universe when it comes to timeshares. The *St. Petersburg Times* reports the Sunshine State's attorney general received more than 2,700 complaints about the timeshare resale industry during a recent year, up from nearly 1,000 a year prior. That's almost triple the number of complaints year over year.

The crooks typically ask for money up front for advertising, title searches, and other administrative fees. You might even be told you'll get your money back if your timeshare isn't sold in ninety days. That's a big fat lie. You won't get anything back except a lighter wallet. But there's more than one level of danger here; there's also the element of what's called a reload scam. Crooks in this field routinely share the names and numbers of people who they've already successfully ripped off. That way other criminals know who is an easy mark and can be hit up for money several times over.

Here's the real truth: Anyone promising you more than a few pennies on the dollar for what you originally paid if you bought a timeshare new is lying. Salespeople should receive commissions only at the time of the sale, not a second before.

## Get rid of your timeshare—but it may cost you

I've received many calls over the years from people who are stuck with a timeshare they can't sell. Timeshares are extremely difficult to unload no matter what you paid for them or when you bought them.

Even if you love your timeshare, sometimes your circumstances change and you need to sell your week. The trouble is that there is no solid, active secondary market for selling timeshares because they lose about 80 percent of their value the moment they leave a developer's hands.

For the last eight years, I've guided timeshare owners who wanted to get rid of their obligation to donateforacause.org (DFC). Historically, this group allowed you to donate your timeshare to charity and claim a tax deduction of up to $5,000 with no costs involved on your end. The process eliminated all maintenance fees, taxes, and any special assessments from your life.

After the transfer of ownership, you would get a receipt for your donation and the proceeds would go to a nonprofit organization of your choosing. The American Cancer Society, Feed the Children, and National Public Radio are just a few of the possible recipients working with DFC. Be sure to discuss the tax issues with your accountant before you claim it as a deduction.

Today, though, there's a postscript to this story. Before the economy tanked, DFC was able to take on the majority of timeshares that people brought to them to unload. Recently, however, I've gotten complaints on my show from listeners who said they were either getting the brush-off from DFC or being asked to pay big money, which is a red flag in my book.

So I got in touch with DFC and spoke to Crystal Foss, the company's president. Foss explained the timeshare resale market is so broken that they accept less than 10 percent of the properties people contact them about. To deal with the more than 90 percent that they can't do a thing with, DFC set up a guaranteed for-profit operation. For a charge of $2,500, DFC will now take a timeshare off your hands.

Make sure you don't owe any money against the timeshare you want to get rid of—including outstanding maintenance fees—or it won't even be considered. DFC still offers their original no-cost option too, but the reality is that the donation is contingent upon resale of the property during a 120-day period . . . and there ain't no way that's happening in today's market! In fact, I have very serious reservations about whether the timeshare market will recover at any point during my lifetime.

At first glance, it might seem counterintuitive to include a tip in this book that's going to cost you $2,500. But when you consider that maintenance fees, taxes, and any special assessments on a timeshare can add up pretty quickly—not to mention the interest you're paying if you took out a loan to buy your timeshare—well, I think you'll agree this one can be a real money saver.

So this remains a legitimate way to get rid of your timeshare, but I know it might prove cost-prohibitive for many people. And I realize that it's like adding insult to injury if you already paid big once to get your timeshare. In the end, I think the best advice I can give is, if you have a timeshare, try your hardest to get out there once a year and enjoy your week.

# PROTECTING YOUR WALLET ON THE ROAD

## Purchase advance travel with a credit card

So many airlines have gone bust in just the past few years. There were a number of factors that led to their demise: the drop in leisure travel throughout the recession, the reduction in business travel overall since 2001, and then the final nail in the coffin—a spurt in oil prices.

Every rise or fall in the cost of jet fuel (kerosene) makes a massive difference in the cost structure of the nation's airlines. They see an almost instantaneous benefit from just the tiniest drop in oil prices. So you can imagine the financial hurt they felt when oil rose to nearly $150 a barrel after it had been around $100 a barrel just a few months earlier!

I recall getting a lot of questions on my show about the one-two punch that affected travelers when two airlines that served Hawaii—Aloha Airlines and ATA Airlines—failed within months of each other. Both failures left thousands of Hawaiians stranded on the mainland and thousands of mainlanders stranded on Hawaii. (Well, you can't really have too much sympathy for the latter group, can you?)

These kinds of failures always highlight a weak spot in how some people choose to purchase their airfare. People who paid in cash, by check, or with a money order or debit card got burned and had no recourse to get their money back. Those who used a credit card, on the other hand, were eligible to get their money back. All it required was contacting their credit card issuer and doing a charge back within sixty days of the original date of purchase. Now that's the way to book smart and safe!

## Don't use a debit card when renting a car or checking into a hotel

Plastic can often be a traveler's best friend. Have you ever tried booking a rental car or a hotel room without a credit or debit card? It's impossible. But as in other areas of your finances, the type of plastic a traveler chooses to pull out is very important.

Debit cards are an overwhelmingly inferior product to credit cards for a number of reasons. The worst weakness is that hotels and rental car companies will put a hold on your checking account if you use a debit card to make a transaction. If you have other checks floating around that someone tries to cash, that could throw you over into insufficient funds land and result in heavy fees.

But there are other, less publicized dangers in using a debit card at the car rental counter or even at the front desk at a hotel during check-in. Pamela Yip of *The Dallas Morning News* found that it's standard practice (and completely legal) in the industry for car rental companies to do a hard inquiry on your credit report, often without your knowledge or consent. Why would they do this? They're trying to protect themselves against auto thieves that love to use debit cards as a low-risk method to get rentals that they can steal. But that inquiry can drastically lower your credit score in the process. The simple solution is to use a real credit card instead.

## Use a no-fee credit card overseas

Using a credit card overseas can be easy and cheap or it can be fraught with a lot of heavy and unnecessary expenses. Several years ago, a reporter for *The New York Times* called major credit card issuers and asked about the fees for using a credit card overseas. The reporter wrote that it was not easy to get answers, but the funniest responses were why the fees existed at all: The most honest answer was that the bank needed to make more money.

Traditionally, you were charged for the bank's foreign-currency buying rate (aka the wholesale-bankers' buying rate) plus a 1 percent conversion fee when using a credit card overseas. But last decade, banks started charging up to 5 percent for absolutely no reason. I want you to find out your credit card's conversion fees before traveling overseas. It's not the most exciting thing in the world, but you need to call your issuer and see what kind of rate they charge.

Banks have to tell you the fees they charge for overseas charges or they can be sued.

Most credit card issuers charge 3 percent if you use their card outside the United States. Capital One, however, has no fees at all on their credit cards when used internationally. Many smaller issuers and credit unions will not charge rip-off fees. Use those cards if you can. In addition, USAA has no foreign-transaction fee, though there is a 1 percent MasterCard/Visa fee associated with their cards. (See "If You're a Veteran, Get USAA" on page 162.)

Using ATMs abroad is the most effective way to get money when traveling. But some banks will charge a foreign-currency rip-off fee that usually starts at $9 or $10 per transaction! That's outrageous. If you're with a big bank, check to see if they are part of any alliance where you can use ATMs fee-free in other countries. Simply tell them what country you're going to and they can tell you if there's a fee-free alliance partner bank there. You can also get fee-free ATM transactions abroad with most Capital One cards.

## Make cheap international cell calls while traveling

After traveling recently in Europe, I was reminded how expensive it can be to call the United States. While in Venice, Italy, I overheard an American woman telling her friend how she got ripped off on calls back home. She was charged $68 for a five-minute call to family and $10 for a one-minute call to check her voice mail. So I told the woman I was paying only 5.8 cents a minute and offered to let her use my cell. Well, she probably thought I was a con artist because she didn't take me up on my offer!

So what's my secret? I heeded a listener's advice and used a service called Pingo.com. This is *not* a free service; you have to pay $12 to sign up and are immediately credited with $5 in calling time. So the net initial cost is $7. But the payoff is in the great rates. I even found an online coupon to receive bonus minutes when I first signed up.

Since then, I've learned about a couple of newer services called CallArc.com and Ring-Plus.net that promise free international calling.

Both services require you to listen to ads in exchange for free talk time. We'll see how these services play out over time. Let's hope they don't end up in Clark's Graveyard! (See page 241.)

The cost of international calling changes at light speed. And the rates keep going down and down. You might find things that are not exactly free, but so cheap that it will feel like it's free! Visit ClarkHoward.com for my updates on the latest and greatest deals.

Aside from that, there are a couple of different ways you can avoid getting eaten alive on charges from your wireless carrier when you're overseas. For starters, you can enroll in your carrier's own international calling plan and use your own phone. If you choose to go this route, make sure you get an e-mail confirmation of your enrollment with the terms and conditions before you travel.

But to go even cheaper, you've got to start with an unlocked world phone that uses Global System for Mobile (GSM) technology. T-Mobile will unlock your existing handset after ninety days, while AT&T requires you to complete your contract before they unlock you. When I was in England and had to get a new world phone, I went to the Carphone Warehouse chain and bought an unlocked phone for $14. You can also try going on eBay and buying an already unlocked world phone on the cheap.

Once you have the unlocked world phone, you should buy a prepaid SIM chip for it online. You might want to use GoSim.com or Telestial.com, which are both good for when you're doing a single-country trip. Check out RangeRoamer.com if you're going to be traveling to multiple nations. If you're going to Europe, you should know about Lycamobile.com. They sell ultra-cheap chips that you can use to call back for practically zilch—some 6 or 10 cents per minute.

One aside here, for those taking an action-adventure trip in uncharted territory, I'd recommend buying or renting a satellite phone from Telestial.com. It will still cost less per minute than the usual charges from your carrier.

Remember, your wallet will be destroyed if you use your standard U.S. cell phone while traveling overseas. And I don't ever want to see that happen.

## Block international calling with your cell provider in case of theft

Not too long ago people used to line up in airports at endless banks of pay phones. The mad rush for pay phones in the pre–cell phone days gave rise to a dangerous crime called "shoulder surfing."

Criminals would pretend to videotape family members near the gates, but they'd really be filming people punching in their long-distance calling card numbers. The crooks would turn around and sell those codes all around the country within minutes of filming.

The days of shoulder surfing are long gone, but the threat of having someone run up thousands of dollars in international calls remains. Today it most often happens when you lose your phone or it gets stolen.

Under current law, you are responsible for those costs even in the case of theft or loss. To avoid a scenario like this, call your cell phone provider and get an international calling block put on your line. That will shut down any criminals who try to dial abroad.

## Ship packages when you travel

The nation's airlines are continually looking for more ways to get in your pocket. A few years ago, Delta and Continental raised baggage fees to the point that it could exceed some ticket prices if you had more than one piece of luggage to check in! Then Spirit Airlines outraged people in 2010 by charging a new carry-on fee that ranges from $20 to $45 per bag.

Southwest Airlines, meanwhile, still has no baggage fees as I write this. Nor will this discount airline charge you to change a trip once you've booked it. Perhaps that's why Southwest keeps gaining more market share while the full-fare airlines watch their shares shrink.

Think Southwest is crazy? Well, I say they're crazy like a fox. Customers who might be on the cusp about taking a trip are probably more likely to book with Southwest because they know they won't get hit with a fee to change a ticket.

But what if Southwest doesn't serve the markets you need? There's another way to avoid baggage fees on the full-fare airlines: Shipping packages with UPS Ground or FedEx Ground can help.

One of my coauthors on this book, Theo Thimou, lives in Atlanta, but both he and his wife are natives of New Jersey. Every Christmas, they travel with their child to visit family in the Garden State. They've found they can ship presents back to Georgia in a medium-sized box (18 x 18 x 16 inches, or 3 cubic feet) for about $20–$25, via a UPS Ground drop-off point that's located inside one of the local big-box office supply stores.

That beats having to pay $100 on Continental or $125 on Delta for a third suitcase. Of course, they could be saving much more if they traveled with no luggage at all, but as a parent myself, I know that can be difficult when you have children.

Visit Kayak.com/airline-fees for a full list of fees pertaining to checked baggage, meals, pets, unaccompanied-minor service, and more.

# Clark's Graveyard

From three-wheeled cars to $9 airline tickets, small-business men and women are always coming up with great ideas about how to do something different, better, or cheaper. But their ideas don't always find a spot in the marketplace, and so the world of entrepreneurship is fraught with the danger of failure.

But failure doesn't make a good idea any less of a good idea.

Here's a partial list of promising websites and services that I've mentioned over the years that went bust and ended up in my graveyard. Each one has its own special place in my heart. May they all rest in peace. . . .

### SaysMe.tv—Exact date of death unknown, but believed to be early 2011
Targeted TV ads had traditionally been too expensive for small business owners to buy . . . until a website called SaysMe.tv leveled the playing field. SaysMe made a business out of buying unloved ad inventory at a fraction of the regular cost and selling it to individuals.

When I checked rates in late 2010, buying an ad spot through Says Me on MTV in the Raleigh, North Carolina, market at 4:00 p.m., for example, cost just north of $180. If you wanted to run your ad before 4:00 p.m., the asking price dropped to a little more than $90 because your target audience was still at school. In smaller markets, you might have been able to get a non-peak ad slot for $20 or $30!

I thought this idea was so great I originally included it in the manuscript of the book you're reading. But my dutiful editors pointed out to me that SaysMe became a corpse sometime in early 2011, while *Living Large in Lean Times* was in production!

### Wesabe.com—Died July 2010

Much like its more popular competitor Mint.com, Wesabe.com offered free online budgeting tools. You gave Wesabe access to all your accounts and it automatically tracked your spending. The unique name apparently derived from *saber*, the Spanish word for "to know," because the goal was to empower consumers with insight into their spending habits. In a good-bye message to users, the company cited lack of funding and poor customer service stemming from understaffing as reasons it went bust.

### Venjuvo.com—Died August 2009

This early "cash for old gadgets" venture offered an online trade-in center that paid you for your pre-owned electronics—everything from cell phones, MP3 players, computers, and cameras to GPS systems and gaming consoles. Shipping was prepaid on the company's dime and users typically received their payment in three business days . . . until the service went kaput.

### JetAmerica.com—Died July 2009

This promising hard discounter was modeled on successful European companies like Ryanair and easyJet. Jet America announced in May 2009 that they'd be offering nine seats for $9 on every flight, with the fares stepping up from there. The plan was to start with one single aircraft per route and add more over time to avoid the risk of growing too quickly. Unfortunately, they never even made it off the ground for their virgin flight.

### SpiralFrog.com—Died March 2009

This site offered free ad-supported music downloads from major label partners such as Universal and EMI. After launching in 2006, SpiralFrog was rumored to have burned through more than $40 million in capital. In addition, some said the service's support of digital rights management—an unpopular restriction that forbids you from taking your music across platforms from one device to another—also helped seal its fate.

**MyRichUncle.com—Died February 2009**

This student loan website analyzed factors like GPA, desired field of study, and the school you were planning on attending to make merit-based loans to students with little or no credit history. But it eventually had to cry "uncle" in the marketplace!

**ZOOTS—Died April 2008**

This high-volume dry cleaner failed after finding out just how difficult it is to crack what traditionally has been a mom-and-pop industry. Among the features ZOOTS offered were twenty-four-hour service, easy online scheduling, and pickup/delivery. The company is being disassembled piecemeal, so you might still see select locations with the ZOOTS name from time to time.

**Eos Airlines—Died April 27, 2008**

The collapse of this all-business-class carrier with service between New York's JFK and London's Stansted Airport came as a surprise. "[It is] particularly regrettable since we have achieved so much, including having a term sheet in hand for additional financing," the airline's website revealed before going permanently offline. The company's advertising tagline was "Uncrowded. Uncompromising. Unairline." Well, they sure got the last one right!

**Skybus Airlines—Died April 5, 2008**

Modeled on Europe's popular Ryanair, Skybus initially launched in May 2007 with one-way fares starting at $10. Skybus ultimately would serve seventeen U.S. destinations before the high price of jet fuel and the slowing economy clipped its wings.

**Steve and Barry's—Died November 2008**

This innovative retailer offered private designer lines at the cheapest prices possible. Most of everything Steve and Barry's sold was around the $10 price point—and that included clothing and shoes branded by tennis player Venus Williams, actress Sarah Jessica Parker, and others. Steve and Barry's Starbury sneakers—the signature shoe from NBA player Stephon Marbury—sold for a mere $14.98. Compare that to upward of $200 for a pair of Air Jordans! But apparently it was the retailer's cheap prices that drove it out of business.

### SunRocket Internet Phone Service—Died July 2007

I was a big fan of SunRocket, a company that offered some of the best deals out there on VoIP service. But people who signed up were not, because they paid up front and, when the company closed, lost all their money. And that included me!

### Automatic vending machines—Died November 2003

I first saw these machines in Europe and Asia, and they were later installed in Washington, D.C. Items in these huge vending machines built into a wall were much cheaper than in regular convenience stores because there was no need for labor. But apparently it didn't work in the States!

### MyFreeCar.com—Exact date of death unknown

This is just one of several car-wrapping websites that have gone under. These companies paid drivers up to $400 each month just to drive around with advertising on their vehicles. Others that have gone by the wayside are FreeMedia.com, UDrive 4Cash.com, and CarWrap.com.

### AllAdvantage.com—Died February 2001

This was a free Internet service that actually paid customers who agreed to view advertising as they searched the Web. For a brief period, I was receiving $12.50 per month. What a great idea it was!

### Freeway—Died February 2001

This once-famed long distance service offered up to two free hours of long distance calling per month in return for listening to ads. Customers had to listen to brief commercials for two free minutes of calls. Now with cell phones, of course, hardly anybody pays for long distance anymore!

## Virgin Connect Me—Died November 2000

This easy-to-use device offered free Internet access and e-mail service for one year. My wife and a couple of the staffers on my radio show all took advantage of the free device, which was initially offered to only 10,000 qualifying applicants. They all had to send the device back, however, when the company died.

## HM Vehicles Freeway—Died July 1982

Back in 1980, I bought a three-wheeled car called the Freeway—no relation to the doomed long-distance service of the same name. This unique vehicle was a true Fred Flintstone putt-putt mobile; it got one hundred miles per gallon on a twelve-horsepower Tecumseh farm engine and had no reverse gear. Once I accelerated too quickly on a highway and the front lifted straight off the ground! Sadly, the last I saw of my Freeway was when I had it hauled off with a tree growing out of it.

# Important Websites

ClarkHoward.com

## HELP ME NOW, CLARK

MissingMoney.com
Unclaimed.org
HUD.gov
Hulu.com
FanCast.com
YouTube.com
Boxee.tv
Clicker.com
Netflix.com
Amazon.com/Prime
GetPeek.com
Kajeet.com
Fidelity.com (800-343-3548)
PenFed.org (800-247-5626)
CUNA.org
FindaCreditUnion.com

StraightTalk.com
MetroPCS.com
VirginMobileUSA.com
Ooma.com
CellSwapper.com
CellTradeUSA.com
crowdSPRING.com
eLance.com
Guru.com
oDesk.com
Fiverr.com
IBRInfo.org
PriceDoc.com
ZocDoc.com
BidRx.com
JointCommissionInternational.org
ZenniOptical.com
EyeBuyDirect.com
GlassesUnlimited.com
GlassesShop.com
RetailMeNot.com

CouponCabin.com
BradsDeals.com
Zappos.com
UPromise.com
BabyMint.com
RedPlum.com
SmartSource.com
CouponMom.com
MyGroceryDeals.com


## CARS

CarGurus.com
ConsumerReports.org
NewCarBuyersGuide.com
AutoSafety.org
ALLDATAdiy.com
PlugInSolutions.net
CARFAX.com
ASE.com
CarsDirect.com
Zag.com
LeaseTrader.com
LowerMyLease.com
Yelp.com
Kudzu.com
DentBetty.com
GasPriceWatch.com
GasBuddy.com
TireRack.com
NICB.org

## COMPUTERS AND INTERNET

Woot.com
1SaleaDay.com
DODTracker.com
LastMinute-Auction.com
DealNews.com
OpenOffice.org
Docs.Google.com
Zoho.com
Office365.Microsoft.com
Gazelle.com
MyBoneYard.com
TechForward.com
EcoSquid.com
ATT.com
Verizon.com
Comcast.com
WhiteFence.com
iFixIt.com
Epinions.com
Bing.com
Safer-Networking.org
MalWareBytes.org
SuperAntiSpyware.com
Avast.com/Free-Antivirus-Download
Free.AVG.com
Microsoft.com/Security_Essentials
Google.com/Chrome
AvantBrowser.com
Opera.com

## CONSUMER ISSUES

Trashwiki.org

DumpsterDiversParadise.com

FreeCycle.org

Yoink.com

Groupon.com

MyDailyThread.com

LivingSocial.com

ScoutMob.com

Glyde.com

Redbox.com

BlockbusterExpress.com

SeatGeek.com

StubHub.com

Zigabid.com

Craigslist.org

Pandora.com

Grooveshark.com

ALDI.com

Save-A-Lot.com

Amazon.com

Alice.com

Cellfire.com

Shopkick.com

PriceProtectr.com

iDeeli.com

BeyondtheRack.com

EditorsCloset.com

Gilt.com

HauteLook.com

RueLaLa.com

Totsy.com

BlackFriday.info

GottaDeal.com

BFAds.net

OKCupid.com

PlentyOfFish.com

Yelp.com

GetHuman.com

Get2Human.com

CharityWatch.org

CharityNavigator.com

IRS.gov


## EDUCATION AND JOBS

Chegg.com

CourseSmart.com

BookRenter.com

ECampus.com

Skoobit.com

Salary.com

SCORE.org

AthenaInternational.org

GreenNote.com

People2Capital.com

USPTO.gov

Lulu.com

Blurb.com

1stBook-Publishing.com

Xlibris.com

iUniverse.com

SCORE.org
ClarkHoward.com (529 guide)
ED.gov
Money-Zine.com
Volition.com
USAJOBS.gov
Grants.gov
Benefits.gov
AnnualCreditReport.com
Give.org
HowStuffWorks.com
InventorEd.org
Invention-IFIA.ch

## HEALTH AND HEALTH CARE

RateMDs.com
Yelp.com
Claims.org
BillAdvocates.com
Recipe.com
Epicurious.com
HopefulHousewife.com
TheFamilyHomestead.com
HillbillyHousewife.com
AllRecipes.com
DiscoverTesting.com
TogetherRxAccess.com
HSAFinder.com
HSAAdministrators.info
Ingenix MedPoint (888-206-0335)

Milliman (877-211-4816)
MIB Group (866-692-6901)
USP.org
CaringInfo.org

## HOMES AND REAL ESTATE

Moving.org
UShip.com
HomeDepot.com
Sungevity.com
TrueCredit.com/Mortgage
Quizzle.com
CreditKarma.com
Credit.com
Reverse.org
EnergySavers.gov/Financial
ClaytoniHouse.com
ZetaCommunities.com
ASHI.com
NIBI.com
ePropertyWatch.com

## INSURANCE

Insure.com
InsWeb.com
NetQuote.com
Edmunds.com
KBB.com

NADA.com

WhatsMyPDQ.org

AMBest.com

FEMA.gov

AccuQuote.com

Insure.com

QuickQuote.com

eHealthInsurance.com

KaiserPermanente.org

HealthCare.gov

KnowYourStuff.org

PersonalReports.LexisNexis.com

ImmediateAnnuities.com

USAA.com

Amica.com

NOLHGA.com

EvaluateLifeInsurance.org (603-224-2805)

## PERSONAL FINANCE

Mint.com

ClearCheckBook.com

Yodlee.com

JustThrive.com

Bankrate.com

MoneyAisle.com

Prosper.com

LendingClub.com

Zopa.com

CreditCardTuneUp.com

NerdWallet.com

Vanguard.com

Schwab.com

TRowePrice.com

IRS.gov (Free File program)

877-SCORE-11 (to buy Equifax FICO score for $7.95)

Credit.com

CreditKarma.com

Quizzle.com

AnnualCreditReport.com (877-322-8228)

NFCC.org (800-388-2227)

Deathswitch.com

AssetLock.net

LegacyLocker.com

MyWebWill.com

WeRemember.org

FDIC.gov/EDIE

NCUA.gov

CDARS.com

OCC.gov

NAAG.org

FTC.gov

## TELEPHONES AND TELEVISION

Net10.com

Google.com/voice

Wi-Ex.com

magicJack.com

AntennaWeb.org

Netflix.com

Vudu.com

TVersity.com

Sezmi.com
800-FREE-411 (800-373-3411)
800-YELLOWPAGES (800-935-5697)

## TRAVEL

HomeExchange.com
Airbnb.com
HomeLink.org
ExchangeHomes.com
JewettStreet.com
SabbaticalHomes.com
CouchSurfing.com
HospitalityClub.org
EvergreenClub.com
Travelzoo.com
AirGorilla.com
Mobissimo.com
Kayak.com
Momondo.com
Yapta.com

InsureMyTrip.com
DonateforACause.org
Pingo.com
CallArc.com
RingPlus.net
GoSim.com
Telestial.com
RangeRoamer.com
Lycamobile.com
Kayak.com/airline-fees
Priceline.com
Hotwire.com
BiddingforTravel.com
BetterBidding.com
QuikBook.com
VRBO.com
BestParking.com
LongTermParking.com
BoltBus.com
MegaBus.com
TUG2.net

# Acknowledgments

Many people contributed to this book, and I'd like to thank them for everything they did. Let me start with the person who is responsible for the title. We were struggling a bit with what to call this book. We wanted something that encouraged people to be frugal, but with an upbeat tone. So we put out a call to my audience, and they had some great suggestions. The one we chose came from Dan Runnells. Thanks, Dan. I really appreciate it.

Other listeners and viewers played an important role. In this book, we feature some of their stories about the way they've used my tips to save money and score great deals. The stories are fun and funny to read, and they add wonderful real-life color.

I want to thank my longtime agent, Laurie Liss, who introduced me to my new friends at Penguin, thereby rebooting the Clark Howard book franchise. Laurie, I appreciate your faith in me.

It's been a pleasure to work with the people at Penguin, including publisher William Shinker, publicity gurus Lisa Johnson and Lindsay Gordon, editors Megan Newman and Miriam Rich, and copy editor Sharon Gonzalez. Thanks for your dedication, great ideas, and diligent eyes. Thanks also to Andrea Ho and Amanda Dewey for your artistic design sense, and Linda Cowen for your legal expertise.

And thanks to the entire Clark Howard team, the people who work every day to make my syndicated radio show and my HLN TV show successful. Special thanks to executive producer Christa DiBiase for the many, many things she does.

*—Clark*

# Index

timeshares, 233–35
Together Rx Access cards, 105–6
toning shoes, 118–19
travel. *See also* air travel
    bus transportation, 229–31
    car rentals, 152, 231–32, 236
    credit card fees on foreign
        transactions, 237
    home exchange, 222
    hotel complaints, 221–22
    hotel payment with debit card, 236
    hotel price bidding, 217–19
    lodging with strangers, 220–21
    medical tourism, 15–16
    timeshares, 233–35
    trip protection insurance,
        227–28
    vacation rentals, 219–20
Twitter. *See* social networks

unclaimed money
    FHA-backed mortgage premiums,
        2, 132–33
    search for, 1–2
    tax refund scam, 200

vacation homes
    purchase, 129–30
    rental, 219–20
    timeshares, 233–35
vacations. *See* travel
veterans, insurance for, 149–50, 162–63
Voice over Internet Protocol (VoIP), 11,
    209–10

warehouse stores
    bulk produce, 71, 76
    deals at, 76
    prescription drug prices, 105–6

warranties
    cell phones, 202
    credit card extension of, 9,
        55, 202
    extended, on cars, 34–36
    extended, on electronics and
        computers, 8–9, 55
    home-builder warranties, 137–38
    home operating systems, 142–43
water, 117–18
Web resources, 246–51
women
    inventors, 96
    small-business owners, 98
    toning shoes for, 118–19
work-at-home opportunities
    legitimate, 12–13, 91
    scams, 60–61, 91–92
    small businesses, 98–99